'*Workstyle* is a brilliant book. Lizzie and Alex are the experts on autonomous working and make it easy and exciting for us all to understand and apply.'

Helen Tupper, bestselling co-author of
The Squiggly Career *and* You Coach You

'This book – a manifesto on how to make work actually work for the people doing it – shouldn't have had to be written, but I'm so glad it has. *Workstyle* recognises our individuality as workers, and gives us permission to break free from the 9-5, while also explaining exactly how to do so.'

Rebecca Seal, bestselling author of SOLO: How to Work Alone (and Not Lose Your Mind)

'Lizzie and Alex have turned an idea, a principle, into a global movement and a successful business. *Workstyle* provides a privileged insight into their real-world experience and offers a framework for anyone thinking about what "organisation" means in contemporary business. An accessible, inspiring, and timely contribution to any leader's library.'

Matt Meyer, CEO, Taylor Vinters

'Whether you are an individual looking to understand your place in the future of work and how to optimise your life, or you are a business looking to harness the real value of the people you work with, this book offers an indispensable guide. Presenting a genuinely novel and brilliant concept this book is jam-packed with academic research, anecdotes, and practical guides to take you from clueless to expert without ever wanting to put the thing down. Who said you can't be more productive and happier...?'

Albert Azis-Clauson, Chair of the Association for the Future of Work and CEO of UnderPinned

'The concept of "workstyle" wins in a modern world! Written in a hugely engaging way, this book explains how the workstyle approach can have a positive impact not just on the person, their health and wellbeing, but on our businesses enabling us to generate superior results, and also on wider society. One day we will look back and wonder how we ever worked any other way!'

Jon Marlow, Managing Director, Divine Chocolate

'An incredibly empowering read which made me reflect on changes I could make to improve my opportunities to learn, grow and have lasting impact through the way that I work. Packed with practical advice and lessons we all need to adopt to move to a more inclusive and productive way of working, I will be recommending this book to EVERYONE.'

Sarah Salter, Global Head of Innovation, Wavemaker

'Lizzie and Alex have spearheaded the conversation around autonomous and asynchronous working for over a decade, bringing innovative ways of working to change the world of work.'

Caroline Arora, VP People and Culture, Blinkist

'*Workstyle* is an important and relevant book that should not be missed, especially in the post-Covid era.'

Jon Younger, Investor, Teacher and Forbes Contributor

'*Workstyle* is a practical guide to a radically new way of working, as we all move into new work environments post pandemic. It is easy to read, has plenty of practical tips and encourages a work-life integration approach to the new world of work. Great value for those who want support in their quest for workstyle changes.'

Professor Sir Cary Cooper, ALLIANCE Manchester Business School, University of Manchester

'To say that I REALLY enjoyed this book does not fully give it the credit it deserves! Lizzie and Alex have truly captured what is wrong with our broken approach to work, and underlines the need for work to serve our chosen lifestyles and not the other way around. Added to that, their personalities shine through their writing to make this book even more enjoyable. Everyone should own a copy of this book.'

Dr Rochelle Haynes, Senior Lecturer in Global People Management and CEO of Crowd Potential

'If you care about creating a future of work in which everyone can belong then *Workstyle* is a must read. Lizzie and Alex have been pioneers of new ways of working long prior to the pandemic. In order to hold on to what we have gained in a pandemic which personally and professionally cost us so much, this book is vital, urgent reading.'

Nicola Kemp, Editorial Director, Creativebrief

'Trust Lizzie and Alex to write this cracker of a book that redefines how we work and how older workers can take their rightful places on intergenerational teams. Love it!'

Susan Flory, creator of The Big Middle *podcast*

'At long last, a genuinely new view of the world of work. Lizzie and Alex bring insight, experience and, crucially, imagination together and offer us a tried and tested solution. This book will make you change how you work but more importantly, it will show how we will all benefit from radically rethinking how we live our lives. A new way of working would be gamechanging for fathers, their partners, their children and society.'

Will McDonald, Trustee, Fatherhood Institute

'Lizzie Penny and Alex Hirst have been in the vanguard of this movement for a decade. Their message from the frontline is insightful, wide-ranging, practical – and readable. In a world of full employment, businesses that win will have to meet their colleagues' workstyle expectations – this is a guidebook for where those are heading.'

Philip Almond, Executive Director Fundraising & Marketing, Cancer Research UK

'It's time we all recognised the deep and enduring prejudices which exclude millions of people from equal participation in society. Now, perhaps more than ever as we put Covid behind us, it is vitally important to not only think big, but to think outside the box and not be constrained by what has been done previously. The world is changing so fast, and so is the way we live in it. But one principle is surely timeless: everyone should have the opportunity to realise their potential and do their best work. I really hope the extensive work that has gone into producing *Workstyle* and its thoughtful recommendations will attract the attention they deserve.'

Lord Kevin Shinkwin, peer and disability campaigner

'In this fascinating and insightful book Lizzie and Alex draw on their deep experience of changing the way they worked – to provide a guide on how to change the way you work. With both practical wisdom and research insights they build a convincing argument for change.'

Professor Lynda Gratton, bestselling author of
Redesigning Work *and* The 100-Year Life

Workstyle

Workstyle

A revolution for wellbeing, productivity and society

Lizzie Penny and Alex Hirst

First published in Great Britain by John Murray Learning in 2022
An imprint of John Murray Press
A division of Hodder & Stoughton Ltd,
An Hachette UK company

1

Copyright © Lizzie Penny and Alex Hirst 2022

Illustrations © Josh Edson

A CIP catalogue record for this title is available from the British Library

Hardback ISBN 978 1 399 80294 9
eBook ISBN 978 1 399 80299 4

Typeset by KnowledgeWorks Global Ltd.

Printed and bound in Great Britain by Clays Ltd, Elcograf S.p.A.

John Murray Press policy is to use papers that are natural, renewable and recyclable
products and made from wood grown in sustainable forests. The logging and
manufacturing processes are expected to conform to the environmental regulations of
the country of origin.

John Murray Press
Carmelite House
50 Victoria Embankment
London EC4Y 0DZ

www.johnmurraypress.co.uk

Together, we can create a happier, more fulfilled society through a world of work without bias.

Contents

Foreword   xiii

Hello, workstyler!   xv

PART I: IDEA

Chapter 1: Introduction   3

Chapter 2: Our workstyle stories   9

Chapter 3: A broken system of work   19

Chapter 4: Why 2014 was a magical year   43

Chapter 5: One word to change the world   71

Chapter 6: Proving the impact of workstyle   97

PART II: WORKSTYLE ELEVATES YOUR WELLBEING

Chapter 7: What is wellbeing?   115

Chapter 8: Mind   121

Chapter 9: Purpose   137

Chapter 10: Learning   151

Chapter 11: Connection   165

Chapter 12: Body   181

↻ **PART III: WORKSTYLE STEP-CHANGES YOUR PRODUCTIVITY**

Chapter 13: What is productivity?   197

Chapter 14: Energy   205

Chapter 15: Clarity   221

Chapter 16: Mastery   235

Chapter 17: Trust   247

Chapter 18: Environment   263

↻ **PART IV: WORKSTYLE HAS A LASTING IMPACT ON SOCIETY**

Chapter 19: How could workstyle impact society?   283

Chapter 20: Inclusion   289

Chapter 21: Attitudes   313

Chapter 22: Collective intelligence   333

Chapter 23: Change the world, and your life, today!   351

Foreword

Sixty years ago I was a pioneer of computer software. I was also, though neither I nor anyone else realised it at the time, a pioneer of a different kind. Today, as I approach the age of 90, I find the rest of the world has caught up with me.

In 1962 the company I founded, Freelance Programmers, employed only women working from home. My own career with two conventional employers had been stymied by the prevailing sexism of the times, and I reasoned that lots of other women must have had the same experience. Others had chosen (or in some cases been obliged) to give up their jobs when they married or had children. They constituted a pool of highly-qualified and highly-motivated staff just waiting to be usefully employed.

Eventually my company proved an enormous success (though not before well-meaning equal opportunities legislation in the 1970s meant we had to offer jobs to men as well as women). Along the way we developed new, flexible ways of working for our new, flexible workforce – people who wanted to fit their work around their lives, rather than adhering to the rigid timetables and structures of conventional employment.

We offered a smorgasbord of benefits. You could work for us part-time or full-time. You could opt to put more of your remuneration package into a pension, or take more holiday for less pay (counterintuitively, we learnt that when you offer staff the freedom to take as much holiday as they want, they tend to take less). We were forerunners of today's gig economy, offering zero-hour contracts to women who valued the freedom such arrangements gave them to combine work with caring for children or elderly relatives.

Today, as Lizzie Penny and Alex Hirst show, working from anywhere at any time has been made possible by advances in technology unguessed at when I started out, back in the era of pencils and paper, typewriters and telephones. What the authors call 'workstyle' is as revolutionary today as the flexibility my company offered was all those years ago.

There is, it turns out, nothing set in stone about the way we work. Patterns of work have often been reconfigured and reimagined. The five-day working week, for instance, was introduced by Henry Ford in 1926; but in Britain public service jobs came down from six to five days only in the early 1950s. Today some UK businesses think in terms of a four-day working week, and there is a general trend towards shorter working hours on the grounds that they deliver greater productivity. Yet none of these changes advocate for individual choice, nor do they bring about the radical change at work that our businesses and our society really need.

With workstyle many of us will have almost complete freedom to choose when and where we work. Where will that freedom take us? How can we use it to benefit older workers, carers, those struggling with ill-health, those who identify as neurodiverse or those who feel burnt-out by years of commuting?

There is much to celebrate, though there are also grounds for caution. The pandemic accelerated pre-existing trends, and introduced many more employees and employers to radically new patterns of work. But it also saw women slipping back in the workplace, as more women than men (pro rata) were furloughed or lost their jobs completely. Women also took the brunt of domestic responsibilities, in particular home schooling.

One thing that won't change is the importance of work. I am a workaholic, someone who admits to being defined by my work: to me, it's not just something you do when you'd rather be doing something else. Thomas Carlyle called it 'the grand cure of all maladies' and Picasso 'the ultimate seduction', and as I get older I understand this kind of thinking better.

For most people, of course, their work is not the entirety of their lives. Yet as Stephen Hawking observed, work is what gives many of us meaning and purpose, and life would be empty without it. Today we have the chance to develop a healthier relationship with it for the benefit of ourselves as individuals and society as a whole: Lizzie Penny and Alex Hirst show us how.

Dame Stephanie 'Steve' Shirley CH 2022

Hello workstyler! (:wave:)

In 2014 we each had separate life-changing events happen: Alex went through burnout; Lizzie had a baby. Quite different experiences you might think, but oddly they led us both to a singular conclusion – that the traditional way of working wasn't working for us and that we, and everyone else in the world, should be free to choose for ourselves when and where we work.

We have spent the past eight years testing, and proving, that work plays a much healthier role in your life if you have the complete freedom to choose when and where you do it – an idea so revolutionary, it turns out, that there wasn't even a word for it, so we created one: workstyle. We love our work and are now dedicating our professional lives to spreading the word of workstyle – as you'll discover, it's something we are extremely passionate about. It's why we decided to write this book.

Not only have we ourselves worked in our individual, regularly changing workstyles for the past eight years, we have helped more than 2,500 workstylers to set, project and respect their own workstyles, and have set up our own longitudinal study of research into it. Having also built a successful business based on workstyle, the two of us have got to know this world well, and we believe that wider society would be a much more inclusive, and happier, place if everyone could have the opportunity to work in the individualised way we do.

In this book, we are going to explain what workstyle is, why now is the right time to move to working in the workstyle way, and the impact it can have.

In the same way as Sir Robert Owen ('Sir Bobby O' to those of us who are megafans) inspired the reform of working practices during the industrial revolution, our ambition is for this book to do the same and create its own revolution today. We hope to inspire you, and show you how workstyle can elevate your wellbeing ('be well'), step-change your productivity ('work better') and have a positive impact on society for ever ('do good').

Workstyle has been transformative for us. We hope it will be for you, too.

PART 1

IDEA

ONE

Introduction

One word to change your life... workstyle

In the UK we say that all the best ideas start in the pub. So it is appropriate that, as Brits, in late 2014 we came up with the word 'workstyle' in a pub on the corner of Shepherd's Bush Green in London. We had both had a tough few months at work and were complaining about being judged on the time we spent at our desks rather than the work we actually delivered. 'What if...?' we pondered over our 2-for-1 cocktails (yep, we're also classy). 'What if everyone could be judged on their output rather than when and where they work?' What if there was a word not loaded with prejudice like 'shirking from home' or 'part-timer' or 'flex pest' that everyone could use to describe their individual way of working? What if we had a work equivalent to designing your own lifestyle? What's your *workstyle*? Light bulb. Moment. :bulb:

Our lives are divided into before that moment and after. The next cocktail tasted different somehow – the sweet taste of finding your purpose in life, perhaps. Since then we have dedicated our careers to proving that individualised workstyles can replace one-size-fits-all working practices – both for ourselves and for others. We have built a business that engages its 1,000-strong workforce entirely through workstyle, and we campaign for others to do the same. We have directly helped more than 2,500 people work in their own workstyle and have apparently inspired thousands of others. So, other than being a new word that we invented in a pub in 2014, what actually is 'workstyle'?

Put simply, workstyle is the freedom to choose when and where you work. It exists in order to create an individualised system of work. The important thing here is to have the true freedom to decide for yourself rather than to be told. This is more than just moving away from working in office blocks or sticking up two fingers to the 9-to-5. It's more than flexible working. This is about fundamentally redefining our psychological contract with work; thinking about fitting our work around our lives rather than fitting our lives around our work. It is about thriving through our work, not in spite of it.

The transformational power of workstyle

The autonomy of living and working according to your own workstyle can be transformational – or certainly it has been for us and the other workstylers we have got to know over the past eight years, many of whom have tried flexible, hybrid and remote working and have found nothing to be as impactful as workstyle. This is about being able to adapt to the less glamorous but hugely important aspects of life – being a carer, a parent, living positively with a disability, managing mental health conditions or feeling fulfilled while living with a terminal diagnosis. It's also for people who simply want to change their relationship with work, who want time to manage their household chores, see their friends or play sport during the day. For people who want to be free to move countries every three weeks or work from the beach (their #ViewFromMyDesk photos are always the ones that really take our breath away!). There are many ways that workstyle changes lives, but in this book we're going to focus on the three areas where workstyle has the most impact:

- Workstyle elevates your wellbeing.

- Workstyle step-changes your productivity.

- Workstyle can have a lasting impact on society.

We are writing this book to inspire you to try workstyle for yourself and spread the word of its transformative effect so that together we can create a revolution in working practices. In the same way as Sir Bobby O did just over 200 years ago with the conception of the eight-hour working day, we believe that this is the start of the next revolution in how we all work. In this book we are going to expand on each of the three ways above in which workstyle changes lives and we invite you to join us in creating the biggest change to working practices since 1817.

The structure of this book

We have divided this book into four parts – first the idea of workstyle itself, then its impact on wellbeing, on productivity and on society.

The first part – the idea – is what you're reading now. In this section we'll explain why workstyle is so important to us personally and highlight the most relevant points in the history of work. We will also explain why the conditions are now right for the widespread adoption of individualised work, and more specifically workstyle. We conclude this section with a summary of our research findings into the link between autonomy (workstyle), wellbeing and productivity. This section may feel like a bit of an information overload but it is important context for the sections that follow.

The second part – impact on wellbeing – explores the ways in which we have found workstyle elevates our wellbeing. We look at five elements of wellbeing and the differences that workstyle has brought to our lives in each of them.

The third part – impact on productivity – explores how we have become more productive through working in a workstyle way. It's an idea that is fundamentally created to benefit people but it is also better for the work we do, as we explore across this section. There are five elements to this, too.

The fourth and final section – impact on society – looks ahead towards the greater opportunities workstyle presents to change our world. First, through the revolutionary change it can bring to inclusion and to individual people's lives; second, through the attitudinal change that could reduce discrimination more broadly; and third, through the opportunity that a truly diverse workforce brings to our ability to solve the world's most important and complex challenges as a result of our improved collective intelligence.

Across all four sections we have included short chapter summaries that provide the opportunity for you to reflect on the themes, to take action and to help inspire others behind the idea of workstyle.

Before we get any deeper into the first section and the idea of workstyle, you should know that we are both geeks. Yes, we're afraid you can expect some geeking-out throughout this book because we think everything surrounding the subject of workstyle is fascinating. :nerd_face: It's not only us who think so. You'll be pleased to hear that we have invited a group of brilliant experts in their fields to go deeper into some areas which we think are particularly interesting. Their 'geek boxes' are spread throughout the book and are hopefully as fascinating to you as they are to us.

We also love people and are fascinated by their stories – it's the inspirational stories of workstylers that have made the past eight years so enjoyable and fuelled our commitment to this idea. We have chosen a handful to include in this book as 'Workstyle Stories'. They are all stories from real-life workstylers already living the workstyle dream, intended to show the breadth of this revolution and the true impact it can have on human lives. If these inspire you, there are many more at WorkstyleRevolution.com.

The other thing you'll notice we use throughout the book is the 'wordmoji' (another word we've made up!), which is the word description of an emoji. This is because we have become so accustomed to our digital-first ways of working that we are now seemingly incapable of writing prose without the addition of emojis to add character and humour to how we write. Since writing a book feels like more of a word place than an emoji place, we've used wordmojis throughout. :smiling_face: If you don't find these funny, which we're confident many of you won't, please just skip over them and focus on the serious words.

The purpose of writing this book is to change the world through the widespread adoption of workstyle, which means that, while our first objective is to convince you, the reader, that workstyle is the future, the second aim of the book is to inspire you to talk to other people about it. To make it easier for you to tell your friends about in the pub (*other meeting places are available), throughout the book you will find hand gestures like the one below which go alongside the narrative so you can remember the case for workstyle more easily, but also so you can look really cool to your mates :wink: and be ready for cross-examination from the naysayers. :ninja: The 'W' for workstyle was our original hand gesture, and workstylers will tell you we've been honing this one for years, but our hope is that you can remember all the others, too, and help spread the word of workstyle.

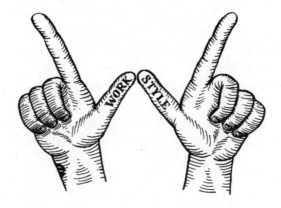

Workstyle is all about creating an individualised system of work, but it is one that needs our collective action to succeed. So, we hope you enjoy the book, but, above all, we hope you join the workstyle revolution and help spread the word so that together we can make much-needed changes in working practices that can create a happier, more fulfilled society.

TWO

Our workstyle stories

Before we get into the details of workstyle, we think it's important that you know our stories and why this is something that is so close to each of our hearts. We like paraphrasing Teddy Roosevelt's quote: 'I don't care what you know until I know that you care.' We're guessing you're the same, and we think it's important that you understand, right at the start of this book, why we both care so profoundly about this cause.

Workstyle story: Lizzie Penny

Mum, entrepreneur, social butterfly, cancer survivor, workstyle campaigner and swimmer

In 2014 I think it would be fair to say I had a bit of an identity crisis. I'd just had my first child (my son, Finn) and had gone from living a harmoniously equal life with my brilliant husband, Nick, to suddenly feeling a bit lost and lonely as a new mum.

In what seemed like an overnight transition, I went from 'Lizzie: entrepreneur, overachiever, organiser of the group and the friend who never forgets a birthday' to simply 'mum'. Doctors, nurses, even people I'd worked with for years, suddenly forgot my actual name and instead used the one I thought only my children would ever call me. Perhaps it was supposed to be a compliment, like a badge of honour for the previous nine months of growing a new life. Don't get me wrong, I loved and still love being a mum – there is nothing in the world like it for the joy it brings. But being suddenly labelled as only a parent stripped me of everything else that I was and made me into something new and alien to me at the time.

When I started to return to work, there were new challenges. To be clear, when I say 'return', I mean opening the door a little bit to dip my toe in the water and slowly build up to three days a week. I was ready to do my job again, but now I also had a family I wanted to look after and I, like so many parents, wanted the perfect mix. The problem was, the world and my particular role weren't set up to work that way. It felt like the most important meetings were always on the two days a week I wasn't in the office, and that I was constantly playing 'catch-up' compared with all the full-time employees. I felt an immense amount of internalised pressure for not dedicating my entire week to work, despite the fact that I was arguably more committed to my work than ever because I was determined to make both aspects of my life work together.

Knowing what I had to give up in one area of my life in order to make another work brought into sharp focus for me the inequalities that existed in the working world. I'm embarrassed to say I'd been mostly blind to these before having children. I started looking around me for others in a similar situation and, unsurprisingly, realised that, even just within my own circle of 'mums', the story was often the same.

There was one friend in particular, an amazingly talented woman, let's call her Philippa, with a career as an HR consultant. I remember her saying she would give up her hard-fought career and take any job doing anything at all if it meant she could work two days a week and be the mother she wanted to be to her son.

And so, as though I could see for the first time with true clarity, my eyes were opened to inequality in work everywhere and the unbelievable injustice and wasted talent of those who, for whatever reason, couldn't work 9-to-5, five days a week in an office. So many people were being denied a fulfilling career, just because they couldn't (or wouldn't) fit into the 9-to-5 mould. More than that, it just didn't make sense to me that companies were wilfully excluding such talented people from their workforce.

That's when Alex and I had a meeting of minds over a few Dark 'n Stormies :cocktail: and the idea of workstyle was born.

The couple of years that followed were a whirlwind of excitement – starting a business to prove workstyle can really work, learning how to be a mum with Finn, barely getting any sleep (on account of the baby), but loving every minute of it.

And then, as if life wasn't busy enough, I found out I was pregnant with twins! After the initial excitement (and sickness) of it all, we started to have a number of complications with the pregnancy. One of those was twin-to-twin transfusion syndrome, a condition where one foetus receives all of the blood from the shared placenta and the other receives none, putting both twins in serious danger. I had surgery when I was 23 weeks pregnant to laser the placenta as the only hope to save both of their lives.

The nine weeks that followed were like nothing I'd experienced before. I was on bed rest, with a husband at work, a toddler at nursery and two baby girls fighting for their lives inside me. And I felt powerless to do anything about it. It was such an awful, but thankfully brief, period of my life. I was physically exhausted and anxiety-ridden, but workstyle work was my escape for what would otherwise have felt like a very long and lonely time each day. It meant I could rest and give the pregnancy as much of my physical self as I could, but at any point during the day I could choose to open my laptop when I had the energy to escape into my workstyle world of work. I wasn't pitied or judged, I could choose to share or not share what was going on in my life, and no one was any the wiser that I was lying in bed, with debilitating morning sickness as well as anxiety, and taking a nap when I needed it. In those moments, I couldn't have been more grateful for workstyle work and the incredible community of workstylers that Alex and I had built – it played such a huge part in getting me through what in many other respects was a truly miserable time. I felt useful, distracted and, in spite of everything, fulfilled.

I will spare you the finer details, but against the odds both our daughters survived. The day Zoe and Megan came home from intensive care and we couldn't fit the double pram through the front door of our London flat was the day Nick and I agreed that, after years of discussion, we would move out of 'the big smoke' to a slightly smaller one – Bristol. We moved across the country without it having any impact on my work life, affording Nick the time to find work – it was exactly what we'd hoped for. Workstyle wins again.

Fast-forward three years to 2020, with three amazing children in tow, our family faced yet another challenge – out of the blue I was diagnosed with breast cancer. To say it was a shock would be an understatement. It was something I was completely unprepared for as a seemingly healthy 38-year-old, and it turned my world upside down.

This next part might not come as news to you, but it did to me: chemotherapy was brutal. It ravaged my body. Name the side effect and I had it. No amount of positive mindset could overcome this one. I've never known anything like it. Sometimes the worst part about being hooked up to a machine for five hours watching the drugs pump into my bloodstream was the sense of apprehension, knowing the awfulness that was to come. And again workstyle work was my outlet – I could escape into my digital working world to contribute as much or as little as I felt up to that day or week. It certainly helped to pass the time in the chemotherapy chair, and it also helped the cancer diagnosis not to define me, nor to completely take over my thoughts as I was so determined it wouldn't. When the radiotherapy started, I changed my workstyle again and Alex and I had a 20-minute chat every day while I drove to the hospital. It gave me something specific to look forward to and filled my head with all sorts of brilliant work stuff, from the taxing to the mundane, to think about during the treatment. When you're feeling at an all-time low, being alone with your thoughts can be exhausting. Having something to focus on, a positive source of progress, helped me through it one day at a time.

That was February. In March the kids went back to nursery and school, and I was back by myself again, but not really back *to* myself, so I worked a little bit, giving myself time for counselling and to process everything that had happened in the past year (there was the small matter of a global pandemic in among this mayhem, too, that had meant the family had all been isolating at home for five months). In April my hair started to grow back. A pixie cut was never in my plan but the quick drying time was a definite bonus and helped motivate me to start swimming regularly again.

By May I was ready to look again at my workstyle in order to fit a little more work around my new life and priorities. I talked to Nick, and to Alex, and reflected on how I wanted to divide up my time. I decided that in the morning I would do the school and nursery run, then go for a swim, then tidy the kitchen before starting work (tidy kitchen, tidy mind :woman_in_lotus_position:). On Wednesdays I would spend the day with Megan and on Thursdays be with Zoe. I would work three short days a week, starting at 10.30am and stopping in time to pick up Finn from school, with a bit of tinkering with messages for an hour a couple of evenings a week. The kids are now all at school, and I update my workstyle one school term at a time, adapting as my medication dictates my day, and fitting work around my health and my family. Gradually I am returning to my energetic and eternally optimistic self again.

From the beginning of my workstyle journey, I have always preached that life changes and your workstyle should change with it. But I couldn't have predicted how dramatically my own life would change over the following few years to really put this to the test.

What started as a way to make work fit around parenting Finn has carried me through having three children, two life-changing illnesses and a move across the country. So many things that, according to society, would have made me a poor fit for a successful and fulfilling career, and yet, thanks to embracing workstyle, I feel like I'm thriving.

Workstyle story: Alex Hirst

Dad, husband, entrepreneur, mental health advocate, village dweller, workstyle campaigner and occasional magical unicorn

I've always been what psychologists would call a 'highly sensitive person'. My genetics mean that I have a heightened capacity for processing information and can therefore feel everything more deeply. It's part of what makes me a good leader, helping with planning and decision making from a position of total awareness, but it's also partly responsible for the emotional overwhelm that caused me to burn out.

Back in 2012 I had a leading role in a start-up creative agency, working ten hours a day and commuting two hours a day, five days a week.

When I look back on it now, I was completely entrenched in presenteeism – the outdated 'bums on seats' notion that values time spent 'at' work over anything else. I'm ashamed to say that I was one of the people who perpetuated the idea of being present but would soon come to understand the negative impact it can have. I always like to think of myself as someone who leads by example, by actions rather than words. This was no different. I made sure I was the first in and last out of the office, feeling I wasn't giving everything I could give unless I was in the office for a full 50 hours a week. I could lie and say it was a terrible time, but for the most part it wasn't. I loved my job and the feeling of importance it gave me. Working in a start-up, I knew that my every action had a direct impact on the business – it fuelled me and I felt I was 'succeeding'.

Two years later everything changed and I fell out of love with work. I became completely disconnected from what I was doing and a less enjoyable person to be around. I was barely able to string a few words together to answer even a simple question like 'What shall we have for dinner?' I became increasingly ambivalent to the highs and lows of life and work. Not even winning the office foosball competition could shift the numb feeling that had replaced my usually heightened emotions.

Having been on fire, I was now burned out.

I still can't pinpoint why it happened. It might have been that I was too emotionally invested, the flip side of the coin within start-up life. Maybe it was hitting a low after the intense high of marrying my wonderful wife, Sarah. Mostly, though, I think it was that my relationship with work was based on how many hours I spent in the office without really understanding why. Eventually I reached breaking point.

Sarah sat me down one evening to voice her concerns about my work life and my mental health. She said I'd become a 'shadow of my former self' – words that have really stuck with me. And she was right.

I had let my relationship with work come before every other relationship in my life. Now that even work wasn't fulfilling me, I didn't have a lot left to give. I was detached 24 hours a day, and even a fully switched-off holiday to Spain to escape everything couldn't rectify my state of mind, as much as Sarah and I both wanted it to. To this day I still can't tell you much about that holiday. I barely remember it and it's upsetting to know that during that time I was so detached from the present that I wasn't forming any actual memory of it.

I came to the realisation that many of my struggles came from my own thoughts about work itself, and in talking it through with Sarah I found that I needed a new psychological contract with work which valued the quality of my output instead of the hours of input. Airing that idea with Lizzie one night in the pub has become one of the most defining moments of my life and was the beginning of what we now campaign for.

In the year that followed, Lizzie and I started Hoxby, a social enterprise where everyone has the complete freedom to choose when and where they work. I felt personally connected to the work we were doing for the first time in a long time. My success was, and continues to be, measured on the number of people working in a workstyle way and living their best lives. The number of hours I spend at my computer now has absolutely no relevance. I've found a truly sustainable way to fuel my motivation every day.

Since adopting my own workstyle in 2014, my mental health has improved with every year that has passed. At first it was due to the control

I had over my own schedule – I'd never felt as free from pressure or bureaucracy as the first time my workstyle allowed me to go to the dentist on a Tuesday at 2.30. :ouch:

Sarah and I took that freedom of control further towards fulfilling our dreams when we decided to travel the world with our eight-month-old daughter, Olivia. A trip of a lifetime that simply couldn't have happened without the freedom for me to work while we travelled. Our time in Australia, Singapore and Hong Kong was liberating. To the point that, when we returned, we knew we could take the bold step to uproot our city lives and move from London to the countryside, fulfilling another life ambition to raise our children in the peace of village life, closer to our families.

It was revolutionary for us. Workstyle enabled us to lead a family life that gave each of us the best of each other. I would take Olivia and my son, Tate, to school in the morning and then work until Sarah returned home having picked them up. I chose my workstyle so that I could be available to both of my children; when they were at home, I was at home with them. We would hang out together as a family until they finally went to sleep. I had the time to be their handyman, their man-mountain, their cycling instructor, den builder, paint-brush cleaner and occasionally their magical unicorn friend. It was priceless time spent in the company of my favourite people that many dads simply never get, so I was more than happy to trade it for a little time spent working in the evening.

I am beyond grateful to have been present for every milestone moment that I, like most parents, almost missed out on: their births, their first steps and first words (even if Tate's was, somewhat disappointingly, 'Mama'). Together, Sarah and I continuously evolve our workstyles so that we can both continue to enjoy our work while always being available for our kids' every need – and there are many!

Inspired by our travels with Olivia, we are now planning to use the school holidays to explore the world. Why wait until retirement when we can work from anywhere with wifi and a good cup of coffee, modelling the life we promote every day? Who knows how that will go, especially with two unpredictable young children, but it's our choice to make and our journey to take, together.

It is ironic that it took a toxic relationship with work for me to realise that the most important things to me are my relationships – with my wife, my children, Lizzie and everyone else around me. I make sure I stick to the workstyle I've set for myself so that I can be the best version of myself for them, whether that's as a present partner who shares an equal load, a friend to talk to, a leader who understands life's challenges or, on occasion, a magical unicorn.

Parenting, cancer, travelling, illness, mental health and rural living have all played a role in our workstyle stories. As you will see from the other workstyle stories throughout this book, there are many others with very different but equally impactful changes to their lives that have been helped by having a workstyle of their own.

Hopefully now you can understand why we care so deeply about this subject and are therefore eager to understand what we've learned about workstyle along the way. Read on, workstyler...

THREE

A broken system of work

The current system of work has run its course, and there are loads of reasons why. We could write a whole book on this alone, but we're eternal optimists and want to stay positive, so instead we're going to focus on just a few pivotal things that make the case for workstyle: the origins of work, the conception of the eight-hour day, the changes over the 200 years since, and why flexible working could actually be hindering progress for all of us.

The origins of work – let's journey back 12,000 years

It makes sense to start 12,000 years ago, right? Of course it does! Our modern-day understanding of work began around then with the first agricultural revolution. As our hunter-gathering ancestors turned their hands to farming, they created a whole range of tasks to be done, not only to survive but also to navigate the literal feast-or-famine nature of their work. :lots_on_your_plate:

Hunter-gatherers had generally viewed their environment as eternally provident and typically 'worked' for only three to five hours a day to meet their immediate needs. By work we mean gathering berries, making tools or hunting wild animals, which ironically sounds more like a non-working day with the children to us. However, the ancient farmers who followed them had to work much harder to turn their land into a productive environment during the good months to feed themselves. And because of the small number of crops and livestock they depended on, they became much more vulnerable to changes in climate, pests and disease, which meant they had to produce more than was necessary in order to store some to survive in tougher months (has the phrase 'make hay while the sun shines' been around for 12,000 years? :thinking_face:).

In such times, there was no shortcut to producing more food from the land. Until the introduction of technology many thousands of years later, the fact of the matter was that your output was entirely dependent on the time that you put into the process. The more you put in, the more you got out – literally reaping what you sowed. The trialling of new methods was a life-threatening risk and a potential waste of precious resources, and so 'painting on the cave wall' brainstorming sessions to come up with new ideas probably wouldn't have been encouraged by the village elders. Forcing the environment to produce enough to sustain you and your immediate family was pretty tough going, and so the idea that hard work equalled output – and subsequently that individual success is a reflection of the amount of time you put into your work – is perhaps the most obvious of the first agricultural revolution's many social, economic and cultural legacies.

As you can see from the chart, over the next few thousand years population growth was slow, and it was slow progress on the evolution of work, too, so we're going to skip all of that period and leap forward

THE WORKSTYLER'S GUIDE
TO WORKING REVOLUTIONS

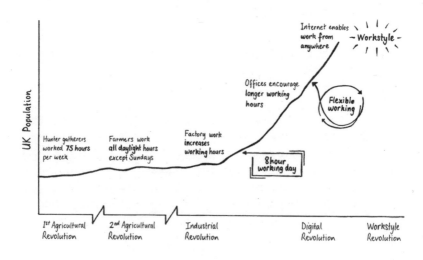

to our next piece of relevant history, a time where the population started booming and work really turned a corner.

Introducing, Sir Bobby O...

Just over 200 years ago Sir Bobby O conceived, and led, a crusade that fundamentally changed the world of work. Robert Owen (1771–1858) – as he was actually called – was a great social reformer who not only had progressive ideas but was also in the privileged position of having his own manufacturing mill where he could test them. (We were thinking of setting up our own cotton mill but decided that launching workstyle through providing professional and creative services was more appropriate for the 21st-century service economy we are living in. :laptop:)

To give some context, life 200 years ago was tough. Drought and famine were common, and a predictable, stable wage was appealing to hundreds of thousands of people who gave up a rural life and moved to cities during the industrial revolution to work in factories. A lot of our working practices which were established in that era are still in place in some form today, from clocking in and clocking out to Taylor's scientific management principles which advocate for there being one 'right' way to do each task independent of any human judgement,[1] and even the fact that football matches start at 3 p.m. on Saturday, which allowed people to get to kick-off after the 2 p.m. finish time for factory workers introduced by the Factories Act of 1850. Though we might think of them as our 'rights' today, concepts such as the weekend, holiday allowances and the leisure industry are not innate to our human existence but instead have been fought for over the past 170 years, and developed and codified in our language and culture as a direct response to industrialisation.

Slowly, however, as the workforce became more prosperous and confident, they started to question some of the working practices they had earlier chosen to accept. Over time, workers clubbed together to make incremental gains in claiming back the time lost to the factory floor and working in servitude to the titans of industry. To give you an idea of the cultural norms of yesteryear, some unscrupulous mill owners would make their factory workers work longer than they were paid for by winding back the clocks an hour without them knowing it.[2] Not cool!

Enter Sir Bobby O, an early version of Alex and Lizzie but in silk jersey pantaloons and a frock coat, who saw the bigger picture of work and life. He believed the 24-hour day should be divided into three equal parts and came up with the concept of 'eight hours' labour, eight hours' recreation and eight hours' rest'. Governments and factory owners at the time thought this was outrageous. In the context of the Lanarkshire mills this was revolutionary, and in the absence of social media to spread the word, Bobby's essays, talks and most importantly actions in his own mill eventually sparked a complete rethink of how people worked.[3] By testing his ideas in practice, he was able to prove not only that his concept was better for people but that treating people better was also beneficial for business, improving wellbeing while also increasing productivity.[4]

Legislation restricting the working day to 'just' ten hours was introduced in 1847, but this was limited to women and children (any whiff of gender equality and the overdue outlawing of child labour were some way off at this point). In response to a rising tradition of worshipping 'Saint Monday'[5] (absenteeism on a Monday to cope with weekend hangovers), factory owners made a deal with their male workers that they could leave early on a Saturday – around 2 p.m. – as long as they promised to return not too hung over and ready for work bright and early on Monday morning. Workers banded together to campaign for more leisure time and were rewarded for their efforts by claiming an extra half day for themselves. Perhaps most importantly, they gave it a name – the weekend – which was added to the *Oxford English Dictionary* in 1878 (workstyle will surely be added soon to further bolster the importance of the 'w' section!).

Bank holidays and public holidays came into existence around the same time, which allowed an increase in leisure time and even spawned entire new industries, with music halls, theatres, weekend escapes and tourism all giving rise to the 'hair being let down' era which has continued ever since. :partying_face: Henry Ford gained fame and popularity as the first industrialist to instigate the 40-hour work week in his factories in 1914 along with a huge increase in average pay, and by 1920 the average working week was down to 'just' 50 hours (!). It's no coincidence that life expectancy in the UK increased sharply at this time[6] – changing the way we work not only changes our quality of life, it also affects how long we live. More on that later. :elixir:

So Sir Bobby O's eight-hour day was transformational for the workforce at the time. He was one of the first social reformers to recognise that work should not be the entirety of people's lives, and that it may even be more productive for people not to be consumed by it. But we think he would be turning in his grave to know that more than 200 years later we are still following the same principle of an eight-hour, 9-to-5 working day. Society, technology and the work we actually do have changed beyond recognition in that time but working practices haven't. It's mind-boggling when you think about all the progress we've made over the past two centuries that we haven't taken greater leaps forward in the way we work.

To really hammer this point home, we want to give you a rundown of some of our favourite inventions and innovations. Since 1817 humans have invented electricity. This spark of ingenuity gave us the light bulb to stop us burning the midnight oil. We traded horses for automobiles and landed on the surface of the moon. Greenwich Mean Time coordinated us across the world, while aeroplanes could take us around it. Planes defied gravity and no doubt inspired the invention of underwired bras which did the same. Telephones liberated us to speak to someone beyond the length of our cup and string while radio enabled us to broadcast to everyone. Penicillin and many other medical breakthroughs doubled our average life expectancy.[7] Personal computers, mobile phones and the internet switched our analogue world for a digital one. We made staplers, then made stapleless staplers. We made plastic and then wished we hadn't. We replaced light bulbs with

LEDs and replaced the entire manufacturing economy with a service economy. Isn't it embarrassing to think that through all this human progress, our collective imagination has only managed to conceive of adding a little more flexibility to the basic 9-to-5 way in which we work?

Why flexible working is our nemesis :horns:

When we talk about workstyle it is often confused with flexible working, so there's one more element of the history of work it's important to include here. Let's fast-forward to the 1950s to look at flexible working and how it is holding back the true individualisation of work.

Flexible working has been around for more than 70 years. It was the brainchild of the great industrialist and cereal maker W. K. Kellogg (1850–1951), who allowed his workers to change their shift patterns to six hours rather than eight hours each. So far, so progressive, but President Franklin D. Roosevelt's dictate during the Second World War that all factories needed to be operating at full capacity brought the initiative to an abrupt end. It was revived in West Germany in the 1960s by management consultant Christel Kammerer and first implemented by aerospace firm Messerschmitt-Bölkow-Blohm in 1967 because traffic was so bad around the factory that workers were frequently turning up late, harming productivity. (Kammerer, like us, hated nothing more than sitting in traffic – she probably had children who liked listening to the *Frozen* soundtrack on repeat, too. :eyes_rolling:)

Initially called 'gliding time' or the German *Gleitzeit*, the idea was for management to agree to a period of time in the morning within which employees could choose to arrive, and a window in the afternoon during which they could leave. Initially, this period was between 7 and 8 in the morning and between 4 and 6 at the end of the working day. So, the first foray into flexible working barely allowed an hour either side of the typical working pattern, and things haven't improved a whole lot since.

The exceptional trailblazer Stephanie 'Steve' Shirley set up an organisation for women working flexibly and exclusively from home in 1962 that grew to 8,500 employees – why her crusade didn't inspire many more organisations to follow suit completely baffles us. Instead of the revolution this should have inspired, evolution prevailed and growing traffic congestion and the oil and gas crisis gradually increased the demand for flexible working and 'telecommuting' in the 1970s and 1980s. It was only in the 1990s that legislation was passed for flexible work in the US, and only in 2014 that the UK introduced the universal right to request flexible working (after 26 weeks of continuous employment with the same employer). Even now, this right is just to *request* flexible working, not for employers to have to grant it.

When we talk about workstyle people often exclaim, 'The 9-to-5 has been dead for a long time!' or 'Loads of people I know work flexibly.' And on the surface that seems like a good thing. Yes, people are working more flexibly, but it is actually slowing down our progress towards a healthier, more productive life and a more inclusive society.

Forgive our negativity here, but we want to lay out clearly the three main reasons flexible working isn't the answer:

1. It is flexing around an outdated, industrial-age system.

2. It isn't creating change fast enough, or at all for huge groups in society.

3. It is creating dangerous divisions between flexible workers and everyone else.

We're going to look at each of these in a bit more detail.

1. It is flexing around an outdated, industrial-age system

Without question the furthering of flexible working comes from the right motivation, to give people the freedom to adjust their working hours to fit their individual circumstances, but it is only doing so in a very limited way. It is, at best, a soggy sticking plaster on the more fundamental wound that society is still endorsing a trumped-up, one-size-fits-all system of work. In short, *flexible* working requires an *inflexible* system of work in order to exist.

Starting work an hour 'later', not working Fridays or working from home on a Tuesday – flexible working is always characterised by how it varies from the 9-to-5, five-days-a-week, office-based regime that is a nasty hangover from the industrial era. :headache: And it is always just that – a variation on the 200-year-old system rather than a radical departure.

Do any of your friends who work flexibly only work during their baby's nap times? Or just work term time? Or live in the depths of a Czech forest? It turns out that flexible working doesn't have quite that level of flexibility. Workstyle does. :drops_microphone: Flexible working is anchored in the traditional working mindset and can never be the individualised system of work that we believe is necessary now that we are in the globally connected and universally accessible digital age of work. We are often reminded of how different the mindset of a workstyler is from that of someone who works flexibly when we talk about working three days a week. A workstyler might respond, 'That's great, what do you do with the other four days?', but even the greatest champions of flexible working usually say, 'That's great, what do you do with the other two days?'

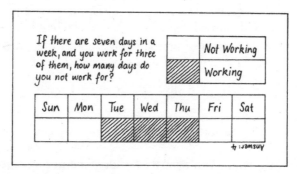

If there are seven days in a week, and you work for three of them, how many days do you not work for?

	Not Working
	Working

Sun	Mon	Tue	Wed	Thu	Fri	Sat

Answer: 4

Even with flexibility, whole tranches of society remain excluded from work, and even many of those who are included are unhappy.[8] More on this later. The idea that flexible working is the solution is in fact the biggest risk for the progress we need. What we desperately need now is to make wholesale systemic change to move from something masquerading as individualised to a new and truly individualised system of work. We have been held back from more revolutionary change by organisations believing 'tweaking work at the edges' through flexible working is enough. It ticks the box, shows they are doing something, allows them to maintain the status quo, and lets them off the hook of needing to fundamentally change working practices to be more inclusive and more fit for the time we live in.

Geek box: The legacy of the agricultural revolution and industrial age in how people think about work

By Richard Donkin, author of The History of Work *and* The Future of Work

Over the past 350 years economists, politicians and social commentators have often predicted the number of hours we work would fall thanks to advances in technology, efficiency and productivity. In 1776 Adam Smith thought that 'pretty machines' would in time 'facilitate and abridge labour' (Smith, 1776)[9] and a few years later Benjamin Franklin opined that four hours a day ought to be enough to produce 'all the necessities and comforts of life' (Butterfield, 1951).[10] In 1930 John Maynard Keynes infamously predicted that by the early 21st century, technology would bring us to the 'promised land' of material prosperity without anyone needing to work more than 15 hours in a week (Keynes, 2010),[11] leaving abundant time for leisure. But Smith, Franklin, Keynes and their peers failed to consider the forces of economic expansion, growth of consumerism, establishment of government institutions and other elements of human behaviour. We are creatures of habit with complex social needs – to be recognised, to influence others, and to feel a sense of purpose and belonging.

So it is no surprise that the legacy of agricultural and industrial work still dominates our way of working today, underpinned by three flawed but fundamental understandings that create or overlook a range of inequalities:

1. The belief that people need to work together at the same time in the same place (synchronously).

2. A preference for measuring work in dedicated blocks of time – the tyranny of hours.
3. Working hours, place of work, even the way people should dress are governed by employer dictate and other social constructs.

First, the idea that we all need to be together at the same time, working synchronously, is rooted in the natural rhythms and physical requirements of agriculture, such as the harvest season or state of the tide. It's why we still have long summer holidays, because children were needed to gather crops and couldn't be allowed time off to go to school (Hall, 1989).[12] The factories that replaced cottage industries in the industrial revolution could house larger machinery, were closer to a source of power and had better transportation links (Griffin, 2018).[13] Since then we've struggled to break with the notion that work is a place we need to go to.

Second, while timekeeping may be as ancient as the seasonal clock of Stonehenge aiding agricultural practices, the industrial revolution transformed our concept of time, away from the rhythms of nature towards tightly organised 'shifts' where we worked in blocks of time to operate machinery. Pre-industrialisation, work was barely formalised and occurred on a needs-must basis. With the invention of factories, employers borrowed precepts from the military to co-ordinate people into regimented production lines. Technological advancements propelled these changes. Taking advantage of more precise timekeeping devices (the pendulum clock was invented by Christiaan Huygens in 1656), factory owners insisted their workers 'clock in' and 'clock out' and regularly docked them up to two days' pay for turning up late to work (Clark, 2005).[14] Workers in an Arkwright mill in the late 18th century worked six 13-hour shifts a week and this was only limited to 10 hours for women and children by the Textile Factory Act in 1844 (Suzman, 2021).[15] While working conditions and hours have improved dramatically since, the pattern of working a daily shift, and our preference for measuring work in blocks of time as the easiest way to quantify remuneration, lives on.

The third influential legacy of the industrial revolution is the control that workers gave up to their employers when working in a factory.

Not only were shift patterns set by factory managers (Suzman, 2021),[16] but thanks to Frederick Taylor and his 'Principles of Scientific Management' (1919),[17] workers were commoditised and corralled into cubicled offices like battery chickens. Tasks became routinised and standardised in the name of efficiency, with a manager's role being to ensure compliance with the 'one best way' of doing things despite limited evidence of its effectiveness (Dignan, 2019).[18]

Fundamentally, the industrial revolution kickstarted economic growth, stressed the prioritisation of profits and established the principle of consumer-led growth, consolidated now in modern politics and policy, which influence how work is done. This has become especially apparent during the Covid-19 pandemic. While easier transfer of information through the internet has liberated us from the need to go to a fixed place of work, attitudes and habits are ingrained in our governance. As governments are based in cities, the leaders of society see half-empty restaurants, half-empty trains and less consumption, and fear that is bad for the economy. So government policies are designed to encourage working together, in the same place, at the same time, to support an economic system designed for the industrial age.

All of these historical factors shape our attitudes, structures and ways of doing things. But while the legacy of industrialisation is persistent, its power is fading and the way we think about work, consumption and the wider environment is shifting, not to that of a once-hoped-for leisure society but to a society framed by greater choice in its relationship with work and greater responsibility in its relationship with the environment.

2. Flexible working isn't creating change fast enough, or at all for some people

Flexible working is here and yet there are huge swathes of society who are still excluded from work. Flexible working isn't working.

The statistics speak for themselves – flexible working has been around for 70 years, but the gap for those with autism who want to work and those who do is actually widening[19] and unemployment for those with mental health problems is worsening, too.[20] The majority of retiring workers would prefer to keep working in some capacity but leave because of ill health, caring responsibilities or redundancy, when they could have been supported to stay in work.[21] The list goes on... While the incremental change that flexible working seeks to drive may be helping specific groups, namely working parents (though even this is a more complex debate[22]), it is not solving the problems of many groups who continue to be fundamentally excluded from work for other reasons. This is not just a case of 'any progress is good' – we've tried that and flexible working hasn't changed things in any meaningful way for these important groups who together make up a large proportion of our society. In fact, for some excluded groups it hasn't created any change at all.

The reality is that flexible working is not equally available for everyone. It depends on your circumstances, the organisation you work for, and often whether you can write a 'business case' for it. This is not just about policies or supportive legal frameworks; often it's also ultimately dependent on your line manager – whether they can empathise with your desire to work flexibly, how far they are happy to support you in reshaping your responsibilities to fit with flexible working, and whether they have the time and headspace to help you to fit your work around your life. What this means is that flexible working is still the preserve of the few, and particularly parents, or those with very specific requirements meaning they need to work outside of the 'norm', but even then they often need to be 'flexible' about being flexible. :cap_in_hand:

For those with full-time jobs who have the right to *request* flexible working, this is not a guarantee that it will be agreed to. In fact, so long as they treat all individuals in the same way, which really only means being seen to follow due process, most organisations are within their rights to refuse these requests for various subjective business reasons, ranging from the burden of additional costs to a perceived detrimental effect on quality or performance.[23] This explains why just 30 per cent of requests for flexible working were accepted in 2019, while flexi-time was still unavailable to 58 per cent of UK employees, according to the TUC.[24] There are countless more people who don't even try to get flexible working because the onus is on them to make a case for it and they don't have the confidence to ask – one survey found this to be true for 43 per cent of women,[25] and we're confident many men would be lacking in confidence, too.

Experimenting with four-day working weeks and shorter working days is seen as progressive, but it continues to miss the point that we're all individuals and so any hours-based working system that is unilaterally imposed doesn't have room for individual circumstances or individual preference and therefore falls short of the leaps forward we could make. The costs that we are seeing for individuals and society call for much more of a radical shift in how we work.

Geek box: The slow progress of flexible working in driving inclusion at work

By Dr Laura Radcliffe, Senior Lecturer in Organisational Behaviour, University of Liverpool Management School

In the UK parents and carers have had 'the right to request' flexible working arrangements, which are policies and practices designed to offer greater control over when, where, how long and how much they engage in paid work, since 2003, and this was extended to all employees with 26 weeks of service or more in 2014. However, in 2021, following experiences during the coronavirus pandemic, a Flexible Working Bill proposing flexible working as a day-one right was discussed in Parliament.

While this seems like a potentially positive step forward, it is also a particularly pertinent time to reflect on what we already know about the real benefits of such flexible working. These policies and practices have promised, for quite some time now, to fix an array of organisational and societal problems, from levelling the playing field for men and women in the workplace and more broadly enabling more inclusive organisations, to enabling a better work–life balance for all. Research does indeed report some benefits, such as increased employee satisfaction (Wheatley, 2017),[26] employee engagement (Anderson and Kelliher, 2009)[27] and an improvement in organisational performance (Beauregard and Henry, 2009).[28]

However, despite these positive findings, other studies reveal a much darker side to flexible working. Indeed, much research demonstrates how, on many counts, the UK's flexible working narrative has over-promised, underdelivered and, worse still, actually exacerbated existing problems, while also creating entirely new ones. For instance, research highlights how flexible working can in fact lead to an increased workload, extra stress and the inability to 'switch off' from work (Kelliher and Anderson, 2010).[29] Where flexible working is considered predominantly as a way to benefit the business's bottom line, allowing employees to work flexibly, meaning they can work any time and anywhere, is all too often commensurate with ensuring employees are 'always on'.

This leads to extensive working, where employees are simply never 'away' from work, now infiltrating all times and spaces in employees' lives, thus depleting, rather than enriching, employee work–life balance (Putman et al., 2014).[30]

Similarly, rather than acting to increase equality and inclusivity at work, flexible working has often been shown to deepen and exacerbate workplace inequalities (Radcliffe and Cassell, 2014;[31] Chung and van der Horst, 2020[32]), with gender and maternal stereotypes affecting those who are encouraged and/or permitted to make use of flexible working (Chung, 2020),[33] accompanied by stigmatisation of those employees for taking advantage of what is viewed as an exception to the norm and an employee perk (Gatrell et al., 2014;[34] Stovell et al., 2017[35]).

Studies have also pointed out that flexible working policies and practices as they currently stand are limited, ironically, in terms of their flexibility, preventing them from being truly useful to diverse and shifting employee and societal needs. For instance, when considering the ageing workforce (Loretto and Vickerstaff, 2015),[36] changing generational expectations (Families and Work Institute, 2005),[37] health challenges and changes across the life course (Griffiths et al., 2013),[38] and the transitory and complex nature of today's families (Schaefer et al., 2020;[39] Radcliffe et al., 2021[40]), current flexible working practices leave much to be desired. Such studies point to the need for a much broader conceptualisation of 'flexibility', alongside a shift in the nature of how work is organised altogether. Importantly, reconceptualisations need to be born out of a genuine desire to support inclusivity at work, and a healthier society more broadly, moving beyond narrow and short-term 'bottom line' mindsets.

In summary, what existing research shows is that current flexible working policies and practices, and the way in which they are implemented in organisations, are problematic and rarely deliver on the promises they make. Further, it suggests that, if we are to truly develop more inclusive workplace cultures, which embrace varied and fluid individual circumstances, a real shake-up of the world of work such as the workstyle revolution would be required to make this a reality.

3. It is creating dangerous divisions between flexible workers and everyone else

In a previous job, when Lizzie worked flexibly (three days as a managing director in the office, four days as a mum at home), she always felt she missed out on all the most important stuff. The celebration of a new client win, a big announcement, someone debuting a new hairstyle, or the draw for the next-royal-baby-name sweepstake. In reality it probably wasn't all important, but she *felt* like it was. Even the silly or fun things affected how much she felt part of the team at work. This is in-group, out-group dynamics in action; Lizzie felt like she wasn't part of the 'main' group because she missed out on these moments of cultural inclusion.

Flexible working is saying that the 'normal' way to work is a traditional 9-to-5, five-day week and that those who work 'flexibly' by varying that are different or special in some way. In some businesses this is explicitly stated, in others it isn't, it's just how it feels. This creates an 'out-group' dynamic where the flexible workers are seen as less valuable employees by others and feel less valued themselves. This is important not only for the individuals but also for businesses: 93 per cent of employees who feel valued say they are motivated to do their best at work, whereas of those who don't feel valued, only 33 per cent would say the same.[41]

'Hybrid' working, a trend that started to emerge following the coronavirus pandemic, where everyone has a 'blend' of working and may, for instance, be mandated to be in the office two days a week, is the same. It creates two groups – those that are in the office and those that aren't. When we say flexible working is our nemesis, hybrid working is that nemesis's younger sibling. In both flexible and hybrid working there is a dominant group – for the former it's those who work 'full time' and for the latter it's those who work in the office (nobody wants to be the only one joining a meeting via video call when everyone else is in the room together :billy_no_mates:). But the point isn't *which* is the dominant group, it's having a dominant group at all which in itself creates tension and can lead to toxic behaviour. What we need is a system that gives individual choice to each person across the whole group – it's the same for everyone, because everyone can choose. It creates the much-needed level playing field and the level of inclusion we ought to be aspiring to.

Geek box: 'In-group, out-group' dynamics and the damage they can cause to individuals and businesses

By Joanna Wong, chartered occupational psychologist

The study of group dynamics and processes has a long history in the world of social psychology. This involves trying to understand the social process by which people interact and behave in a group environment. One of the early and most influential studies was Sherif's 1954 Robbers Cave experiment (Sherif et al., 1961).[42] Sherif looked at the way that intergroup conflict developed between groups of schoolboys, arbitrarily organised into two groups, the 'Rattlers' and the 'Eagles', while at summer camp. His research, and subsequent research by others such as Tajfel (Social Identity Theory[43]), tells us that even just being allocated into separate groups appears sufficient to generate stereotyping, competitiveness, conflict and suspicion of the 'out-group' – a deeply human reaction which can be difficult to overcome. While this study is old, it has helped us to understand how easily 'in-groups' and 'out-groups' can form in our societies and indeed in business. The way we respond to 'out-groups' is likely hard-wired through evolution, an innate preference for what is known and familiar, and the imperative to favour the survival of one's own 'tribe' – in-group 'favouritism'.

Applying a group dynamics lens to work enables us to see how easily well-intended policies to create flexibility for some within the workplace may inadvertently create unhelpful in-group and out-group dynamics. Leader Member Exchange theory further illuminates this domain, showing us how leaders and managers in businesses may inadvertently foster toxicity through allowing in-groups and out-groups to form among the individuals they lead, in part owing to their responses to different styles of behaviour. The bias towards favouring those 'like ourselves' threatens to further elevate bias and stereotyping, with significant detrimental effects on both individuals and the businesses they operate within.

It is easy, therefore, to see how some well-intended flexible working policies may have exaggerated existing in-group and out-group biases in the workplace. Those with flexibility, and those without. Those at home, those in the office and so on. Traditional organisational structures, particularly those within corporate behemoths, may unwittingly create multiple layers of siloed in-groups and out-groups. Today's movement is towards more inclusive, collaborative, even 'holacratic' (decentralised, self-organising, non-hierarchical) working practices, but structurally many organisations have not innovated to tackle some of these 'invisible forces' which seem to pull groups apart within their organisations rather than glue them together. Some of the sticking-plaster attempts organisations have made to implement 'flexible working' practices have tended to create more 'special groups', when really more systemic change and challenge to existing working structure, culture and norms might be required – creating a more 'workstyle' approach for all rather than special situations, more subgroups and associated antagonism for the few.

An example

Nowhere has the power of the group process been more apparent to me than during the pandemic. As was common in most schools in the UK, at the peak stage there was a mix of 'key worker' children and 'non-key worker' children in and out of school. In my son's class, 18 out of 30 children were 'in'. This created a host of group dynamics to handle. The school is an excellent one, but it is large and traditional. They did their best in the circumstances, however, and continued with known approaches – essentially full teaching for those in school and full school curriculum delivered to parents to 'teach' at home. This approach meant huge disparity between those 'in' full time and those 'out', and at times there is still a whiff of discord between key worker/non-key worker school groups which would not have been present pre-pandemic. Contrast this with an alternative approach. The school that adopted the digital-first policy. All children were taught live via video call. Those children of key workers, those without access to technology, and children with specific needs were able to join the video call in a classroom at school, while all the other children joined from home. A full shifting of the paradigm in this school enabled much more even participation for *all* in almost full education. This approach reduced the degree of disparity between groups and enabled everyone to focus on the singular unifying purpose of establishing a sufficiency of education for all.

I share this example because, while we can't always do much to get rid of in-groups and out-groups in the workplace, we can use technology and new thinking as a powerful lever in minimising their negative effects and consequences. Enabling everyone to define and fulfil their workstyle (not just the few), supported by technology and agile working practices, appears to offer a significant step towards the more participative and inclusive cultures we are striving for.

Individualised working, not compromise

And so our whistle-stop tour dissecting just a few relevant elements of the history of work comes to an end. Though the eight-hour day was a breakthrough in its time, the industrial system of work and the beliefs that accompany it are a relic of a bygone era which is creating a huge amount of unseen harm.

In the 70 or so years since its conception, flexible working has made progress only for some excluded groups and is now distracting the conversation from the more radical change that is needed. However widespread its adoption, it will never create the leaps forward in working practices that we need. We have a unique opportunity over the next decade to create a true revolution – a fundamental change in how we all work. But if we all keep feeling grateful for working 'flexibly' – coming in a bit late, leaving a bit early, or not working on a Friday – then we will miss the chance to be part of something far more transformational for us all.

We need to stop trying to evolve the industrial system into something better. It's time to rip it up completely and start again.

Chapter summary

- The premise of more work in, more yield out is grounded in our ancestors' experiences 12,000 years ago. Hunter-gatherers typically 'worked' for 3–5 hours a day, and then in the first agricultural revolution more structured working began to appear.

- The eight-hour day is more than 200 years old. It was first proposed by the social reformer Sir Robert Owen (Sir Bobby O), and at the time it was a progressive approach, but we think he'd be turning in his grave to know the majority of people are still working in this way more than two centuries later.

- Flexible working was first conceived of 70 years ago. While it comes from a place of positive intent, it isn't effective in three ways. First, it's flexing around an industrial age system rather than proposing more radical change to how we work. Second, it isn't creating change fast enough, and in some areas of inclusion we're actually moving backwards. And third, it's creating 'in-group, out-group' dynamics where it actually increases discrimination for some and makes many of those who work flexibly feel different from the norm.

From the mouth of a workstyler: 'I joined the workstyle revolution because... flexible working was a huge leap forward from my previous experience, but now in retrospect it was still much more rigid than workstyle working. Thirteen years ago, after having my second son, I went the whole workstyle hog and started working for myself, doing what I love in a way that works for me (and my clients). It feels great, and I'm really hoping that more employers start to change their mindset so they can attract, reward and keep the amazing amount of talent out there who want a workstyle that's right for them.' Katherine, London, UK

Fact to remember: The fundamentals of work are 12,000 years old,[44] the eight-hour day is more than 200 years old[45] and flexible working is 70 years old.[46]

And finally... Clearly Kammerer's children pre-dated *Frozen* by the best part of a century. We wonder what cassette they would have insisted on playing on repeat... :chewed_up_tape:

Play your part in the workstyle revolution

Reflect

☐ Reflect on the assumptions that underpin the way you work. How many can you identify?

Consider these questions:

1. *How much freedom do you truly have to fit your work around your life?*

2. *Which groups do you think could be excluded by the default working structure in your organisation or working group?*

3. *Are you in an in-group or an out-group at work? Are your assumptions and behaviours perpetuating the exclusion of some individuals or helping to create accessibility and inclusion in the workplace?*

4. *Does the way you work serve your life or are you working this way because that's how it's always been done?*

Act

☐ Now that you are aware of your assumptions, consider three ways that you could start to tackle these. For example, if you identified the assumption that meetings must be conducted face to face, can you experiment and run a meeting remotely? Or if you assumed that you must work 9-to-5, the same hours as your colleagues, can you try changing your working hours to see how it impacts your productivity, happiness and ability to collaborate?

☐ Read more about Sir Bobby O's social reform and ideas at WorkstyleRevolution.com.

Inspire

☐ If you identify with the in-group at work, talk to someone who might be in the out-group about how you could work together better. How can you break down the silos? If you identify with the out-group, talk to someone in the in-group to do the same thing.

☐ Do you have any friends that are currently excluded from work? Why might that be? Is there anything you can do to help? (One thing you could do is to give them this book when you have finished reading it, or keep it for yourself and buy them a less dog-eared copy!)

FOUR

Why 2014 was a magical year

Over the years we've pondered why we didn't start the workstyle revolution earlier, but in truth, even if we'd wanted to, the conditions we needed wouldn't have been there.

The year 2014 was a magical one in lots of ways – Lizzie had her first child and Alex got married, #NoMakeUpSelfies raised millions for Cancer Research, Conchita Wurst won the Eurovision Song Contest and Malala Yousafzai became the youngest ever winner of the Nobel Peace Prize. Meanwhile, not making the headlines, we noticed some important changes taking place that created the opportunities that exist today to fundamentally change the way we all work, for ever. This is a great chance to introduce you to our first complex, scientifically grounded hand gesture to help you remember the 'triangle of opportunity'. :nerd:

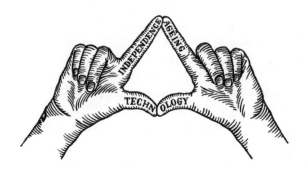

In 2014 there were three big changes afoot: the ageing population was getting more attention, technology was starting to redefine how we could collaborate and communicate, and our independence in how we worked was undergoing a fundamental shift. We're going to look at each of these factors in more detail as they paved the way for the creation of workstyle.

OPPORTUNITY ONE: The ageing population requires us to change how we work

Worldwide, people aged 60 years or over increased from 8.6 per cent in 1980 to 12 per cent in 2014, and this figure is projected to rise to 21 per cent in 2050.[1] Since 1840 our life expectancy has been increasing by roughly 2–3 years every decade[2] as a result of some pretty incredible scientific progress, as well as improvements in health awareness, sanitation and nutrition. Today reaching 100 is no longer the monumental event it once was, and in the future it's likely to become a common occurrence – 100ths will be the new 40ths. :cake_overcrowded_with_candles:

Demographers forecast that, if these trends continue, half of the children born today might expect to live until they are 104.[3] Yes, it blows our minds, too. The British monarch, who writes a letter to anyone who reaches 100, may need to review their duties to make more time for letter writing (while upholding one's workstyle and ensuring one spends enough time with the corgis, of course).

In 2014 Lynda Gratton and Andrew Scott were writing their book *The 100 Year Life*,[4] explaining how this fundamentally changes how we view our lives and the stages of life that most people will go through, highlighting the requirement to reshape how we work and how we view our careers. When we are all living longer, unless each of us radically increases the amount of money we save (which is simply not going to be possible in practice for many of us with increasing costs of living as well as mortgages, student loans and other debts to repay), then it's fair to assume the ratio of the years we work to the years we spend in retirement will need to remain approximately the same. Gratton and Scott argue this means that in the past, where we might have retired at 65 expecting to live until we are 75 (funding a 10-year retirement from a 45-year-career), if we're now expecting to live to 100 and entering the job market at 20, all else being equal we'll need to be working until we're nearly 85. And yet in 2018 it was estimated that more than a million people aged over 50 who wanted to work were prevented from doing so by outdated work practices and age discrimination.[5] Keeping us all in work until we are 85 requires a radically different working system.

As the population ages, a higher proportion of the workforce is nearing retirement. This creates major issues for businesses, too. In 2014, 25 per cent of BMW workers were less than 15 years away from retirement – a figure that was expected to rise quickly to more than 35 per cent by 2020.[6] As the case study below highlights, Unilever is in the same predicament, with a significant proportion of its workforce nearing retirement. For the first time it is becoming a business imperative to find new ways of retaining workers as they get older. There simply aren't enough people to do all the jobs that need doing if they don't.

Better retention of those over the age of 60 also leads to improved knowledge retention and lower recruitment costs, as well as better value through access to the best talent across age groups.[7] Productivity gains can also be made through intergenerational working that teams industry veterans and learned experts with intelligent naivety and fresh enthusiasm.[8] :chart_with_upwards_trend:

And the upside is significant – $3.5 trillion could be added to OECD economies simply by encouraging older workers to stay in the workforce for longer (including a 5 per cent boost in GDP for the UK alone[9]). The UK economy is facing a predicted 2.6 million labour shortfall by 2030, due largely to the number of older people leaving the workforce.[10] It makes for a pretty compelling case to reshape how we work around our demographic changes to find new ways to help older people to engage in work for longer.

Case study: U-Work – how Unilever is retaining experienced talent through the freedom to choose

By Placid Jover, Vice President of Human Resources Latin America & New Employment Models, and Morag Lynagh, Global Future of Work Director, Unilever

At Unilever, we see that the world of work is changing and want to do the right thing for our business and our people. In the UK we recognised that almost a third of our workforce would reach retirement age in the next five years, while millennials want to experience working for other organisations and people are increasingly looking for a more personalised employment experience. These changes are the driver behind us creating and pioneering new employment models.

First launched in the UK and now rolling out in other markets, U-Work is an example of this. We pay a retainer and in return the employee commits to working a minimum amount of time each year. As well as additional pay at the rate for the job for each assignment worked, employees receive a benefits package (e.g. medical cover, pension, funds to pay for their learning). This is different from the package that regular employees receive but still provides security. It's available to existing Unilever employees and alumni, giving the individual flexibility with security and Unilever access to a talented pool of people who know our business. This satisfies both older, more experienced workers who are increasingly choosing to work for longer but wanting to gradually reduce how much they work, and also younger people who are looking for meaningful jobs with more flexibility. So far we have 75 people working in the U-Work programme globally, most of these in the UK where U-Work was first launched.

Heidi, who worked for Unilever for 16 years before leaving and starting her own furniture restoration business, has returned through U-Work. She says, 'I wasn't looking for regular full-time or part-time employment. U-Work employment can run alongside my lifestyle and business while allowing me to stay connected to

Unilever. I feel loyalty is built into the concept as people feel part of the family.'

Models like these we're trialling at Unilever are surprisingly rare. We're not aware of any other large organisations doing anything like this. In a fast-moving world, U-Work supports our move to a more agile way of working and resourcing. In return the employee has a minimum guaranteed amount of pay every year, and this is increased depending on how many assignments the employee chooses to work on.

U-Work is different from part-time employment; it's a lifestyle choice. How each person works is agreed by the assignment line manager and employee based on the needs of both parties. Employees dip in and out of assignments, usually with a break in between. It works for employees across all generations who are looking for the freedom to work in the way that suits them best – for those who want to phase into retirement, or have family commitments, or who want to study, travel or be more entrepreneurial and work for other organisations, too. We are proud to be pioneering this initiative to reinvent work and are moving towards working in a more workstyle way.

There are also broader societal implications if we fail to adapt to the ageing population. In the UK the number of people of 'pension age' is increasing at almost triple the rate of people of 'working age'.[11] As the ratio of dependants to workers increases, the support system that has helped past generations will no longer be sustainable – there simply won't be enough tax income to fund the pensions and social care that will be needed. And at the same time the threshold for a 'living pension' is getting higher as the cost of living increases.

As our life expectancy increases, where a nation state can't fund pensions and social care, and families and communities can't give the support they need, older people will *need* to continue working in order to remain financially independent for longer and this, in turn, creates a requirement to reshape our system of work to facilitate an older workforce being able to fully participate in it.

Geek box: Why we need to retire the idea of retirement!

By Michelle Hawkins-Collins, ageing well specialist, gerontologist and founder of The Wisdom Space

Stephen Hawking once described life as being empty without work because it gives meaning and purpose. It is no surprise that people therefore find it difficult to accept that they need to retire because they wake up one morning and hit the chronological age that some-one, somewhere, at some point in time, deemed to be 'old'. The word 'retirement' comes from the French word *retirer*, which means 'to with-draw', and in this case withdraw from something that gives your life meaning and purpose. The whole concept of retirement is not only damaging for individuals, it is damaging to society.

Let's start with some context on why chronological age should not define us. Global life expectancy has increased steadily over the last 200 years. When the UK state pension was introduced in 1907, life expectancy at birth was 40 years for men and 43 years for women. By 2017 this had more than doubled to 84 and 87 years respectively (PPI, 2017).[12] This means that 65-year-olds today have a whole new phase of life that didn't exist for many people a generation ago. We simply cannot compare a 65-year-old today with a 65-year-old even a few decades ago. And yet, despite these gains in health and longevity, retirement and pension ages have barely changed since the concept of retirement was introduced over a century ago.

Add to this the fact that we become more diverse not less diverse with age given our different experiences and expectations, and you start to realise how misguided it is to design work and pension policies around chronological age as a proxy for how well people function. All it serves to do is perpetuate ageism, and fail to capture the benefits of fuller working lives for individuals, businesses and society.

For individuals, there are three key benefits:

1. *Meaning and purpose.* As the quote from Hawking suggests, work often gives us the chance to be part of something bigger than ourselves and

to accomplish something purposeful. This both creates and sustains wellbeing (McKnight and Kashdan, 2009).[13] The challenge is to ensure that work *is* meaningful for older people and that it is individualised enough to support other meaningful occupations such as the critical role of caring that many older people provide.

2. *Social connection.* This is a major determinant of health and wellbeing and a lack of social contact through feelings of loneliness increases the risk of early death by as much as 50 per cent (Holt-Lunstad et al., 2010).[14] The current cliff-edge nature of retirement poses an additional challenge to this, and we need to help people to transition to a different kind of work which may be unpaid, part-time or seasonal but which is meaningful and maintains social contact.

3. *Financial stability.* For many, working in later life isn't a choice, it's a necessity. Because we're living longer, the amount we need to save during our working lives also needs to be higher. The average Brit currently needs more than £260,000 to retire without money worries (Royal London, 2018)[15] and one in four older people in the UK struggles financially (Age UK, 2017).[16]

For businesses, older workers are a valuable, transformational asset. They bring cultural continuity and cognitive diversity both from accumulated experience and from the different ways in which an older brain works (Jeste et al., 2019).[17] And people of all ages *want* to work in intergenerational teams – in a large study of 2,000 people aged 18–99, more than four in five wanted to mix with people of different ages (The Age of No Retirement, 2018).[18]

Finally, **for society**, enabling people to continue in meaningful and individualised work reduces the demand for public services such as health and care through better individual health and wellbeing and through supporting older people as carers. It also increases public finances through continued tax contributions. With the number of people of state pension age and over projected to increase by 32.5 per cent in the UK between 2015 and 2039 (ONS, 2016),[19] finding new ways of engaging older people in meaningful occupations is a social and business imperative. Defining their value not by age but by contribution through a system such as workstyle will literally change lives.

On top of all of the important elements outlined above, this is also about choice – more than half of those working beyond state pension age are doing so because they are not ready to stop working.[20] If work is

structured in the right way, it's a source of enjoyment, connection and stimulation. And it has proven health benefits in itself – working longer reduces the likelihood of getting dementia,[21] and postponing retirement by as little as one year increases life expectancy by around 11 per cent.[22] :astonished_face:

In 2014 it dawned on us that as the population grew and changed to a significantly older demographic, we urgently needed a new model of work that was fully inclusive for older workers. Without this, there would be huge implications, with businesses simply not having enough workers to meet their needs, and with society not being able to provide the necessary care and support for those who had retired.

OPPORTUNITY TWO: Technology allows us to work in an entirely new way

We are both 'geriatric millennials' – what a flattering title – which means we remember life before the internet and are therefore comfortable with both analogue and digital forms of communication. Do you remember your landline number or your BT Chargecard number? We do. We felt the impact of clip art and the first brick of a mobile phone which Lizzie's family shared and took in turns to use when they went out (flawed when two of them went into town and wanted to rearrange when or where they were meeting! :face_palm:). Nibbles on MS-DOS, *Chuckie Egg* on BBC Micro, *Pacman* on Amstrad or *Tetris* on the Game Boy... these were all 'breakthrough' technologies that other geriatric millennials will no doubt remember with joy, along with the *Mavis*

Beacon program that taught workstylers Jessica and Laura to touch-type long before they realised just how valuable the skill would be. :qwerty:

Technology has a history of transforming the way in which we live and work. Developments in farm machinery prompted people to head to urban centres for higher-paid factory work. The advent of the steam engine and automobile had a transformational effect on the way people moved around, and food refrigeration meant food could be transported further distances, allowing city populations to soar. And in 2014 the accessibility of wifi was catapulted forward thanks to a new innovation, while computers became even more portable and breakthrough software was invented that would facilitate truly accessible collaboration for the very first time.

By 2014, 78 per cent of people in the UK had high-speed internet at home,[23] with 39 per cent of the world having access to the internet (a number that was growing fast) and 76 per cent of the developed world.[24] That same (magical) year mobile network Three introduced the personal hotspot feature on all pay-monthly plans in the UK for the first time, enabling us to access the internet by tethering to our mobile phones – from cafés and hospitals to beauty spots and trains. Suddenly, we were liberated like never before and an opportunity to work from anywhere presented itself.
:Beach_with_parasol:

This was coupled with restaurants and bars starting to offer high-quality free wifi. We started Hoxby from various Pret a Manger restaurants around London (we remember the passcodes to get into the toilets of the one on Hyde Park Corner if you're desperate!), using their '_TheCloud' excellent free wifi and fuelled by superfood salads. Pret was ahead of the game, but others followed suit and more and more public places introduced free wifi, from parks to shopping centres, opening the door for vast choice in where we work.

The real power to redefine how we worked was this prevalence of wifi, coupled with the portability of hardware. The year 2014 marked the 30-year anniversary of the introduction of the Apple Macintosh computer, and in that time it had progressed from the original desktop weighing 7.3 kg to a laptop with a much more palatable weight of 2.0 kg. We were personally delighted at the advent of computers that were small enough to carry around without causing long-term damage to our shoulders – laptops that slotted into your handbag and smartphones that fitted in your pocket. This provided new opportunities to re-evaluate how we worked, eliminating the need to go to an office and further facilitating individualised working.

With newfound freedom to access the internet from anywhere and the tools to do so, it was the turn of co-creation software and new communication programs to redefine the way we worked together online. Hours of trying to re-read, copy and re-order Post-it notes from a meeting room wall and the practical impossibility of global simultaneous collaboration on single documents was instantly made more efficient with the arrival of software such as Mural, Miro, Microsoft Office Online or Google Apps.

CASE STUDY

Case study: Buurtzorg Web – how Buurtzorg are using technology to enable autonomy, revolutionising cradle-to-grave care in the Netherlands and beyond

By Jos de Blok, founder and CEO, Buurtzorg

The Buurtzorg model is all about autonomy and agency for both our staff and those we care for. This is what sets us apart and is also the source of our success. Our approach is to empower nurses (rather than nursing assistants or cleaners) to deliver all the care that patients need in order to maintain their independence. All our teams are self-managed and entrepreneurial. They decide how they organise the work, share the responsibilities and make the decisions.

Buurtzorg launched in the Netherlands in 2006 and scaled very quickly from 1 team to 850 teams in just 10 years. Our current turnover is around €0.5 billion. This scalability would not have been possible without the technology that underpins all that we do.

It is my strong belief that systems should serve people and not the other way around. During my career I have seen first-hand the damage caused by taking the latter approach. Back in 2006 the systems we needed to enable our approach did not exist and so we created an IT company and, in collaboration with nurses, built from scratch an integrated system as a platform for all of our needs. Our aim was to reduce bureaucracy, increase productivity and improve the quality of care, always keeping the emphasis on simplicity. Buurtzorg Web was born, underpinning our knowledge sharing, learning and development, collaboration, scheduling, payroll and billing.

The technology we use brings many advantages, both in terms of facilitating our day-to-day operations as well as supporting our approach to care provision. The simple, fully integrated platform means we can operate efficiently with a back office of around 50 staff serving over 15,000 people, keeping overheads low. This frees up the rest of the organisation to focus on care for our patients.

The professional freedom and responsibility our staff have, which is unusual in an industry characterised by fixed shift patterns and lack of choice, would not be possible without Buurtzorg Web. When someone is able to make their own decisions and can see that they have the power to effect change, the impact is very positive and far reaching, influencing personal lives, too.

Our platform and the power of technology also allow for considerable agility, supporting the application of our model to a wide range of care needs – we are growing at pace within mental health, youth care, maternity care, primary healthcare and have exciting longer-term plans for a new approach to care homes for the elderly.

At Buurtzorg, we know from years of hands-on experience that a more holistic, autonomous and patient-centred approach to health-care yields better results all round. Our client satisfaction rates are the highest of any healthcare provider, and staff commitment and contentment are reflected in the many awards we have won. These accomplishments stand out in an industry that faces considerable challenges in terms of both carer and patient wellbeing.

We want to show that the amazing results we have seen in the Nether-lands and beyond can be achieved anywhere in the world. Working in different regions (Buurtzorg is currently active in 24 countries), we have discovered that the problems are the same. The message every time is to start again from the patient perspective and simplify the systems. This is the philosophy behind the revolutionary model of care we have created, a model that brings independence and improved quality of life to both our patients and our staff.

When humanity triumphs over bureaucracy, we believe community care gains the most. We are proud to have redefined the provision of care for all age groups by pioneering the use of technology coupled with autonomy to create the kind of environment where humanity prevails.

Technology was fundamentally redefining the way we work together. In 2014 Google Apps was being rebranded and relaunched as Google Suite for users to join forces the world over to co-create documents, spreadsheets and presentations. Version control nightmares in organisations around the world were finally over. :grinning_face_with_big_eyes: And perhaps more importantly, with its wide compatibility and ease of use, truly diverse, distributed teams could collaborate in ways not previously possible.

Following a year of testing behind closed doors, online community tool Slack launched publicly in February 2014 (yep, still a magical year ... :wand:). The business grew at lightning speed and became a 'unicorn'[25] (not the kind Alex pretends to be with his children – the kind where a start-up is valued at over $1 billion in its first year) and allowed people to collaborate in a truly accessible and inclusive way that had not been seen before.

Slack claims to reduce emails by 32 per cent and meetings by 27 per cent.[26] While the specifics of these statistics will of course vary by individual (we're confident it's reduced our emails by 95 per cent, for example), there is no question its invention, alongside other similar systems, has ushered in a new era of effective online collaboration for work. Within just two years Slack was hosting over 30,000 communities and was one of the fastest-growing start-ups of all time.[27] And for communities like Hoxby it didn't just replace the need for email, it created a digital environment for human collaboration that replaced the need for a physical one. New programmes such as Threadit, a video exchange website created by Google's Area 120 innovation lab, and 'clips' in Slack provide more new ways to build deeper personal relationships and collaborate in remote teams while working at different times.

Geek box: How platforms like Slack make collaboration more accessible and inclusive

By Brian Elliott, Executive Leader, Future Forum and Senior Vice President at Slack

From its inception Slack was designed to support a more flexible, inclusive and connected way of working. The team behind *Glitch*, a multiplayer online game, originally built Slack as its own internal communication and collaboration tool. With employees distributed across three locations (Vancouver, San Francisco and New York), they needed a way to stay in sync during the workday and used Slack both to co-ordinate on projects and to feel connected as a team.

When the game didn't grow as planned, the company pivoted and Slack as we know it today was born with a mission to make work simpler, more pleasant and more productive. Over time the Slack product expanded with the addition of new capabilities like voice and video calls and a platform for integrating the thousands of software tools that teams use every day.

Over the years the company grew up but maintained an ethos of 'work hard and go home' that helped people find balance. But still Slack, like most companies, was office-centric. The headquarters in San Francisco grew and whole departments, like engineering, had nearly everyone working in that building every day. Executive reviews happened around a table in a conference room, and if you were dialling in from Denver, Dublin or Pune, you often had a hard time tracking what was happening.

The pandemic shifted life at Slack, as it did for many. Suddenly, office-centric assumptions went out the window, replaced by a scramble to establish new digital-first policies, which created short-term chaos but long-term gains. In the face of such enormous challenges – parenting while working, caregiving for family and friends, illness and more – we needed to enable more individual ways of working. Teams found ways to accommodate the clear need for widely varying schedules.

The old concept of 'headquarters' also shifted dramatically. In May 2020 a senior leader in Denver declared, 'Slack is now our headquarters.' It wasn't a marketing slogan – it was a declaration from someone who had made too many trips to San Francisco in order to be 'in the room where it happens' and who, amid the pandemic, felt more connected to his teammates than ever before.

A few months into the pandemic Slack founded Future Forum, a consortium to research what works, and what doesn't, for people at work. Every quarter we survey over 10,000 knowledge workers – and with every quarter the picture has gotten clearer. The vast majority (78 per cent) of knowledge workers want location flexibility at work – they want to come together occasionally for connection and camaraderie, but nowhere near five days a week (Future Forum, 2021a).[28] Even more striking is the fact that 95 per cent of people want schedule flexibility – not 9-to-5 days packed with meetings, but a more limited set of hours when they are in sync with their teams, with other times reserved for heads-down focused work at a time that works for them (Future Forum, 2021a).[29]

Our research has also shown that the autonomy Slack can facilitate presents an opportunity to improve inclusion at work. In the US Black, Hispanic/Latin and Asian/Asian American employees have reported a higher sense of belonging during the pandemic, because new working structures help cut down on the code-switching and micro-aggressions that are more prevalent in the office (Future Forum, 2021a).[30] In both the UK and US women with children say they value schedule flexibility more than men with children do, since they often bear more of the burden when it comes to caregiving (Future Forum, 2021a).[31] Across countries, employees that worked outside of their company's headquarters pre-pandemic report that they no longer feel like second-class citizens within their organisations now that teams are more distributed (Future Forum, 2021b).[32]

All employees crave connection. With Slack, companies can be built around a digital headquarters that all employees have equal access to, no matter when or where they work. Still, it's important to understand that going digital-first doesn't mean you never meet in person. There's tremendous value in holding a new team formation event that's more about building social ties and psychological safety than 'getting work done'. In fact, 80 per cent of employees surveyed say that the primary reason they want to visit the office is for connection, like camaraderie and team-building (Future Forum, 2021c).[33]

The evolution in how we work – making work better for people from all walks of life – is just starting. Technology has a key role to play as an enabler of this transition. But it's up to all of us to seize this moment as a once-in-a-generation opportunity to design a better way to work.

Leaps forward in technology have revolutionised the way we can communicate and collaborate within organisations (if organisations choose to adopt and embed them, of course). With this came the opportunity for true global and 'asynchronous' working, where borders and time zones became immaterial and teams could work together seamlessly even if they were on opposite sides of the world or online at completely different times.

In 2014 we saw the opportunity to stop thinking of work as a place we went and to start thinking of it as a thing we did, whenever and wherever we could access wifi or find space for our laptops. We realised that online collaboration and communication meant we could choose to do this in a way that best suited each of us as individuals. One size no longer had to fit all.

OPPORTUNITY THREE: Independence is paving the way for a new working world

When we weren't working from Pret restaurants, you'd find us crouched on train platforms or working-from-tree, and it's safe to say we attracted a few sideways glances. :pair_of_weirdos: But even in those early years a short hop on the Central Line to the Hoxton Hotel in Holborn would see us surrounded by people working like us. The open-plan reception, dining, cafe, bar, foyer area that became our sanctuary felt like it had been carefully tailored to enable such co-working to happen. It was a beautiful, vibrant place to work, and more and more locations for informal co-working were popping up and people's expectations of work were starting to change.

CASE STUDY

Case study: Blinkist – how we built a business to meet the new expectations of work

By Holger Seim, co-founder and CEO, Blinkist

When we founded Blinkist, we had a strong desire to make it an engaging and cool place to work and recognised that attitudes to work were changing. We wanted to build on the start-up vibes we had heard about and seen at other companies, and as first-time founders we knew we needed to experiment and learn. Despite this desire, when we started Blinkist we got it all wrong: we focused heavily on the commercial side and didn't put conscious effort into culture and organisation. Fortunately, we learned from our mistakes early on and, having listened to what our people wanted – trust and freedom – we started working in a holacratic way, with an emphasis on self-organisation and empowering people to deliver their work however they see fit. Empowerment has been a thread throughout our history and continues to be a key way of working. We do not have 'managers' at Blinkist; we have leads focused more on coaching and developing individuals to learn and grow rather than managing their day-to-day work.

We now have 17 million users in more than 140 countries listening to powerful ideas from books and podcasts with Blinkist, and we have evolved our ways of working over the past nine years, from holacracy to our own 'Blinkist Operating System' and now 'The Blinkist Way'. Throughout that change we have maintained our principles of empowerment, enablement, accountability and strong autonomy in decision making. It's a journey for us as we grow and drive towards our goal of being one of the most engaging places to work in Europe. We don't always get things right, but we're proud of our unique culture and continuously high engagement score of more than 75 per cent.[34]

Less through design and more through doubling down on the inherent trust we have in our people to deliver business outcomes, we provide flexibility for people to be able to produce their best work when it suits them. We recognise that this isn't always at one desk between the hours of 9 a.m. to 5 p.m. So we have a flexible schedule to enable people to deliver their best work when they are at their best. We have our headquarters in Berlin and have colleagues in the US, UK, Finland, Serbia, Spain and Italy, including members of our leadership team located across these countries.

It's all we know to operate this way – it's how we have always worked since starting Blinkist in 2012. My fellow founder, Tobi, and I will always care about our culture. Enabling people to have an outstanding experience working here is a strongly held desire for us both. Plus it makes business sense. We have significantly higher retention than in the market of Berlin start-ups and pride ourselves on consistently gaining exceptional reviews on Glassdoor as well as being named in best workplace awards.[35] We firmly believe that our long-term success is supercharged by a strong culture and outstanding employee experience that is fit for more independent and trust-based approaches to work.

Independent working was on the rise in 2014 as more ways to earn a living were emerging. Individuals who previously may have looked to a traditional job with an employer to provide a monthly salary started to find they could earn income from new sources and create portfolio careers for themselves.

Platform businesses such as Airbnb and JustPark began giving people the opportunity to generate income for themselves from their property if they had one. Other platforms enabled people to monetise a following on YouTube or Instagram, for example, while others found freelance work through platforms like MyBuilder, Upwork or Fiverr, and creators were selling their wares on Etsy, Amazon or eBay. More and more professional services companies, from the 'Big Four' accountancy firms to learning and development companies like MindGym, were beginning to use freelancers and benefit from the adaptability they provided to smooth out periods of high and low demand. All of these factors changed attitudes and brought unprecedented choice in how to work and what we might choose to piece together to earn the income we need.

The draw of such independence and the rising idea of a sharing economy provoked what some call the gig economy, with self-employment booming across Europe. IPSE research showed that people were moving into freelancing for overwhelmingly positive reasons: the freedom to choose where they work (83 per cent) and when they work (84 per cent) and for improved work–life balance (73 per cent).[36] The last decade has seen a rapid evolution in the freelance population, with more than 4.6 million people now self-employed in the UK, fast approaching the 5.4 million in the public sector[37] and therefore soon to be the biggest 'group' in the workforce (if you were to view freelancers as a group, which is all too rare in our opinion). In the US nearly a third of workers are self-employed.[38] People are moving in their droves to work this way so as to take back control and reassert their independence.

Geek box: The changing nature of work and the rise of the project economy

By Professor Andrew Burke, Dean of Trinity Business School and Chair of Business Studies, Trinity College, Dublin

Developed countries' success in the 21st century has been due to their effectiveness as innovation-driven economies. Corporate growth and innovation alongside entrepreneurship are the vehicles delivering the outstanding economic growth. The firms involved rely on expertise beyond the confines of their employees to deliver projects which drive innovation and growth. While there has been huge negative press and focus on the freelance gig economy, the real action in the flexible labour market is actually taking place elsewhere in what is termed the project-based economy. This relates to businesses where innovation, agility, growth and the ability to manage uncertainty and risk are the keys to competitive advantage and success. In order to perform at this dynamic level, these firms need to draw on independent contractors to access expertise beyond the confines of their employee base, respond rapidly to changing market and technological requirements, and manage innovation and growth on an agile and lower-risk project basis. The impact of this boost to economic performance is the finding that the net effect of freelancers on employees is more strongly one of helping to create and sustain jobs for employees than competing for the same work (Burke and Cowling, 2020).[39]

Our research (Burke, 2019)[40] has shown that in high-skilled work, the UK project-based economy is five times larger than the gig economy. We also find that highly skilled freelancers earn more than twice the earnings of equivalent employees. Recently, we found similar effects for another dynamic economy, namely the Republic of Ireland. This latter study (Burke et al., 2021)[41] also explored the roles of age and gender, finding that the freelance labour market displays much less discrimination than that which occurs in the employee workforce. Our research finds that the experience of older freelancers is highly valued to the point that older freelancers – including the over 60s – earn more and charge higher day rates than younger freelancers. We also find that the earnings differential between men and women is 72 per cent less among freelance workers than it is in the employee workforce. The same study found that high-skilled freelancers had considerably higher levels of job and life satisfaction as well. Other research has found similar findings on life and job satisfaction for other countries, too.

The 2019 report also finds that, while digital platforms have played a major role in promoting gig economy working, they have also made a very big impact in promoting project-based freelancing. In some cases, online communities, such as Hoxby, have enabled highly skilled freelancers to organise themselves into co-operatives and collectives which have enabled them to adopt collective management techniques to reduce the risk and lack of welfare support typically associated with freelancing. In addition, by collaborating and hence combining their skills and business contacts, digital-based collectives have enabled freelancers to tackle more market opportunities than would be possible for freelancers working on their own. Combined, these benefits can enhance worker wellbeing by enabling them to choose a freelance career that better matches their work–life balance, allowing them to work on projects that they personally find more life satisfying, have less isolation and loneliness, and have less risk than is normally experienced with the often precarious nature of a self-employed career choice.

Combined, the research highlights the very significant economic importance of the high-skilled, project-based freelance economy. This is by a significant margin the largest single freelance economy generating the most value added for businesses as well as the highest earnings for freelancers. This important economic and societal movement needs greater recognition and nurturing in particular areas. This requires public policy to adopt a differentiated – that is, not a 'one-size-fits-all' – approach to the freelance sector. Our research indicates that pairing high/low skills with project or gig economies is likely to be a practical and useful method to use. In short, when work is low skilled and in the gig economy, it is more likely to require worker protection or support. By contrast, when it is highly skilled and in the project-based freelance economy, it is more likely to need enablement and legitimisation by government. Regardless, what is very clear from the findings of these studies is that not only have attitudes to working structures changed but the performance of the innovation-driven economies requires both a sufficient supply of and the freedom for firms to utilise freelancers on a project basis.

With an increasing demand for freelance work, and similarly increasing need for freelancers' expertise, many people began to think of themselves as individuals with multiple strings to their proverbial career bow. The diminishing risk of self-employment (alongside the increasing insecurity of traditional employment) gave rise to the idea of a side hustle, that could quickly evolve into having a 'portfolio career', as popularised by the author Emma Gannon in her defining book *The Multi-Hyphen Method*.[42]

This made a lot of sense to Alex, who had spent much of his career to that point experimenting with different forms of work to satisfy the different aspects of his personality. In fact, prior to 2014, Alex had worked in no less than 20 jobs over a 17-year pursuit of fulfilling work. It seems he was never destined for the traditional, linear career path that he'd imagined he would have. Perhaps all the more remarkable, then, and testament to the power of workstyle working, that he's managed to stick with working with Lizzie for eight years! :grinning_squinting_face:

As human beings, we are too capable, talented and diverse a species to restrict ourselves to one form of work, and the idea of a job for life that has served previous generations is no longer the norm. The ease of self-employment and the desire to have multiple aspects to your work identity just as you have multiple aspects to your personal identity have enabled us to develop more rewarding, fulfilling careers. Take workstyler Bernardo, who is a professional singer, podcaster, black-belt karate teacher and author of three books. Or Yacob, a workstyler whom you will meet later, who is a qualified accountant, hypnotherapist, psychotherapist, aromatherapist, massage therapist, NLP practitioner, proofreader, cricket coach and Nordic walking instructor. (Yep, I think we can all agree that Yacob takes the prize for most impressive portfolio! :trophy:) He has also completed projects and commissions as a writer, photographer and seascape painter and has written award-winning poetry. :yacob_of_all_trades:

Portfolio careers support independence in how we work, meaning we can insure our careers away from a dependency on a particular industry or organisation and perhaps most importantly allow work to reflect the full spectrum of our creativity, strengths, interests and personality to feel as fulfilled at work as we do in life. Through a mixture of elements, not just one.

So in 2014 (:wizard:), as we began to think beyond the bounds of traditional employment and find ways to build portfolio careers, we found that with greater independence came greater responsibility. If we are planning to work longer and have multiple careers in our lifetime (either one after another or concurrently as a portfolio career), we each need to become more accountable for managing ourselves. By letting go of the 9-to-5 construct that had been the norm for centuries, the 'working day' lines previously drawn to segregate work and life needed to become lines that we defined, and importantly regulated, for ourselves.

In 2014 a booming population of freelance workers and platform businesses gave rise to portfolio careers.[43] This brought independence and a newfound responsibility for self-management. We realised that many more people were earning and working through their own individual portfolios, and that those still in more traditional employment were looking for different qualities when choosing who to work for.

The ageing population gives us a burning platform to change the way we work, the digital revolution has made the traditional, industrial era system of work feel starkly out of kilter with the dynamic and connected world we live in, and our independence in our approach to work has evolved to a point where we are all ready for the next revolution in working practices.

The year 2014 was part of a defining period of change across demographics, technology and independence. In all three areas our world was transforming in revolutionary ways that would enable us to see the opportunity to create a new system of work that could last long into the future alongside our rapid evolution.

The big opportunity that connected these three changes was that of enabling individual choice. For the first time there was the opportunity for a working system that could give individuals the complete freedom to choose when and where to work. One where we can fit our work around our lives rather than the other way round.

Over that last Dark 'n Stormy cocktail in 2014 it felt like everything came together and we could create a very different, and much improved, working world for future generations as well as for our ageing selves. Conditions were perfect for a new, individualised and inclusive system of work to be born. For a revolution to begin.

Chapter summary

- In 2014 there were three big changes that created the conditions for the conception of individualised work through workstyle. We call these the 'triangle of opportunity':

  o **Ageing** – We realised that, as the population changed to a significantly older demographic, we would need a new model of work that is fully inclusive for older workers. Without this, there would be huge implications, with businesses simply not having enough workers to meet their needs and with society not being able to provide the necessary care for those who have retired.

  o **Technology** – We stopped thinking of work as a place we went to and started thinking of it as a thing we did, wherever we could access wifi or find space for our laptops. We saw that online collaboration and communication meant we could choose to do this in a way that best suited each of us as individuals.

  o **Independence** – We noticed that people were increasingly earning and working through their own individual means rather than through the comfort of traditional employment. This booming population of freelance workers would give rise to portfolio careers and, with this, independence and a newfound responsibility for self-management.

- All of these factors came together to create the perfect opportunity for a new, individualised system of work to be created. It was time for a revolution to begin!

From the mouth of a workstyler: 'I joined the workstyle revolution because... I wanted to have a portfolio career on my terms. I am a PR consultant, graphic designer and sculptor, exploring 3D design and animation and making jewellery as a hobby.' Eleni, London, UK

Fact to remember: Three facts for three opportunities in this chapter.

- Ageing – 21 per cent of the worldwide population will be over 60 by 2050.[44]

- Technology – Using the right technology can reduce the need for meetings and emails by almost a third.[45]

- Independence – There are 4.6 million self-employed people in the UK[46] – soon to be the biggest group in the workforce.

 And finally... In 2014 Alex realised he was unemployable, having had more than 20 jobs over a 17-year career, so he set about starting a business with Lizzie. :plan_U:

Play your part in the workstyle revolution

Reflect

☐ Consider how the triangle of opportunity has, and will, impact your life now and into the future.

1. *Do you know someone who has retired since 2014? At what age do you think you would like to retire (if indeed you want to retire at all)? What would your ideal transition to retirement be?*

2. *How are you using technology differently from how you used it in 2014? What have the implications of this been on how you spend your working and non-working time?*

3. *If you were working in 2014, how have your attitudes to work changed since then? Are there other opportunities for you to earn a living in new ways that weren't possible then? Are you more independent in your approach to work?*

Act

☐ Write down five things that interest you that are not currently part of your job. This could be an artistic hobby, blogging, doing yoga, bee-keeping... Would it excite you to turn any of these into a side hustle that creates income? If not now, would it at some point in the future as your life changes?

☐ Read *The 100 Year Life* by Lynda Gratton and Andrew Scott and *The Multi-Hyphen Method* by Emma Gannon for further inspiration.

Inspire

☐ Start a group at your company or in your working community to discuss the implications of the triangle of opportunity and consider ways that the organisation can and should respond to these changes.

❐ Suggest changes in your organisation to make it more accessible to all age groups. Introduce new technologies that support a digital-first approach to work and to empower individuals to work more independently.

FIVE

One word to change the world

And so we're here! This is the chapter where we get to talk about our favourite subject. Here we're excited to explain the idea of workstyle and are going to do so in the style of an interview with your inquisitive self. Imagine you are sitting on a sofa not dissimilar to one you might see on breakfast television and we are chatting to you from home on the screen next to you. So buckle up, this is where the workstyle ride really starts. Enjoy the adrenaline rush as we answer all your burning questions, kicking off with, erm, a dictionary definition... :still_geeks:

So what does workstyle mean?

In short, workstyle is the complete freedom to choose when and where you work.

noun: workstyle

plural noun: workstyles

Workstyle ushers in an era of individualised working. The word 'workstyle' is used to describe someone's completely self-determined way of working and is derived from the word 'lifestyle', which is used to describe someone's way of living. It was created during the digital revolution by Alex Hirst and Lizzie Penny (while sipping 2-for-1 cocktails) in response to the newfound ability for individuals to choose when and where they work for themselves, such that their work fits around their life.

Its conception marks the start of autonomous working in a way that is cohesive and united, as part of an individualised system of work that replaces the traditional 9-to-5 working day and the five-day 'working week'.

So tell us, Lizzie and Alex, how did you come up with workstyle?

Workstyle is a word we invented during a particularly giddy word-association game because there wasn't a word for what we were trying to say. :zany_face: There wasn't a word that could be universally used to describe choosing your own individualised way of working and in so doing change the basic operating system of work to something more fit for purpose – a complete reprogramming of the way we think about our work. There were words that existed to help people describe how they work in relation to the 9-to-5 system but nothing that could replace the system itself. We could see that changes in ageing, technology and independence were creating the perfect conditions for a new system of work, for individualised working to replace the one-size-fits-all approach, and for each of us to have autonomy over when and where we work. Workstyle is the word and the idea we came up with that makes it possible.

Surely there's a hand gesture to go with it?

Yes, there is, how funny you should ask that! This is our original hand gesture and the one that workstylers are most familiar with. The two hands come together like this to form the letter 'w', for workstyle.

And where did the word 'workstyle' come from?

Having struck upon the idea of individualised working, we explored all the possible ways in which we could support people working individually, from apps to campaigns, but could see from the evidence that words were the most powerful way to enact change (read on for our geekery around the importance of language). Some of the words we came up with before last orders were too terrible to admit to, but at the time we couldn't pinpoint why. So, with the bell about to bring our night to an end, we brought our thinking back to what this is all about: our goal is to give people the language to choose when and where they work for themselves. If everyone is free to make choices in their lifestyle, we believe they should be free to choose their own workstyle, too.

Currently, too little of many people's lives is within their control to design because when and where they work have been predetermined by organisational policies and underlying cultural norms which don't take into account their needs as individuals. Each of us is different. We may have things in common with others – Lizzie knows others who swim every morning and Alex knows others who take their kids to school – but the combination of elements in our lives – families, hobbies, living arrangements, eating habits and sleeping patterns – is completely unique to us. Individuality is what work is missing.

At the heart of our conversation in the pub that night was our desire to create a word that would normalise individualised working. One word to give everyone the freedom to work in their own way and collectively create a new and fully inclusive model of work. Our goal throughout this journey has always been to create a happier, more fulfilled society through a world of work without bias. It is the individualised nature of workstyle that removes the bias in our system, but it wasn't until the trends we shared in the last chapter all started to come together in 2014 that it became possible to see the solution that would give us hope for a happier world. :hugging_face:

You might be someone who is living with a disability and can't commute to an office, or have caring responsibilities that mean staying at home or going to an elderly parent's house each day, or you may have a terminal illness or suffer from poor mental health. You might be someone who is just fed up with sharing a crowded train on the commute to work each day. If you have the freedom to choose when and where you work, then work becomes more accessible to you and everyone else than if we all have to get to an office or place of work to do a job on a fixed working schedule.

This is the higher, societal opportunity that workstyle aspires to, but it is also an opportunity for everyone, right now. We could all have more autonomy to lead our lives on our own terms. Being able to work from the hairdresser's can be a great use of time for a multitasker like Lizzie, but how we choose to fit our work around our other priorities in life is unique to us all – whether that is caring for someone, surfing during daylight hours, spending meaningful time with a young family or choosing to learn French on a Wednesday afternoon.

Rather than feeling glued to a desk or stuck in a predetermined shift pattern while life passes us by, the freedom of workstyle allows us to breathe new life into our existence. We've lost count of the number of times workstylers have told us they downed tools on a sunny day to get outside to sunbathe at the beach, do some gardening or hang out a load of washing in that perfect drying weather. :Rock_and_roll: They seize the moments that arise, moving their work time to when it pours with rain at the weekend or in the evening after the sun has set. Our productivity and mood are lifted by working when it's raining[1] and our eyes aren't drawn to staring longingly out the window when the sun's out. :shades:

Woah there! Surely that won't work for everyone?

While we are dreamers and revolutionaries, we are realists, too. And we recognise that the perfect utopia of workstyle that we have described so far might not be immediately achievable for everyone, in every type of work. There are a couple of the big questions that come up whenever we talk to someone new about working this way. What about shift work, manual work and jobs where others rely on workers being physically present? What if you can't afford to say no to paid work just because it doesn't fit your workstyle? How can you meet client deadlines if you work only when you want?

A WØRKSTYLER'S GUIDE TO FITTING WORK AROUND LIFE

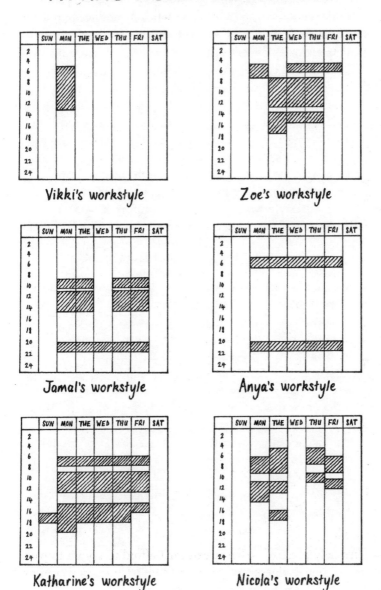

Vikki's workstyle

Zoe's workstyle

Jamal's workstyle

Anya's workstyle

Katharine's workstyle

Nicola's workstyle

It is true that retail workers need to be on the shop floor at certain times, factory workers need access to heavy machinery, and police, teachers and healthcare professionals need to be at certain locations in person. While the Buurtzorg case study in the previous chapter shows that workstyle thinking can be applied to some of these industries, there is no question that workstyle is best suited to knowledge work (thinking work that can be done anywhere, any time). There are 2.5 million businesses[2] in the UK knowledge economy. Globally there are estimated to be more than 1 billion knowledge workers,[3] so this way of working could impact a great number of lives, even if only applicable to knowledge workers in the first instance. Our ambition, in time, is to take workstyle to all forms of work, but even in the short term we know that elements of workstyle can be used to improve all work for all people. What is important is that we approach the design of work in a workstyle way rather than assuming it won't work in certain situations and therefore ruling it out entirely. Think of it as a sliding scale where the benefits can be unlocked even by taking small steps to incorporate workstyle thinking to some degree.

For many of the industries in which choosing where to work isn't possible, there is still scope for more openness to individual preference in when people work. For example, in professions that rely on shift work, such as midwifery or manufacturing, technology now makes it possible for companies to move away from strict shift patterns, instead allowing the team to autonomously decide among themselves who works when – meshing their workstyles to achieve the required level of cover. Consider how this individualised approach might help alleviate the critical shortage of workers currently experienced in certain sectors. And in the future even things that we think today must be done at a certain time and in a certain place might be done virtually or 'asynchronously' (not working at the same time). Teachers running their classes remotely during the coronavirus pandemic was a great example of this. Workstyle – and the individual freedom to choose – is about questioning whether the way it has always been done is the only way, and whether it can and should be done differently.

Of course, it could be argued it is only those in a position of some privilege who can say no to work that doesn't fit their workstyle. The complete freedom to choose for yourself depends on a certain level of confidence or support. Because workstyle is not currently embraced by all organisations, it can limit your options in the short term (although we would argue it creates limitless opportunities in the long term). But change has to start somewhere, and for those of us who do have the confidence or support to work in a workstyle way, we must embrace doing so, become vocal supporters and drive the revolution forward so that one day everyone can work this way.

We recognise that workstyle is a total rethink of society's approach to work. We have faced lots of challenges during our time working in a workstyle way and through our work at Hoxby, but we have also found solutions to all of them. We know that working this way is possible and that the end result is worth it. Workstyle won't work perfectly for absolutely everyone and every type of work, but we would argue it's still a vast improvement on the traditional way of working which simply doesn't work for huge groups of society. We should all question whether we can take steps to move towards workstyle working and reflect on how we can each play our part in creating an individualised system of work that is better for each of us and more inclusive for everyone.

And what's the impact on the work you deliver?

If you're wondering how workstylers can work whenever they want, wherever they want and still be sure to meet client deadlines and deliver exceptional work, it's important to consider this in the context of an individualised system of work. Workstyle is about enabling people to work in the way that is most conducive to their own best performance, empowering them to be self-starters, giving them ownership and individual accountability over their work and their environment, and providing support instead of exerting control. Workstyle is also about producing better outcomes than working in a traditional way, and our research has found that people working this way feel more accountable for delivering higher-quality work. More on this in the next chapter.

A large part of the answer to this question comes from the way workstyle works in practice. When we started Hoxby, we believed in complete freedom not just for when and where work should be done but also how. So we let Hoxbies choose which tools to use, how to create documents and how to manage projects for themselves. But we found very quickly that you need to provide some foundations – defined structures and processes – that underpin a workstyle way of working. Workstyle still needs parameters and some active management. So we moved to mandating certain ways of communicating, collaborating and working. This vastly improved efficiency, productivity and enjoyment for all of us working this way. This, balanced with the high levels of accountability workstylers feel, makes for exceptional output from diverse teams, delivered on time, in a workstyle way.

Workstyle requires that we focus on how work is delivered as well as the work we are delivering. As teams we must work together so that between us we have everything covered and collectively uphold the workstyle approach. There are three golden rules to doing this:

1. Workstylers need to **take accountability** for fitting our work around our life so we can each still achieve what we want in our careers and produce work we're fiercely proud of. Part of doing this is only taking on work where we know we can excel and deliver to a high standard within our workstyle, and being confident to say no to work we can't deliver brilliantly within these parameters. Client deadlines in knowledge work are a condition of the work you do and workstylers are keenly aware of that.

2. Workstylers **set up projects to take workstyles into account**, considering client needs and deadlines to maximise our efficiency either through working in teams across different time zones, having someone available for a client when they need them, or having team members with overlapping workstyles for short-turnaround projects. Clear project planning from the outset and great communication are crucial skills for anyone leading a workstyle project.

3. Workstylers **support each other**, substituting in when needed so the team output is never compromised but unexpected circumstances can still be covered (remember that for some people short bursts of work will be a desired part of their workstyle and therefore substituting at short notice is something they actively choose).

We'll cover all of these in more detail at various points in the coming chapters.

Tell me, how has the way we talk about work evolved?

The language we use to talk about work has shaped how we think about it, and so it stands to reason that, if we want to change the way the world works, we need to change the words we use to talk about it. We will always need to create new words if we are to evolve. Using them may feel alien to us at first, but they grow on us quickly, like when people formed a 'bubble' during Covid lockdown or explaining to someone that they need to 'unmute'. Words that are intuitive stick. Many of those words are created in response to the prevailing changes in our world, but there are others that make those changes happen.

Take, for example, Sir Bobby O's memorable message of 1817 – 'eight hours' labour, eight hours' recreation, eight hours' rest' (catchy :simple_smile:). While this wasn't new vocabulary, it was a powerful articulation of the idea that work should be balanced with allowing time for life outside work.

Reflecting on this compelling narrative more than 200 years later, we can still agree on the need for 8 hours' rest (though this may be a pipe dream for readers with young children), but what is less clear-cut now is our interpretation of work as 'labour' and that it is something that necessitates the need for 'recreation'. Back then labour was physical, it was unpleasant, something to endure until such time as we could find recreation. Recreation comes from the Latin word *creare* – to create – and *re* – to begin again. This word we use for our non-working time is derived from a basic assumption that we need to create again, or renew ourselves. Use of the word and its meaning to 'refresh oneself by some amusement' was first recorded around the year 1400 and is defined today as something we do when we're not working. :fun_fair:

Our work, and therefore our need for recreation, has changed but our language hasn't. If you're wondering why this matters, it's worth checking out the work of Lera Boroditsky, a cognitive scientist who has worked at Harvard and MIT, and her research team, who have discovered over the past 20 years that the way we use language shapes

how we think about the world.4 Lera references how this is clearly demonstrated by an Aboriginal people in Western Australia, the Kuuk Thaayorre. This people has a language that contains no words for right, left, forwards or backwards because instead they use compass directions to describe movement and position. It seems impossible to imagine, but because they use the same linguistic approach for all situations, it is entirely normal to them. It is simply their language to say 'There's a wasp on your north-west ear', and so the common greeting among members of the Kuuk Thaayorre is not 'hello' but 'Where are you going?' It is a form of communication that places emphasis on position and direction in space rather than on the person. This means that members of the Kuuk Thaayorre are much better than English speakers at staying oriented and keeping track of where they are, even in unfamiliar landscapes or inside unfamiliar buildings. What enables them – in fact, forces them – to do this is their language. Having their attention trained in this way equips them to perform navigational feats once thought beyond human capabilities.

The way that we speak has the ability to shape fundamental concepts like movement as well as dictate how we interpret specific situations. Lera tells the story of a man knocking over a vase, but since we aren't big vase-shop visitors we feel this is a more relevant example for us: in Spanish, having observed a child (possibly your own) single-handedly devouring a box of chocolate cookies and then smearing a shop window with their chocolate-covered fingers, you might say: 'The window is now dirty.' In English, you are more likely to say: 'That child has made the window dirty.' Even these small differences can impact the way the event is recollected – studies suggest English people would be more likely than Spaniards to remember who dirtied the window rather than details about the action itself.[5] The moral of the story here is that, as well as being more relaxed taking our messy children out for the day in Madrid rather than London, by changing our language we can change what we pay attention to without conscious awareness. This has the power to reframe how we think about the world, or specific areas within it.

This was our fascinating starting point for thinking about the working world we wanted to create. We pondered why work–life balance wasn't called life–work balance. We sought to understand why holidays at work are called 'annual leave entitlement', and determined that much of the language used at work seems to have been created by the custodians of that work – companies, rather than the people who do it. It became apparent to us that many people have never sought to challenge the conventional wisdoms of work, accepting it as being something they simply don't have the power to change. So we did a little more digging into the work of original ancient farmers (:spade:), where we found an implied assumption that work is hard and a negative part of life. The word 'work' is one of the oldest words in the Western languages. Descending from the Germanic word *Werk*, it is generally accepted to mean to do something that takes effort. Excited by this discovery, we sought to excavate the complete origins of other words we use to describe work that make us think of onerous activity, of toil, stress and being forced to do something against our will. The French and Spanish words for work – *travail* and *trabajo* – are derived from the Latin *trepaliare*, meaning 'to torture and to inflict suffering or agony', which sounds brutal but we've all had at least one job where that felt not too far from the truth! The word 'labour' originated from the Latin word *laborare*, meaning to 'plough the earth, or to accomplish anything with difficulty or struggle'. Wow, with this history it's not surprising that work has such a poor reputation!

This underlying relationship with the word 'work' extends to the present day. When people ask how work is going it's unusual to hear the response of 'I love it!' or 'It's awesome!' because mostly people tend to focus on the negatives, often responding in terms of how busy they are. This response has been normalised such that many people now say it without thinking, with some even wearing it as a badge of honour. It's a sign of an unhealthy relationship with work that can give the impression that work is more important than anything else.[6]

The same is true when we talk about non-traditional ways of working. 'Part-timer' is often used as a derogatory term, and working flexibly is often perceived as being less committed to your career. The reality is that those who work in non-traditional ways are often fighting doubly hard to juggle everything in their lives while going against the 9-to-5 norm, and should be applauded for their dedication on all fronts. Working in a different way doesn't mean that we have a lesser impact than those with a 'full-time' work schedule. We are measuring the wrong thing – we're tracking time and presence rather than output and impact. Using descriptors of the time and effort we're putting into work rather than those of effectiveness and outcomes also makes us more likely to focus on the negative elements of work.

Given all the negative words we use to describe it, it is no surprise that we think work is hard and something that we might want to avoid wherever possible. We pity the 'workaholic' who works in the evening without considering that they may have chosen to be with their children all day (:raised_hand: it's in both of our workstyles). Historically, to question whether hard work is an indisputable fact of life might have labelled us a 'shirker' – and those of us who work from our kitchen tables would almost certainly have been 'shirking from home'. We'd argue the opposite is true – believe it or not, we can put on a laundry load mid-morning and still have an extremely productive and fulfilling day at work. :loads_done:

When toiling on the factory floor to produce basic necessities, or when using primitive tools to push the natural environment to produce enough food to stay alive, these might have been valid beliefs. Today, though, work can play a much more positive role in our lives. If we can afford to, we might choose to change our lifestyle or actively seek out work projects which align with our values and enable us to have a positive impact in the world. When we are passionate about a project, or learning new skills and exploring our curiosities, and working when and where it suits us, work may not tire us out. In fact, it might not feel like hard work at all but actually feel more like recreation. We might focus on what gives us energy from work, what fascinates us, or use work to provide escapism (when sitting in the chemo chair, for example). For work to become a positive part of our lives, we need to create positive language for it.

Words can change the world. Our language shapes our thoughts and feelings and guides our behaviour. If we can change the language that we use to describe work, we might find ourselves able to re-evaluate how work fits into our lives or even – whisper it – fit our work around our lives rather than the other way round.

The word we need in our lives is **workstyle**.

Is there a difference between 'workstyle' and 'work style'?

We knew we were onto a winner when as soon as we started using the word 'workstyle', we noticed people used it back to us in the same conversation. It was a great feeling that we never take for granted, even as we hear people speaking openly about their workstyles now, describing the when and where of their work and how it fits around their life. But we've noticed people starting to use the word in a way we hadn't intended – sneaking it into a standard flexible working policy, or in a corporate blog about personality profiling. If you're going to use the word 'workstyle', and we really hope you will, all we ask is that you use it properly (there's nothing worse than someone learning a new word and then using it wrongly :face_with_rolling_eyes:).

To be clear, workstyle is not the same as flexibility around the 9-to-5. It's not the clothes you wear for work (though *workwear you like* is important to us too :hoodie:), and it's not the way you hold your pen or the computer you like to use. It's not how fast you type, and it is definitely not the pose you make when presenting to a room full of people. :man_dancing:

Workstyle is the complete freedom to choose when and where you work. It's empowering and refreshing in equal measure and the idea of workstyle can fundamentally reshape work for us all. This 'workstyler's guide to the revolution' lays out the key differences between the traditional way and the workstyle way of working:

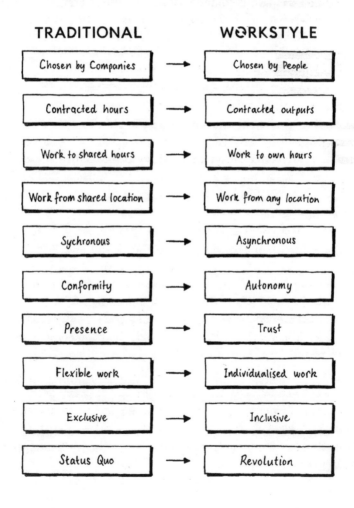

THE WORKSTYLER'S GUIDE TO THE REVOLUTION

TRADITIONAL	WORKSTYLE
Chosen by Companies	Chosen by People
Contracted hours	Contracted outputs
Work to shared hours	Work to own hours
Work from shared location	Work from any location
Sychronous	Asynchronous
Conformity	Autonomy
Presence	Trust
Flexible work	Individualised work
Exclusive	Inclusive
Status Quo	Revolution

This all sounds great in theory, but have you put workstyle to the test?

Yes! People often find workstyle difficult to imagine, thinking it would take pretty major infrastructural change to enable the attitudinal shift we're advocating with workstyle working. So, if you will indulge us for three minutes, we will tell you a bit about how we did it at Hoxby to show that workstyle is entirely possible and has been working for us since 2014. :lab_coat:

Creating a new word comes with its own implications – in just one word, workstyle, we have replaced the assumption that all work is done to a shared schedule in a shared place with an assumption that all work is done to an individual schedule in individual places. This was something we knew we would need to understand deeply and when we came up with the idea, we went in search of a company that was working this way and found none. :stumped: Unperturbed, and in fact excited by the opportunity to get this wrong a few times if it could ultimately lead to something incredible, we set about building an organisation that would serve as the prototype for workstyle. So we set up Hoxby – a social enterprise (and now also a B Corp) – to prove that workstyle could succeed in practice at an organisational and an individual level. :petri_dish: To test the spectrum of work as fully as possible, Hoxby was created to provide all the internal services that a business might need. We would test and develop those services on our own business before then providing them to our clients as an outsource partner. Eight years later Hoxby continues to provide the same broad range of services to clients and has grown from two people in 2014 :wave: to around 1,000 people across the world, each working in their own workstyle in 2022. :chiliad_wave:

When we started this experiment, we worked from each other's houses or nearby cafés and at one point investigated getting a small office space. Then we gave ourselves a slap and remembered that an office was the last thing we would ever need. It was a reminder to us that letting go of the way people have become accustomed to working would be difficult, even for us.

From that moment, we forced ourselves to question absolutely everything about the way people work together within an organisation. We concluded that Hoxby (and many others) could be boiled down to a group of people working towards a common goal. Everything else was up for debate. To really understand the potential of workstyle, we would need to build an organisation that challenged the fundamental elements of the way we work.

So, rather than building a company of employees in an office for fixed working hours, we built a community of freelancers without an office and with no fixed working hours. Members of Hoxby are known as Hoxbies and are spread across countries from the UK to Argentina,

Thailand to New Zealand. They can work any of the 24 hours a day or seven days a week they choose and can change their workstyle as often as they like. There is no accidental pressure to log on at a time that suits someone else. No policies, just a shared belief in workstyle, a mutual respect for one another's freedom to choose and personal accountability to deliver great work on time in order to progress towards our shared vision. Deadlines are fixed, and teams are built around workstyles from the beginning of every project to meet them. Every single member of Hoxby has the complete freedom to choose when and where they work and everyone is encouraged from day one to set, project and respect their workstyle.

What lessons have you learned?

So many! We quickly saw that there was demand for this way of working, which was great, but nobody had any idea how to do it, ourselves included. :thinking_face: :torch:

So, without an office, fixed hours or any employed staff, and with new applications to join every day, we started from a position of chaos. It didn't last long as we quickly started learning what works and what doesn't work – much like many of the companies which experimented under Covid conditions, we imagine, except that for us it was six years before the global pandemic. We were building it from the ground up rather than in response to a crisis, so time was on our side to test, learn and evolve.

At the heart of our culture was a desire to do things differently from how they had always been done, in pursuit of truly individualised work. At first we let everyone use their own systems, had some people co-working in real life, others online, and mostly worked 9-to-5 UK time. That didn't work at all! It was impossible to co-ordinate people or collaborate efficiently, so we concluded that working asynchronously, having a digital-first mentality and nurturing a trust-based culture were key to creating the conditions for workstyle to succeed. In those first few months we learned so much. So much, in fact, that we began to understand why nobody else had tried this. :intrepid_adventurer: Three lessons have stuck with us ever since.

LESSON ONE: Work needed to be done asynchronously, not synchronously

From the start we set about creating working practices to enable more asynchronous working. Asynchronous working sounds horribly like jargon (:sick_in_mouth:), but all it means is not needing to work at the same time as other people. For example, you might say: 'Traditional working is synchronous; workstyle working is asynchronous.' We found that starting with the assumption we're all working at different times meant reprogramming ourselves and having patience to wait for a considered reply rather than going around in circles with immediate reactions in email chains. It also meant learning when and how to schedule more focused productive time rather than allowing constant interruptions. One of the most exciting things we found was that it quickly broke the meeting culture which has long been stopping talented people from getting anything done in so many organisations.

When we started to work to our own individual schedules, we realised that working on cloud-hosted, shared documents at times that suited each of us was highly efficient, knowing that we could pick up where others had left off or collaborate seamlessly and work to our own workstyles.

After 200 years of conditioning to work alongside people for set hours of the day, it felt weird to be apart from each other and our colleagues, so we often met and worked together in cafés and each other's homes. Gradually, as we became more familiar with the technologies and behaviours, we became more asynchronous until it became our natural way of being. It has been liberating to work without meetings and unscheduled phone calls. If you need a call (which we would argue you rarely do), you need to plan it in advance because phoning someone out of the blue simply doesn't happen and actually feels highly invasive to members of an asynchronous workstyle-working team. We learned to send a message instead using our work communication platforms, never on text or WhatsApp which we reserve for personal relationships. As leaders, we realised we would have to learn many new skills quickly and set the example we wanted fellow Hoxbies to follow.

LESSON TWO: We all needed to adopt a digital-first mentality

Not having an office felt scary and uncomfortable to begin with, but it forced us to invest our energy into finding the right digital environment to work in rather than a physical one.

When you can work from anywhere, the digital infrastructure of the business is what enables collaboration to happen, not the painted corridors and soulless meeting rooms of old. We turned to Slack as our primary tool for communication and Google Suite (as it was then) for collaboration tools. There were other tools as well, but the most important thing for us was to decide which tools we would use for which purpose, and stick to them ourselves and insist that everyone else did, too. Having multiple tools during those early 'chaos days' was impossible to manage and created confusion. So we stuck to a system and mandated that all internal communications would be done in Slack. This meant every conversation could be seen by those in the channel and email inboxes became practically redundant. :sun_rising_over_horizon: Building this infrastructure is how we operate as a digital-first organisation (rather than physical-first) and it is an essential part of enabling individualised, asynchronous workstyle work to happen. Systems within a digital-first organisation need to be agreed and then adopted universally across the business if they are to successfully replace the old paradigm of assuming that work is done in person and permeate the culture to become new everyday behaviours, as illustrated in Brian's geek box in Chapter 4.

This reset to the assumptions and ground rules of work created a collaboration between people that happens fluidly, efficiently and, we found, joyfully rather than working from meeting to meeting, and required us to place an entirely new level of trust in one another.

LESSON THREE: A trust-based culture underpins workstyle

When we aren't in the same room as someone and can't see them working, we have no choice but to trust that they are doing their bit, upholding their end of the bargain. This is something that was very noticeable to us at the start of the Hoxby experiment – and it wasn't just the two of us that felt it; every member of Hoxby did. Not only were the Hoxbies working in different countries at different times, but also they had often never worked together before. But we set a culture from the start that meant we trusted each other. It's a big adjustment, but when we trust that someone is working, then the only fair appraisal of their work is to look at what they actually deliver rather than any of the more traditional predictors that can create bias at work. It moved us towards appraisal of one another's output and away from even noticing or talking about one another's input. It made us more accountable to one another because we realised that we could only enjoy the freedom of workstyle if we met every deadline and delivered fantastic work. Hoxbies quickly understood that you're only as good as your last piece of work in a trust-based environment – that you can work in entirely your own way, but always make it your best work.

With accountability in the hands of each person, we saw increased levels of communication. That is evident today when Hoxbies work together – they communicate regularly and they are clear and explicit in the words they use in order to make sure they are understood in a digital environment. We came to realise that using corporate jargon from yesteryear had no place in a workstyle world where clarity is key to avoiding misinterpretation. It's why we have a jargon-busting bot within our Slack environment, to remind us that removing ambiguity is a skill we've had to circle back to many times before we could finally run our ideas up the flagpole so we can all sing off the same hymn sheet and begin to grease the wheels of change. :circle: :flag: :choir: :engine_oil: :laughing_face:

Joking aside, explicit communication within Hoxby has led us to higher levels of transparency and openness. People talk openly about their own workstyle as well as resolutely respecting others'. As you will see from the workstyle stories that follow later in this book, the information and feelings shared between people without the pressure of being face to face have gone far beyond anything we had seen in our traditional working lives. This high level of openness is something that we as leaders wanted to reciprocate from the start, sharing as much information about the organisation (as well as about ourselves) as possible with every member of Hoxby over videos they could watch at a time that suited them. Recording videos is another skill we've had to learn that has been key to building trust. To begin with, it felt uncomfortable; they took a long time to get right and even then we never felt truly happy with them. Practice makes perfect though, and whether it's dancing to 'Eye of the Tiger' to motivate the team or delivering a performance update in a green morph suit, we're now much more confident about recording authentic videos, however silly or serious.

When is the right time for workstyle?

The time for workstyle is now.

When we set up Hoxby to prove the idea of workstyle, it was always with the intention to make workstyle something that everyone can benefit from. Workstyle isn't ours, it's yours.

Everything we have done since that light-bulb moment has been to bring workstyle to you on these pages, but it is fair to say that the coronavirus pandemic accelerated our plans. So dramatic was the impact that it had on work that it presented a once-in-a-generation chance to challenge people's most fundamental beliefs and reset everyone's relationship with work.

Because of the pandemic, society now understands that working remotely and on our own terms can be done, but it was tested in all the wrong conditions. Sustaining work during enforced isolation in the face of a global health crisis, with children at home, at a time that was already hugely challenging for people's mental health, is no fair basis for comparison to what it is otherwise like to have a workstyle.

We, and plenty of others, had been working in a workstyle way for six years before coronavirus came along. So Covid-19 wasn't a catalyst for the concept, but, even in hugely challenging conditions, it did take the blinkers off some of the naysayers' eyes and show that work can be done differently when it needs to be. And though the circumstances were incredibly tough, it still inspired many people to think about what we could achieve if we wanted to work in new ways, hopefully paving the way for mass adoption of workstyle.

There are examples throughout history of similar monumental changes arising because of a much-needed catalyst. In the UK the Parliamentary Reform Act 1832 dramatically changed who was eligible to vote and therefore cut the number of MPs with economic interests in the West Indies in half. This enabled the long-overdue Slavery Abolition Act to be passed by Parliament and the long-fought battle to abolish slavery was won. At the same time, the first women's suffrage bill came before Parliament, but the suffrage movement would continue for a further 86 years before the Representation of the People Act finally gave the first vote to women in the UK, just as the First World War was coming to an end in 1918. It was the contribution of women during the Great War that would finally challenge the notion of female inferiority to such an extent as to bring about lasting reform. It would take a further ten years for all women to be granted the vote, but you have to wonder what would have become of the suffragette movement without one of the deadliest conflicts in human history acting as a catalyst to finally create leaps forward for the perception of women in society.

While these examples are in completely different contexts, they are a reminder that there will always be plenty of people who have a vested interest in preserving the status quo and who stand in the way of change until the momentum from such catalysts forces them to step aside. Right now, sandwich shops in urban centres, commercial property landlords and an extensive public infrastructure network that connects the suburbs to skyscrapers are all keen to see people working from offices. Changing our system of work will be disruptive to a number of businesses which stand to lose from such a shift. However, the pandemic was the first opportunity for many people to step outside their normal way of operating and to see the 9-to-5 system for what it is rather than confusing it with an immovable, immutable reality. These affluent voices which have powerful influence of course leapt to promote a 'return to the way things were' following the pandemic, at the expense of progress.

There is also a risk, following an epoch-changing event such as a global pandemic, that we see fragmented and disparate approaches to work as we transition to a post-pandemic world. Whether it's hybrid working, everyone working from home, everyone in the office three days a week, let's not be dumbfounded by trying to find the perfect combination that will ultimately be perfect for no one. There is only one solution that is proven and that is to give people freedom to choose for themselves. This is individualised working. The word 'workstyle' makes it possible.

Today we stand at an inflection point in history. We have a chance to revolutionise our way of working for good, to move forward from industrial-era working practices and beliefs – and to shape the world in a positive new way. Let's use this moment to create a new working system that is right for each and every one of us, fit for the digital age and for future generations. Let's unite behind the idea of workstyle.

Chapter summary

- Workstyle is a word that we invented in 2014 because we couldn't find one that enabled us to talk about individual working patterns in a non-judgemental way. We define it as **the freedom to choose when and where you work**. You might say to someone (and we hope you will), 'What's your workstyle?'

- We know language can change behaviour, and our hope is that workstyle can move us into an era where the prevailing system of work is an individualised one, which is a better fit for the digital age.

- While workstyle is most easily applied to knowledge work, elements of it can be used to improve all work for all people. The onus is on those of us that are able to work this way to embrace and drive the revolution so that one day everyone can.

- We've tested the idea of workstyle in practice over the past eight years through a social enterprise and B Corp we founded called Hoxby. We've learned a lot and are continuing to learn every day from this experimental way of working. Early on we found that there were three important conditions for successfully working in a workstyle way:

  o asynchronous working – not working at the same time (synchronously) but instead each of us working to our own schedule

  o digital-first working – assuming all work and collaboration happens digitally rather than physically (we don't have an office, for example)

  o trust-based environment – trusting one another, being accountable for our own work and assuming others can, and will, deliver.

- We believe that in the future we will all work in an individualised system and that system is workstyle.

- **From the mouth of a workstyler:** 'I joined the workstyle revolution because... all of my greatest adventures happen between 9 and 5!' Laura, skydiving in Switzerland

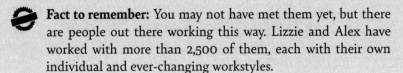 **Fact to remember:** You may not have met them yet, but there are people out there working this way. Lizzie and Alex have worked with more than 2,500 of them, each with their own individual and ever-changing workstyles.

And finally... Lizzie and Alex invented the word 'workstyle' in a pub on the corner of Shepherd's Bush Green in London. A lengthy debate followed about whether it should be one word or two (one of the great conundrums of inventing newwords). We settled on one, on the basis that 'lifestyle' is one word, and if workstyle were two words, then it wouldn't be the new word that the world needs. Or the new world that the word needs, as Alex said to Lizzie as they left the pub.

Play your part in the workstyle revolution

Reflect

❏ Look again at the 'workstyler's guide to the revolution' and reflect on how many of the boxes your work ticks in the left- and right-hand columns.

❏ Do you set your own working hours? Can you work from wherever suits you best? Do you feel trusted to deliver? When did you last go to the hairdresser's during your 'working day'? Are you able to take a break exactly when you need it rather than when break time is 'allowed'?

Act

❏ Say the word 'workstyle' out loud (starting with the cat, perhaps). Describe how you work at the moment, starting with 'My workstyle is...'. Try to include the days and hours you work, where you work, how you take breaks or holidays and the aspects of life you need to fit work around – school pick-ups, appointments, chores, favourite hobbies, etc.

❏ Use the word 'workstyle' in a conversation with a friend or a co-worker and see whether they understand it and repeat it back to you in the same conversation.

❏ Watch Lera Boroditsky's TED Talk 'How language shapes the way we think'.

Inspire

❏ Speak to the leadership team at your organisation about workstyle working. Would they be open to having a discussion about asynchronous, digital-first and trust-based ways of working? And if you are in the leadership team, make it happen. :wink:

❏ Take a photo of the 'workstyler's guide to the revolution' and share it with colleagues or on social media.

SIX

Proving the impact of workstyle

So far we have explained what workstyle is, the thinking behind it and a little of how we tested the idea within Hoxby. From the anecdotal stories we heard (some of which we will be sharing shortly), it became clear to us very quickly on this journey that workstyle was revolutionary and hugely positive for everyone involved. But we also realised that when you came to read this book you would need us to back this up not only with doing it in practice but through first-hand research and data. We wanted to empirically prove that workstyle works. :nerd:

So in 2019 we started measuring the impact of workstyle within Hoxby to understand whether this way of working would be beneficial for businesses and the extent to which it is good for individuals, specifically looking at wellbeing and productivity. In this chapter we explain our workstyle hypothesis, the research we've carried out so far, the results and the implications. To say we are excited to share this with you, now, is an understatement.

Respect the workstyle

We've already written about what we learned in the early days of setting up Hoxby, but as we look in more detail at the research it is important to understand just how ingrained workstyle is in everything we do. Leadership at Hoxby is different from that at other organisations in various ways, one of the biggest of which is that we all project and promote workstyle vigorously within the community. We are disciplined in turning off our notifications when we aren't working. Our statuses and profiles are always up to date with our availability and who to turn to for urgent tasks. Everyone at Hoxby has created their own workstyle document which is available for everyone else in the community to read. As well as the when and where of their work, this document often describes why they work (their values and purpose and where they get their energy from), how they work (the nature of the work they want to do) and what they work on (built around their passions and their skill sets). Communication, prioritisation, shared responsibility and trust are the key to respecting workstyles. #RespectTheWorkstyle is one of our values at Hoxby and we have made sure to illustrate what this means for the community beyond this three-word statement – this is about respecting other people's workstyles as well as our own. We know that every Hoxby is an individual. We can't overstate how important this is – individualised working is the foundation of the workstyle system. We value our differences. We not only respect them but we have also made them the central tenet of our community. We celebrate the ability to fit our work around our lives rather than the other way round with weekly nominations for Hoxby Heroes who have been beacons of workstyle. :lighthouse:

Some fun project planning detail for you: every single project at Hoxby is kicked off with a process that starts by asking the entire project team to reiterate their workstyle and confirm their availability to work on the project. A crucial responsibility of our Project Leads (the Hoxbies who run the projects) is enabling and respecting the team's workstyles while also ensuring each member of the team is accountable for fantastic output, guaranteeing that we can deliver refreshing client work every time through careful planning. And at the end of every project we run a review process where we ask whether those involved felt their workstyle was respected (among other things).

Hoxby is an organisation that has been designed around the idea of workstyle since its inception. :workstyle_egg_hatching: And our longitudinal study (where a subject is studied over a period of time to see changes over the period and collect more robust data) has helped us really understand the social and organisational experiment we have created. Setting up a workstyle way of working takes time and energy – not all organisations can work this way immediately, but our hope is that sharing here what we've learned from the data and the theory will inspire others to adopt this way of working, too, and for the revolution to gather pace.

Autonomy and workstyle

Now, before we could get our geek on, we needed to define workstyle in a scientific context. No formal definition existed (except the one we have made up, of course – one of the challenges of inventing something new! :scientist:), so we needed to find a proxy in the academic literature that we could use to measure whether workstyle was as embedded in the Hoxby community as we thought (and hoped) it was. When we talk about workstyle we talk about fitting work around our lives, about choosing when and where we work, about individual freedom and control. The closest match in existing research is 'autonomy'.

Autonomy is 'the degree to which the work provides substantial freedom, independence, and discretion to the individual in scheduling the work and in determining the procedures to be used in carrying it out',[1] which sounded a lot like workstyle to us. Boom! This is the most popular academic definition, first penned in 1976. (Side note, if we have been talking about autonomy and its benefits for more than 45 years, why has it taken us so long to build it into our ways of working? :disappointed_face:) In 2016 researchers suggested the addition of a new facet, locational autonomy. So now autonomy encapsulates the when, where, what and how of work. For the purpose of our research we also chose two outcomes that had been consistently mentioned by workstylers as needing to be measured: wellbeing and productivity. Wellbeing was defined as the extent to which an individual finds happiness, balance and meaning, and lacks stress in their work. Productivity is defined as the ability of an individual to achieve their goals efficiently and effectively.

Without spoiling the ending, autonomy is amazing. Not just amazing but mind-blowing, in fact. Studies have found that those with more

autonomy take greater pride in and are more emotionally attached to their work.[2] Work–life balance,[3,4] job satisfaction,[5,6] engagement[7] and productivity[8] are all improved, while stress,[9] staff turnover[10] and exhaustion[11] are decreased. Efficiency has also been found to increase as people are able to choose their optimal working conditions,[12] save time and energy by reducing commuting time[13,14] and are forced to communicate more effectively.[15] So the academic literature overwhelmingly supports our anecdotal evidence that autonomy positively impacts wellbeing and productivity. :crosses_finish_line:

Measuring autonomy, wellbeing and productivity in workstyle working

Next we needed to define the hypothesis that we wanted to prove – that it is autonomy which is the key to elevating our wellbeing and step-changing our productivity. Through our research we looked to answer the question: does workstyle working (as practised at Hoxby) lead to higher levels of autonomy, wellbeing and productivity? If we have your full attention, then we'll begin...

In 2019 we ran the first version of our research within the Hoxby community through a survey asking Hoxbies to look at 25 statements about autonomy, wellbeing and productivity and to let us know how much they agreed (or disagreed) with each one using a Likert scale. :lollipop: Over the years we have evolved things a bit and the questionnaire now has 120 questions in total, but these are part of a broader piece of research we do each year at Hoxby (we'll have to write a separate book on that at some point!). The survey takes around half an hour, and we encourage Hoxbies to make themselves a big cup of tea and settle into a comfy chair before they begin. :cosy:

Most importantly, we remind them that they should only complete the survey at a time that suits their workstyle, and to be completely honest with their answers.

When the scores came in, we were thrilled to see Hoxby scored highly for autonomy, wellbeing and productivity (yay!). We also looked at the relationship between the variables and found that they were all strongly, positively correlated. High levels of autonomy were associated with high levels of both wellbeing and productivity (double yay!). The data implies that the Hoxbies who feel most autonomous (and have lots of control over setting and respecting their workstyle) are also happiest and most productive. It felt rewarding to know that everything we believed was proving to be true. This is what workstyle is all about and confirmed in data what we had already seen first-hand ourselves.

From 2020 we expanded our study to capture more responses from the community, building it into our yearly 'passport' process. All Hoxbies must now complete the survey in order to stay in the community and to benefit from the All-Community Profit Share where we share 25 per cent of our profits evenly among all the Hoxbies. This means we have a larger sample size which produces even more valid research. It also prevents participation bias which can artificially inflate results – where only individuals who are having a positive experience (and are likely to score more highly) choose to complete the survey.

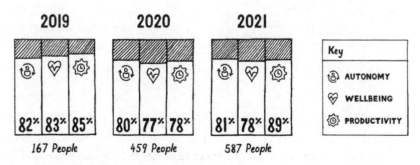

Autonomy–wellbeing–productivity scores at Hoxby

We now have three years of data, and the story has stayed the same – high scores and strong relationships across all three variables. :applause: Given the theory and anecdotal evidence in addition to these results, we can be confident that the workstyle way of working at Hoxby leads to higher levels of autonomy, wellbeing and productivity. :relieved_face: We were particularly excited to see that wellbeing and productivity remained high in a year when a global pandemic challenged people's mental health like never before. We are proud to be able to say workstyle helped protect Hoxbies from the negative effects, with both productivity and wellbeing actually increasing, against the odds.

Importantly, we also found that wellbeing explained the relationship between autonomy and productivity. It is *through wellbeing* that autonomy affects productivity. The implication is that productivity can be increased by improving wellbeing. Creating an autonomous working environment through the setting and respecting of workstyle is one of the best ways to do this – it boosts wellbeing and that in turn is responsible for boosting productivity. When we talk about creating a revolution at work, this is why. Workstyle is making revolutionary progress in improving wellbeing, and therefore productivity, through a system of work which puts autonomy and individualised working at its heart. :heart:

But wait, there's more! When we looked further into the data we also found something interesting within the measure of productivity. Each year Hoxbies have scored themselves most highly for their ability to work as a team, the quality of their work and their ability to meet the expectations of clients. Ironically, these are all the things that naysayers might argue suffer when teams are not based in an office together – if you know one, why not give them a copy of this book and stick a note in this page? :wink: The lowest score within those measured was for Hoxbies' ability to remain focused on the most relevant tasks when working. This is an expected side effect of working in a way where you may be interrupted by someone at the door with a delivery or the dog wanting a walk at a time that doesn't suit you, which could pull you away from the task at hand. We find insights like this so useful as we are now working with Hoxbies to help them tune out the noise, disconnect the doorbell and minimise other interruptions, such as ensuring they have their notifications switched off and can remain focused at the times that best suit them for deep work. We're excited to see more fascinating insights from next year's survey results and the years after that. #AlwaysImproving is one of our values, too.

The dark side

Our research has shown that the workstyle-respecting environment at Hoxby has enabled high levels of autonomy which are associated with high levels of wellbeing and productivity. So far, so positive. But our time spent digging deep into the theory and losing ourselves in the data also hinted at a dark side to autonomy.[16,17,18,19] We came across stories of workers (not Hoxbies, to be clear) who claimed they had full autonomy and were living the work–life balance dream and yet were 'always on', picking up the kids from school but checking their emails at the gate, or staying up until 2 a.m. to make sure a proposal was word perfect.

Therefore we're rounding off this chapter with two conditions that must be met for the full benefits of autonomy to be enjoyed. :notepad:

1. First, experienced responsibility – you must be mindful of the responsibility you feel for your work and how this might cause you to break your workstyle.

2. Second, true choice and autonomy – it must be your choice to work this way. It must be real freedom.

CONDITION ONE: Experienced responsibility

In 2020 we broadened our study to measure experienced responsibility, the degree to which an individual feels personally accountable and responsible for the results of the work they do. The research we read suggested that experienced responsibility tends to be higher in purpose-led organisations like Hoxby and also where people enjoy high levels of autonomy such as that enabled by workstyle. Theoretically, when you align closely with the purpose of your work, you are more likely to hold yourself accountable for the outcome.[20] On top of this, the more you are able to set your own way of working, the more responsibility you will feel for the output.

This was important to investigate as high levels of experienced responsibility are important in order to be diligent workers but can prevent us from respecting our own workstyle. It can make us more likely to go above and beyond to deliver outstanding quality, and we might not rest until we feel truly satisfied with our work. This mindset could encourage us to work extra hours or to work at undesirable times in order to deliver something we feel wholly proud of. As suspected, Hoxby scored highly for experienced responsibility. Knowing this has reinforced the importance of the workstyle-supporting infrastructure and leadership at Hoxby and of educating Hoxbies to be mindful of this potential pitfall. We have come to realise it is not simply enough to say everyone can work in their own workstyle, we need to find ways to help Hoxbies define their workstyle, commit to it, and for others to help them to ensure they enforce it. Workstylers need to be fully accountable for their output without breaking their workstyle, which often means becoming experts at saying 'no'. :person_with_arms_forming_an_x:

CONDITION TWO: Choice and autonomy in real life

The second really important thing to remember is that autonomy won't positively impact your wellbeing and productivity if your workstyle is not representative of your choice. For example, if you are forced to work from home as a result of cost-cutting measures (or a pandemic). Or if an employer gives you the 'autonomy' to work outside of the traditional 9-to-5 in order to improve your work–life balance, but the culture at your organisation makes you feel compelled to work all the time and you end up stressfully sending emails when you should be listening to your friend over coffee. Flexible working is a prime example of this, where, though many people can work in a non-traditional working pattern, they are conscious that the 'norm' in their organisation is to work 9-to-5, Monday to Friday, so they feel obliged to check in from time to time during the whole 'working week'. All of these are slight amendments to the status quo masquerading as autonomy. :elaborate_mask: They are 'autonomy' on paper but not in real life. The company is telling you to design your own working pattern but not creating the right framework for you to be able to do so and respect it. This is not workstyle – workstyle comes with true autonomy.

As a final note, we wanted to mention that we have also spent many hours and days looking for research from other organisations, or any existing data that we could benchmark our results against. But with little success. Frustratingly, it seems there are very few organisations out there willing to put themselves under the microscope to help make the world of work a better place (mind-boggling, we know) and none doing research comparable to ours. For us, the fact there is no comparable study in existence currently serves to reinforce just how important it is that we continue with this study and share the results as widely as possible. :loudspeaker: If you know an organisation that would like to replicate the study with us, we'd be delighted, so please do pass on our number! :scrap_of_paper: :scrawled_on_napkin:

Geek box: The academic literature on autonomy that underpins our belief in workstyle

By Annika Hart, future of work specialist, organisational psychologist and Managing Director of Futureproofing, Hoxby

As far back as 1976, a couple of academics named Hackman and Oldham came up with the Job Characteristics Model of Work Motivation[21] (quite the mouthful, I know). This model includes autonomy as a core job dimension that leads to high motivation, high performance, high satisfaction, and low absenteeism and turnover (Hackman and Oldham, 1976).[22] In particular, autonomy promotes these outcomes via a critical psychological state: experienced responsibility for the work. When an employee has autonomy in their work, success will depend on their own decisions. An employee with autonomy should therefore feel a strong personal responsibility for the outcome of their work, motivating them to perform well, in turn generating positive feedback and creating a self-perpetuating cycle of positive work motivation that drives good performance and wellbeing.

Hackman and Oldham found strong support for the relationship between autonomy and positive work outcomes in their model. In a sample of 658 employees across 62 different jobs and 7 organisations, they found autonomy was significantly positively correlated with motivation, satisfaction and work effectiveness and negatively correlated with absenteeism – a brilliant finding given the breadth of the research and the fact that this was over 45 years ago when the majority of organisations and workers were still in a hierarchical and traditional mindset. They found the same correlations in these four areas were true for experienced responsibility.

Other academics took the work of Hackman and Oldham further with the design of the Job Demand-Control (JDC) (Karasek, 1979)[23] and Job Demands-Resources (JDR) (Demerouti et al., 2001)[24] models (again, not the catchiest of names). Both models describe how autonomy influences wellbeing and productivity through three processes: a 'job strain' process, a 'motivational' process and a 'buffering' process.

Let's start with the 'job strain' process. This explains how a combination of high job demands (for example, work overload and time pressures) and low autonomy will negatively impact wellbeing and performance. Whereas a combination of low job demands (for example, a well-resourced team with realistic deadlines) and high autonomy will prevent job strain and lead to higher levels of wellbeing and productivity. There is plenty of evidence for the strain hypothesis in the research. Working in a high-strain job (with high demands and low autonomy) has been found to be associated with lower wellbeing and job satisfaction and higher levels of burnout (Van der Doef and Maes, 1999).[25]

Next let's look at the 'motivational' process, which is best explained through Self-Determination Theory (Ryan and Deci, 2000).[26] This theory argues that humans have three basic psychological needs that must be fulfilled in order to achieve optimal functioning: autonomy, competence and relatedness. When these needs are met, individuals will experience higher levels of wellbeing and will be engaged and motivated to perform better in an organisational context. The theory explains that autonomy affects both intrinsic and extrinsic motivation. Intrinsic motivation is defined as the doing of an activity for its inherent satisfaction. Autonomy affects intrinsic motivation as individuals feel free to choose to do things that are interesting or personally meaningful to them. Extrinsic motivation refers to behaviour that is driven by external rewards. Autonomy affects an employee's extrinsic motivation through the facilitation of the accomplishment of goals.

Lastly, the 'buffer' process explains how autonomy can protect employees against the negative effects of high demands, so that even in an environment where job demands are high, increasing autonomy can still increase wellbeing and performance. For example, if an employee has the autonomy to choose what to work on, they may decide to engage in challenging tasks and learn new skills – arguably an environment in which job demands are high and therefore their wellbeing and performance should be lower according to the strain hypothesis. But in this scenario, the employee still experiences high job satisfaction as it was their choice to take on the tasks.

In addition to these models, there has been more recent research that shows that a better work–life balance is positively correlated with both autonomy and wellbeing (Wood et al., 2018;[27] Demerouti et al., 2014[28]). There have been two mechanisms suggested to explain this. First, a time-regulation mechanism suggests that autonomy reduces conflict between work and private responsibilities and improves work–life balance. Second, a recovery-regulation mechanism suggests that autonomy over when, where and how an individual works would facilitate recovery through in-work and between-work rest time, preventing work overload and the resulting negative impact on work outcomes (Nijp et al., 2012).[29]

Overall, all these models point to autonomy at work being good for individuals and good for the organisations that implement it – providing a strong theoretical foundation for workstyle.

So to recap, through the longitudinal study into workstyle working at Hoxby we have shown that this revolutionary way of working creates high levels of autonomy, which is associated with high levels of wellbeing and in turn with high levels of productivity. This proves workstyle can succeed in practice at an organisational and at an individual level.

When you have the absolute freedom to choose your workstyle and you are dedicated to respecting your workstyle regardless of any external pressures, you will be happier and more engaged and will perform better at work. It's as simple as that. :green_tick:

Over the following chapters of the book we will look in more detail at how we, and other workstylers, have found working in this way has elevated our wellbeing and step-changed our productivity, as well as highlighting where there is further research over and above our own study to support this. We will then look in more detail at the wider implications that mass adoption of workstyle could have for building a more inclusive society and for bringing diverse groups together to find new solutions to some of society's most pressing problems. Read on as we demonstrate the revolutionary power of workstyle.

Chapter summary

- Hoxby is the prototype organisation we created to test workstyle in practice and see how it impacts both individuals and businesses. We wanted to empirically measure the effects of workstyle so that we could share what we had learned and inspire others to join the revolution – so we set up a longitudinal study that we repeat every year.

- The study looks at the relationship between autonomy (our chosen academic proxy for workstyle as it is a very close match), wellbeing and productivity. Over the past three years we have found that all three of these factors are positively correlated and that it is *through wellbeing* that autonomy improves productivity. This means that productivity can be increased by increasing wellbeing.

- The theory surrounding this area, and the results of our study, have also shown that autonomy can have a dark side. First, it increases the 'experienced responsibility' felt for tasks such that people feel so accountable for their work that they go above and beyond to deliver – prioritising the quality of the work over respecting their workstyle. And second, for all the good we know it can do, autonomy at work won't positively impact your wellbeing and productivity if your workstyle is not representative of your choice: choice and autonomy have to go hand in hand.

- Overall, our research has proved that autonomy through workstyle can enable an individualised system of work that is better for wellbeing and productivity.

- **From the mouth of a workstyler:** 'I joined the workstyle revolution because... sitting in traffic or a cramped train for more than three hours a day and then at a desk for another eight hours just seemed like a huge waste of time and affected me in more ways than I care to remember. Autonomy and having the freedom to choose is everything. Working the hours that suit me, when I'm at my most productive and creative, and still having time to enjoy my life and my family is irreplaceable.' Joana, Sliema, Malta

Fact to remember: Over our three years of researching workstyle working at Hoxby, scores for autonomy, wellbeing and productivity have averaged an incredible 80 per cent.[30]

 And finally... The academic proxy for workstyle is autonomy. Individualisation of work is dependent autonomy. The future of work is all about autonomy. Maybe we should use the autonomy wordmoji here? :autonomy:

Play your part in the workstyle revolution

Reflect

❏ Reflect on your own level of autonomy and how it might be impacting your wellbeing and productivity.

❏ Consider whether your wellbeing would be improved by having more control to decide for yourself when and where to work.

Act

❏ Write down five changes that would enable more autonomy in your work. Dream big and include things you might think aren't currently possible. Keep reading the book to find out how you can make this happen.

❏ Get in touch at lizzieandalex@workstylerevolution.com to find out more about the Hoxby longitudinal study or if you would like your organisation to get involved. We would love to further test the link between autonomy, wellbeing and productivity across as many work contexts as possible and can help you do this at your organisation.

❏ Become an expert on autonomy and read Hackman and Oldham's original research. :future_of_work_maestro:

Inspire

❏ Ask friends how much autonomy they have in their work. Did they know that autonomy is linked to productivity and wellbeing? Do your friends with greater autonomy feel happier and more productive? (We would love to know what you find out. :curious_cat:)

❏ Suggest to your boss (if you have one) that you would benefit from more autonomy at work. Approach the conversation with the statistics and research findings from this chapter in mind.

PART 2

WORKSTYLE ELEVATES YOUR WELLBEING

SEVEN

What is wellbeing?

The term 'wellbeing' can be traced back to the 16th century,[1] but only recently has become something people appreciate they need to consciously care for in themselves.[2] In the context of our longitudinal study we defined it as 'the extent to which an individual finds happiness, balance and meaning, and lacks stress in their work', but wellbeing is about more than just work. The World Health Organization defines health as 'complete physical, mental, and social wellbeing'.[3] In fact, it could be argued that wellbeing is one of the fundamental goals of human endeavour. It's why we're all here. It is a vital component that allows us all to flourish in all aspects of life. The happiest, healthiest and most fulfilled people in life have high levels of wellbeing.[4]

Since wellbeing was first conceived of hundreds of years ago, we've learned huge amounts about the molecular biology of our bodies and our brains (OK, we haven't personally learned this :small_brains:), which has enabled us to extend our lives by developing drugs and technologies that heal and protect us from almost anything nature can throw at us. Amazing human advances have dramatically improved our standard of living, too. Whether it's picking up a prescription drug at the pharmacy to cure an ailment, buying a bunch of healthy bananas for 40p from the local supermarket or going abroad on holiday to relax and boost our mental health, there are many areas in which we have been able to improve our wellbeing thanks to human ingenuity.

And yet, despite all this remarkable progress, people are no happier than they were decades ago[5] and their wellbeing isn't reaping the benefits it could be. When you consider that at its most basic level people are still working the same way they did in 1817, it is possible that our system of work could be the underlying reason why their wellbeing hasn't moved forward as much as it should have. As the story on the next page shows, there are many people who have an unhealthy relationship with work without even realising it. :sleepwalking: All too often their wellbeing is taking a back seat.

Aliens and sandwiches – a short story

 nce upon a time you had to explain your current working day to an alien that landed on planet Earth. That you set an alarm clock to wake you up in the morning before daybreak, training your body out of its natural rhythm. Then you rush out of your nice warm home away from your young children before they wake, onto a crowded train or to spend an hour or more sitting in a motor vehicle, travelling dozens of miles at the busiest time of the day, rushing through the crowds to reach a desk with a screen, perched high in the sky in a truly impressive feat of engineering that we call a skyscraper.

You spend the next ten hours up there – during many months the only hours of natural daylight – staring at this screen, giving yourself back and neck pain in the process, barely moving your body all day, except perhaps to nip back down to ground level to grab a quick bite to eat. Although there are many wonderful culinary delights to sample in this world, you explain to the alien that you regularly choose to eat some processed meat trapped between two slices of bread. This takes less than four minutes to eat and has become so popular among your co-workers that even in just the small island called the UK that you live on, people consume around 3 billion of these each year.[6]

You remain at your desk for the rest of the afternoon, using the wonders of modern technology such as your phone and a laptop to call and even see others who aren't in the same location as you (this takes quite a bit of explaining to the confused alien), until the sun has dropped low in the sky. The alien, who remarkably speaks your language fluently, asks if it's dangerous to be outside in the open air too much, and you reply that actually you love being outside, that fresh air and exercise are really important for our physical and mental health, but you never really thought about it much because everyone accepts this is how we work.

To counteract your lack of movement all day, you explain that when you leave the office you battle the throngs of other humans spilling into crowded rooms to use machines that simulate the land moving under you so you have to run on the spot to keep up. Alternatively, you leave the office just in time to dash for after-school pick-up, arriving hot, sweaty, in a panic and stressed, with little energy left to engage with your offspring. Occasionally, on leaving the office you divert instead into small, overfilled buildings to drink large glasses of alcohol which give you a mild giddy feeling and have the effect of helping you forget about the day you've just had. You arrive back home a few hours later with just enough time to have a quick meal with your family, or heat up the leftovers, before you crash into bed to recover enough strength to do the whole thing again tomorrow.

You explain that you repeat this routine for five out of every seven times the world spins on its axis, so that you can earn enough promissory notes of credit to spend on things like getting other people to cook for you from time to time or listening to them play instruments together. When the alien asks if this is unusual, you explain that the process is replicated by more than 70 per cent of the population,[7] whose combined behaviour has led to a period of abrupt climate breakdown and we are now in the midst of a mass extinction of our own making.

The alien looks at you, bewildered, and you feel you have to justify your part in perpetuating this perplexing state of affairs, so you claim, somewhat feebly, 'Well, we all have to work to make a living.'

Workstyle and wellbeing

So maybe you don't work in a skyscraper, and you always have breakfast with your kids before you go to work. But the point here is that how we engage with our work is critical for our wellbeing and can give us a flourishing, fulfilling life – through having a healthy body and healthy mind, feeling connected to others, being able to learn and grow, and finding meaning and purpose in what we do.

Earning a living is fundamental for all of us – we can't meet our basic needs, like having enough food, a roof over our heads, staying warm and feeling secure, without it – but working to earn that living in the best way for us as individuals is also critical to ensure our own wellbeing. :zen:

Our research proves that workstyle is better for our wellbeing because it provides much greater levels of autonomy. We can personally corroborate this from our own experience, too. We have found working in a workstyle way has transformed our wellbeing. We are happier and healthier than ever before. Alex hasn't had a stress-related vertigo spell or jaw pain since having his own workstyle, and Lizzie is in more of a positive mindset than ever, thanks to workstyle and in spite of her recent cancer.

We have reflected a lot on the different ways workstyle has improved our wellbeing and grouped these into themes over the next five short chapters, reflecting on three ways that we have found workstyle to be of most benefit to our wellbeing in each case. Luckily, these also fit neatly with our next very simple hand gesture. :hand_up:

So this is our take on the five main ways workstyle has improved our wellbeing:

> **MIND** – Having a healthy mind.
>
> **PURPOSE** – Creating meaning in our lives.
>
> **LEARNING** – Directing our own growth and development.
>
> **CONNECTION** – Building relationships with others.
>
> **BODY** – Having a healthy body.

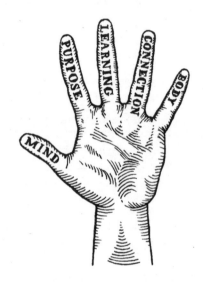

EIGHT

Workstyle elevates your wellbeing: MIND

Workstyle story: Cat Lewis-Shand

Mum, mental health champion, facilitator, trainer and speaker, multimedia specialist, music composer

I remember the moment my life changed for ever. I was sitting at home relaxing with friends. Out of nowhere I felt a huge 'bang' on the side of my head and a feeling of intense pain. It was agonising, but also strange. I even looked round to see if something had just hit me.

The pain went away but not for long. It came back, and it got worse. After seven years of appointments and waiting I was finally diagnosed with occipital neuralgia, a rare form of cluster headache also known as ice-pick headaches. It means that, at worst, I can experience over 20 excruciating lightning-like headaches in one day.

Before the diagnosis I was already coping with depression and down days when I found it hard to focus, find motivation or even get out of bed. The pain was sometimes unbearable and that, coupled with my depression, meant I had to retire from the role I loved, as a teaching assistant for kids with special needs, on health grounds at the age of 46. To further add to the stress, I was originally turned down for the state benefits I was entitled to and had to take my case to court, where the decision was overturned.

But I missed earning a living and the fulfilment of work. I started asking myself how I would ever find a job flexible enough to fit around days when I couldn't work because of my headaches and my depression. I was scared that I wouldn't be able to provide for my family – my wife and my two daughters. That was when I hit rock bottom. The headaches made my depression worse. My depression made my headaches worse. It was the worst kind of snowball effect. Something had to change, and so I set out in search of a way I could fit my work around my mental and physical health.

Thankfully, my life – and work – are very different now. The change from not working to discovering workstyle made me feel like life was good again. Suddenly I was able to work and bring in some money. My self-esteem went through the roof. I found myself smiling again – all the time.

I found work to fit around my unique circumstances within the Hoxby community, and straight away it was fun, rewarding and fulfilling. I could work when and where I wanted and work doing things close to my heart, from being a mental health champion to writing Christmas spoof songs for Alex and Lizzie. It meant I could work around my headaches and depression and also attend things like hospital appointments with ease. And I could earn a living in a way which suited me and supported my family while fulfilling both my passion for raising mental health awareness and my love of composing and performing music. This experience at Hoxby was a big factor in me later being offered a role at mental health charity Mind as their Senior Training and Consultancy Officer for Workplace Wellbeing. It feels amazing to be able to continue to improve so many people's lives and to continue to help workstylers, too, with their mental health alongside my work at Mind.

Workstyle has been life-changing for me. It gives me the freedom to literally work around my pain and depression – to put my life first. I still experience my headaches, but they're less frequent these days because I'm less stressed. I can take breaks whenever I need to. I can work in the evenings or at weekends when it suits. And it's wonderful to once again be able to contribute financially to my family. Not being able to do so before workstyle had really impacted my mental health.

Remember that snowball I talked about earlier? It's gone. Completely melted away. Because now I can take time for myself and look after myself.

I'm grateful and proud to be part of the amazing workstyle community. Community is important because even when you have your own workstyle, you need a connection with other people.

It's no exaggeration to say that workstyle has given me a new lease of life, a newfound sense of belonging and a whole world of new friendships.

The mental health opportunity

According to the World Health Organization, almost 1 billion people are living with a mental disorder.[1] There is a global crisis in mental health.

And work is a major contributor to this problem. Nearly one in six of us are experiencing mental health issues at work.[2] Twenty-seven per cent of those suffering from anxiety say that work is the root cause.[3] In 2019/20 there were 17.9 million sick days taken in the UK because of stress, depression and anxiety.[4] Better support for employees' mental health at work could save UK businesses up to £45 billion each year.[5] And yet very few organisations take meaningful action to truly protect the mental health of their employees.

Many companies are making small interventions to support mental health and awareness of the problem is growing. However, most of these schemes deal with the symptoms of poor mental health rather than fundamentally addressing the root causes at work. Research has shown 97 per cent of professionals feel their employer has a responsibility to support the mental health and wellbeing of staff and 88 per cent consider the mental health policies of a potential employer important when looking for a new role.[6] And yet only half of UK employers have a mental health policy in place.[7]

We believe that workstyle can be transformative for mental health. Whether you're someone who has a diagnosed mental health condition, someone who is experiencing mental health difficulties or someone who is simply looking to improve your everyday mental health, the same principles apply. In our experience of workstyle working, there are three ways in which it improves mental health compared with traditional working practices:

1. **AUTHENTICITY** – Being true to yourself.

2. **OUTPUT** – Measuring your work in terms of what you deliver.

3. **SPARK** – Discovering your sources of positive and negative energy.

1. AUTHENTICITY – Being true to yourself :for_real:

It is a sad reality that most organisations are not a diverse representation of society. In fact, a report by Deloitte and the Alliance for Board Diversity into board diversity of Fortune 500 companies in the US didn't find a single company that reflected the demographic make-up of the US, with the benchmarks of 50 per cent women, 13 per cent Black, 18 per cent Hispanic and 6 per cent Asian/Pacific Islander.[8] Instead, all too often companies are groups of people who look, think and act the same, and those people who don't feel they fit with the majority (which, ironically, is often the majority :thinking_face:) work hardest to conform.

One of the most commonly cited reasons that workstylers give for leaving traditional work structures is to free themselves from the pressure to conform. Consciously or not, people try to fit in and it compels them to make numerous micro-adjustments that help them to conform at the expense of their individuality and their true, authentic selves. Pretending to be someone who wants to wear high heels every day when actually we work best in slippers is learning to stamp out a bit of ourselves.

One example of this is a professional footballer who kept their sexuality a secret until deciding to come out as openly gay in 1990.[9] Justin Fashanu was the first Black footballer to command a £1 million transfer fee, in 1981, and while he certainly isn't the last in this regard, he remains, more than 30 years later, the only prominent player in professional English football to be openly gay. With 3 per cent of the UK population being openly gay,[10] it seems highly likely there are others not feeling they are able to be their true selves at work. Justin later committed suicide, and we are left wondering about the other gay footballers since Justin, whose wellbeing has also likely suffered at the hands of not being able to be their full, authentic selves in their work. Whatever work it is that people do, suppressing who they really are compromises their confidence in themselves and their individuality, at the expense of their mental health.

Research at the University of Novi Sad in Serbia demonstrated this. There are three 'elements' of authenticity – the first is authentic living (living as your true self), the second is accepting external influence (the extent to which you take on the behaviours of those around you) and the third is self-alienation (lacking a feeling of integrity or connection with your true self). The research showed that when these are taken together, they are a statistically significant predictor of psychological wellbeing and overall mental health.[11] Laura's story about her blue hair, nose ring and flamboyant handwriting in Chapter 17 is a great example of how this is being ignored in traditional work and how embracing authenticity can transform mental health and wellbeing.

When we feel we can really be ourselves and are recognised for the individual contributions we make, we are happier. We feel more valued, more connected to our work and enjoy a greater sense of belonging[12] (blue hair and all). :nose_ring: Working in our own workstyle sets an expectation that we protect and express our individuality. And authenticity in your work specifically reduces the risk of two negative elements of wellbeing: boredom and burnout.[13]

The authentic workstyler

Whether going the whole hog or simply adopting some of the principles, workstyle is about openly being your 'whole' self at work. It improves mental health by removing the false dichotomy between work and life. When we make a distinction between who we are in our 'work life' and who we are in our 'real life', the implication is that work is distinct from life rather than an important part of it. Planning your workstyle means looking at your whole life – and considering the role that work plays within it rather than seeing the two as separate. We have found doing this helps to pre-emptively reflect on where burnout, stress or other mental health struggles might happen, which means you can discuss these areas with others and be open about the challenges you face.

2. OUTPUT – Measuring your work in terms of what you deliver :trophy:

Many people still consider time spent working as one of the key measures of success at work. Part of becoming a workstyler and enabling workstyle to succeed is to stop appraising ourselves in these terms. Some people are so entrenched in the idea of working a certain number of hours in a week that they feel as though this is the primary requirement of work. This might be because they are insecure overachievers,[14] working 15-hour days and yet still worrying that they've not done enough work, or perhaps because they're people pleasers, meaning when someone asks them to work late to help on an urgent task, they say yes without considering whether they really should for their own wellbeing.

Evaluating 'success' at work by hours spent doing it also creates other problems. This time-based mentality can be hugely detrimental to mental health, leading to an 'always on' approach, with some people having such a 'fixation of checking and quickly responding to messages' that it is now a named condition called 'telepressure'.[15] Recent research has even shown that recipients overestimate the importance of emails they receive outside of work (because they assume they must be extremely urgent to have been sent during off-hours) and therefore feel even more compelled to respond immediately.[16] This extends to time expressly taken away from work, too, with 60 per cent of people checking work emails on holiday.[17] :switch_off: And yet working long hours leads to 27 per cent of people feeling depressed, 34 per cent feeling anxious and 58 per cent feeling irritable.[18] New levels of connectivity have led to a rise in 'workaholism', which has been linked with both physical and mental health conditions, including headaches, back and joint pain, anxiety, depression and substance abuse.[19]

Until recently, however, rather than being treated as a grave process of addiction, workaholism has been celebrated as dedication to a career. From Silicon Valley's 'sleeping is cheating' culture to the London law firms with sleep pods at the office so employees never have to leave, being all consumed with work can be a subtle but important part of workplace culture that can leave a devastating legacy on mental health.

Before he co-invented workstyle, as Alex explained in his workstyle story, he would work 50 hours a week on the basis that he believed this was how he could validate that he was giving all he could to the job – both to himself and to his employer. It was a thought that ultimately led to his burnout – partly because it was more time than he could feasibly give his best positive energy to work each week, but more importantly because it was a measure of time (in) rather than value (out). We can always work more, or less, but the truth is that our fulfilment and success don't come from how much time we spend working but from what we achieve while we do it. It's why workstyle has a culture underpinning it which is respectful of life, and that when a workstyler is 'off' they should be fully switched off, with others taking on shared work in their absence in order to still ensure high standards are met, deadlines are hit and to achieve the collective goal. In this way, workstyle offers the opportunity to measure our performance by what our working effort delivers. :slice_of_cake:

After all, Parkinson's law tells us that 'work expands so as to fill the time available for its completion',[20] which means that, if you have a number of hours to do a task, it will take you that amount of time. Focusing on the outcome can free us to think more about what needs to be achieved rather than how we will fill the time needed to achieve it.

Workstyle removes ambiguity about success criteria at work and gives individual freedom to decide how each of us will work to achieve a defined output in a way that best suits our mental health. It puts the emphasis of work on what needs to be achieved and focuses the mind on the ultimate output (and outcome) rather than on the number of hours involved or when those hours are worked.

3. SPARK – Discovering your sources of positive and negative energy :high_voltage:

Knowing ourselves and managing our positive energy can be make-or-break for our mental health. Understanding our personal sources of energy, positivity and inspiration can unlock great things, as Cat's workstyle story shows.

We have found that creating a workstyle of your own helps you to understand where you get positive energy from, what makes you feel inspired and how your work can play a positive role in your life, and then ensures your way of working is reflective of that. The power of creating this spark is not to be underestimated. Creating the individual conditions to feel as personally happy, energetic and inspired at work as possible is one of the things workstyle can give us that traditional structures of work can't. Lizzie used to suffer from stress at work – letting positive energy tip over into negative pressure – but since moving to work in her own workstyle she feels much more in control, works the way that is most effective for her, has time for exercise and family, and has reduced her stress levels significantly. :peaceful: But life is a journey, and when building up working time after cancer treatment she found the negative energy creeping back in. She reflected on sources of positive energy, as well as those that were draining it, and created a new workstyle that was fit for that period in her life. Having the autonomy to be reflective about removing stressors (unnecessary video calls) and creating energisers (a fun-filled daily Threadit exchange with Alex) and putting these into everyday practice through workstyle worked wonders for her state of mind and in turn for her overall mental health at what was a particularly difficult time.

As every parent of a young child will understand, setting and maintaining boundaries is incredibly important. We have five between us so we know this acutely well. Boundaries help children to make sense of the world and reduce the anxiety they feel when confronted with the unpredictability and complexity of our existence.[21] Without things like set meals, behavioural rules and bedtime routines, the world is simply too uncertain and unpredictable for children to cope with and is proven to lead to increases in anxiety and mental health disorders. However, while boundary setting has been the subject of much study in child developmental psychology, it's only recently started to be recognised as important in the workplace, in spite of more than 40 per cent of employees saying they are neglecting other aspects of their life because of work.[22] With any kind of work, boundaries are essential, and it's critical to set them in a way that is going to positively impact your wellbeing rather than setting them at the limits of your capacity. Managing your energy means recognising and setting your own boundaries, and workstyle helps us to reflect on this and make decisions to find a healthy balance between life and work wherever possible.

Workstyle gives you the language to talk about when work might tip too far, crossing these boundaries or taking more of your total energy than you're happy for it to. Setting your workstyle invites you to reflect on where your spark comes from and what might cause you to lose it, in order to channel your energy in the most invigorating way and look after your mental health.

Geek box: How organisations that are structured to provide more autonomy at work support better mental health

By Nancy Hey, Executive Director, What Works Centre for Wellbeing

Wellbeing is often associated with leisure – the idea that it encompasses relaxation and a lack of stress. But doing difficult, important things well with other people is hugely rewarding and, in turn, good for mental health and wellbeing. There are many areas of our lives where we might find these beneficial, collective and stretchy challenges: looking after the home, learning, volunteering and, of course, our work. From UK national population data we can see that a commonality between these activities is that they can provide people with a sense of purpose (What Works Wellbeing, 2021a)[23] – that what you do in life is worthwhile. This sense of purpose is an important aspect of wellbeing, one that is independent from and in addition to feelings and emotions.

That work is important to our wellbeing is one of the most robust findings in the literature. A systematic review which pulled together nationally representative surveys from the UK, Germany, Australia and the United States found that, when measuring life satisfaction on a 0–10 scale, the unemployed reported about 0.5 points lower satisfaction compared with those who were in employment (What Works Wellbeing, 2017a).[24] What's even more important is the longer-term impact of unemployment. Many factors affect our wellbeing, some more than others, but mostly we adapt to it. This is not the case with unemployment – it permanently impacts our lives for the long term and spills over into our social and civic lives, too (What Works Wellbeing, 2017a).[25]

But not all work is equal. What the numbers also tell us is that, on average, we are happiest at both 23 and 68 and most miserable during our working age (ONS, 2016).[26] The least 'happy' thing we can do (after being ill in bed) is being at work in the presence of our line manager (What Works Wellbeing, 2021a).[27] These findings correlate with rates of suicide (Statista, 2021)[28] and use of antidepressants (Pennington, 2021)[29] which peak at the same time as our mid-working-life misery. Clearly, then, improving both working life and inclusive work practices should be a high priority for improving mental health and wellbeing.

The Covid-19 pandemic has of course had far-reaching consequences for both mental health and work. The data that has emerged from this period provides us with opportunities to glean new insights into the role work plays in our wider lives. A revealing statistic from the ONS showed that at least 25 per cent of people reported that work helped them cope better during this time (What Works Wellbeing, 2021b).[30] So, work can help improve our mental health.

The research suggests that an important reason for this is having control and agency – factors that working can bestow on our lives. Having a high sense of control is related to positive psychological outcomes and is linked to an ability to feel healthy, whereas decreased control is associated with stress, depression and anxiety disorders. It has been shown that freedom of choice and the locus of control are found to predict life satisfaction better than any other known factor (Verme, 2009).[31] We can see this in many places, for example in South Australia where those who do not have control were found to be more than ten times more likely to have poor wellbeing (What Works Wellbeing, 2017b).[32] Additionally, it has been found that independence and work–life balance, which you could also describe as the freedom to choose, are important drivers of job satisfaction, a measure of contentment (de Neve, 2018).[33]

All this points to the importance of autonomy in supporting better mental health and the role work can play in supporting that. It is alarming, therefore, that a key finding in the 2017 Skills and Employment Survey (Cardiff University, 2017)[34] was that the proportion of workers who confirmed they have 'a lot of discretion over how they do their jobs' reduced from 62 per cent in 1992 to 38 per cent in 2017 – this is a huge drop for this type of measure, one that is both surprising and worrying.

The potential implications of work playing a positive part in supporting our mental health are far reaching – way beyond reducing absences through sickness and increasing productivity (What Works Wellbeing, 2017c).[35] The ripple effect is of great significance. Purposefully designing work to best support mental health has the potential to significantly improve things not just for the individual or organisation in question but also at a societal and national level.

For us, working in a workstyle way has been an opportunity to reflect more on our mental health, and workstyle has also empowered us to make changes in our lives to improve it. When we shed the baggage of conformity that traditional work loads upon us, we can be our individual, imperfect selves and focus the best of our energy towards the things that matter, in life and work. We feel lucky to be our true selves at work, but this shouldn't be a privilege.

Mental health is important to each and every one of us. We all think differently and feel differently and can look after our mental health in different ways, so having the autonomy to design our own workstyles gives us the ability to better care for ourselves. Our lives are unique, varied and constantly changing – our freedom to process that change and to stay on top of the stresses we encounter along the way helps ensure our long-term mental health, while incorporating the work that energises us into our lives is key to helping us to enjoy a happy, fulfilling career. Working towards meaningful outputs helps us to better appreciate our own value and improve our sense of self-worth beyond the amount of time we spend working. It all comes together as we feel confident being our authentic, unique and inspiring selves. To be the real you is to see the power of workstyle.

Chapter summary

- Traditional working is contributing to a global crisis in mental health, which is resulting in millions of sick days each year – a quarter of those suffering from anxiety saying work is the root cause.

  o **AUTHENTICITY:** Workstyle means work is individual to you and you can be your authentic self. This is better for your mental health and wellbeing generally rather than having to conform to societal norms or have a separate work persona.

  o **OUTPUT:** Being judged on your output and basing your success on what you deliver rather than how much time you spend working is better for your mental health and helps prevent burnout because it removes the ambiguity of success criteria and gives you the individual freedom to decide how to achieve an outcome.

  o **SPARK:** Having control over when and where you work is better for your mental health because you have more choice to work in a way that gives you more positive energy.

- Individualising work through workstyle better supports mental health and improves wellbeing because it allows people to be their authentic selves and because of the control it gives people over how they direct their energy at work.

From the mouth of a workstyler: 'I joined the workstyle revolution because... following the sudden death of my seven-year-old daughter, Annaliese, I totally lost myself for a while. Getting back to work felt scary and stressful, and I just couldn't imagine working full time. Workstyle allowed me to pick the work and hours that suited my level of mental resilience and gave me the space I needed to take things slowly. I felt beyond lucky to be able to get back into my groove in this way after such a devastating experience.' Clare, Hazlemere, UK

Fact to remember: Almost 1 billion people are living with a mental disorder.[36]

And finally... Parkinson's law says that work expands to fill the time available for its completion. So we suggest you aim to complete this book within the next seven days and tell us whether Parkinson's law prevails. :speed_reading:

Play your part in the workstyle revolution

Reflect

☐ Reflect on how authentic you are able to be in your work – are you the same person at work as you are outside of work? How much have you changed in order to conform to work norms? Compare your profile picture on LinkedIn with your Instagram profile picture. How different are these two people and why?

☐ Consider your top achievements over the past 12 months. What are you most proud of? What made you happy?

☐ Think about the things that fill you with positivity and the things that drain you.

Act

☐ Identify one way you could be more authentic at work. Implement it today (or whenever you're next working).

☐ For each achievement you listed as the top achievements over the past 12 months, what was the outcome or output? Reframe your work the same way – write down the outcomes and outputs that you achieve rather than the tasks you do. How does this exercise make you feel about your work?

☐ Out of the things that give you energy, pick one and commit to doing it more. Pick one thing that drains you and consider how you could do it less.

Inspire

☐ Choose a friend or a co-worker to hold you to account for your wellbeing. Share with them the actions you have committed to and encourage them to reflect and act in the same way (this also works well in groups).

❑ Encourage your organisation to move to output-based working. Look on WorkstyleRevolution.com for tools to help you do this.

❑ Ask for your next project to be defined in terms of outputs, with a clear brief that outlines the deliverables but lets you approach the work in the way that suits you best.

NINE

Workstyle helps you be well: PURPOSE

Workstyle story: Ed Horrocks

Water baby, dad (of four), husband, traveller, brand strategist, oh – and resident bedtime storyteller

Once upon a time I was living my best corporate life and fulfilling my passion for building and guiding purpose-driven organisations. My success in leading creative teams for world-class businesses had set me on a personal journey, exchanging sun-drenched Sydney for a threadbare train seat into grayscale London for work. A hefty three and a half hours of commuting each day surely had to reap its rewards? And it did. It was an incredible time.

Head of the Creative Studio and subsequently Head of Brand at an exhilarating high-profile firm, I thrived, most of all on the inspiration I took from the CEO who was embarking on defining purpose as an integrated part of the business strategy.

Placing purpose at the core ignited a real spark within me personally and this spark fuelled a move to one of the biggest consulting firms in the world. Long days of presenteeism were replaced by long days with the 'flexible' option of working remotely and my train carriage seat was replaced with the saddle of a Boris bike which made for a slightly more positive commute.

Life felt good, and there was the odd opportunity to take my kids to school, but by no means was I achieving a work–life balance. More of a work–work–work–life imbalance! Home time during the week remained a luxury I just didn't have, and all too often my eldest daughters would sit on the stairs waiting for me to get home and hoping for a bedtime story that never came.

Fast-forward through a redundancy and a consequent dipping of my toe into the world of freelancing and I recall the days that I started to create my own workstyle (not that I knew it as that back then). I began setting my own rules and boundaries which resulted in more time with my family, more presenteeism at school plays, more mealtimes together and, of course, more availability for bedtime stories. I was even able to join the local Masters Swimming Team because I finally had a schedule that allowed space for the training. I felt an immense sense of release and freedom, especially having always assumed this lifestyle was unachievable alongside a successful career.

Having removed the shackles of a traditional corporate role, I then found it hard to find another 'full-time' position that fitted. The value I attached to time at home had become the 'money can't buy' variety and with this mindset firmly on board, I discovered the workstyle revolution and a like-minded community of people. Workstyle helped me identify and fulfil my personal purpose: to inspire purpose in others and make ambitions reality (starting with my own kids).

Today I am filled with pride rather than guilt in responding to clients either side of the school run or even doing a video call in a wetsuit, surf-ready, in a beach car park while our family enjoys our four-week long summer travels. My work and output are the measure of my success, with my wellbeing as the ultimate winner.

Recently, when I was asked to work away for a few days, my son struggled to understand why I couldn't be there to read his bedtime story as normal. This kind of normal suits me just fine. I believe that workstyle will help change the world of work so more people can live their own happily ever after. Workstyle is the future.

The ~~End~~ Beginning.

The meaningful work opportunity

As Ed's story shows first-hand, purpose is critical to living a fulfilling, flourishing life. As a number of wise philosophers and psychologists over the years have identified, humans can survive almost any manner of living if they have a strong enough reason to. We have heard incredible stories of this in practice, too, such as climate activist Greta Thunberg's double crossing of the Atlantic on a boat at 16 years old. Driven by her passion for saving the environment, she completed the carbon-neutral trip with no toilet, fixed shower, cooking facilities or proper beds,[1] enduring hardship and discomfort in the name of her purpose.

Purpose is the cause or belief that drives us. It is the overarching sense of what matters in our lives, a north star to guide our decisions and actions. We experience purposefulness when we work towards something personally meaningful. Individuals who feel their purpose is fulfilled through their life and work are happier,[2] more resilient[3] and healthier.[4] One study even showed that for each one-point increase in purpose on a six-point scale, an individual spent 17 per cent fewer nights in hospital.[5] Remarkable.

When aligned with our purpose, work can not only keep us out of hospital, it can provide huge satisfaction, too. We know ourselves that through our work we are changing people's lives, or at least that's what they've told us, and we feel an enormous sense of fulfilment and increased wellbeing as a result. As we all get better at understanding ourselves and can create the relationship we want with work, we can benefit from great energy and satisfaction. :joy:

The problem is that many people are not working in a way that is aligned with their purpose and their wellbeing is being negatively impacted as a result. Organisations are unclear on their purpose, and even where it is defined, there is a disconnect between what people feel is their personal purpose and the purpose of the organisation they work for. Only 53 per cent of workers in the UK feel their organisation has a sense of purpose,[6] and one survey found that the top priorities of employees were represented in only 11 per cent of organisational mission statements.[7] Some people tell themselves that this doesn't matter, that the things they do for work are not for the pleasure they give them, or the impact they are making on the world. They consider work as serving a function, to earn enough to live and pursue their passions when they're not at work. But many are realising that traditional ways of working don't leave space for purpose outside of work either.[8] Ninety-four per cent of professionals in one study said they work more than 50 hours per week,[9] and another survey found 26 per cent of work is being done outside of working hours.[10] So it is not surprising that 87 per cent of Brits said they are looking for more fulfilment through their work.[11]

Much has been written in recent years about the power of purpose, not just for businesses but for people, too. Simon Sinek has inspired a generation with his book *Start with Why*,[12] and people are now much more conscious of the need to discover their own sense of purpose, and the support exists to do it. Workstyle can help you to find meaning and purpose in work and also help make time for the pursuit of your purpose in your life beyond your work.

We have found that workstyle helps us to live and work with more purpose. There are three ways it does this:

1. **CHOICE** – Doing more of the work you love.

2. **JOURNEY** – Staying on course when life changes.

3. **LEGACY** – Working towards your eulogy.

1. CHOICE – Doing more of the work you love :heart:

Workstyle gives you the complete freedom to choose when and where you work, which means those factors no longer need to dictate what you do. It means that your attention is focused on 'what' you are actually doing and 'why' – your raison d'être – rather than because a particular job happens to have a short commute or because they are the largest employer in your area. Workstyle should mean that when choosing work you aren't constrained by the 'when' and 'where' of that opportunity and you can redefine your psychological contract with work to focus more squarely on what you love to do. Widespread adoption of workstyle opens up new possibilities for individuals being able to work with any organisation, anywhere in the world. This affords us a new freedom to choose for ourselves what we actually want to do for work and means we can choose work that fits more closely with our individual sense of purpose.

With this newfound choice, we can bring enjoyment and passion into our relationship with work. Coming back to our love of language, the word 'amateur' ultimately comes from the Latin *amare*, meaning 'to love'. In the past it was used to describe skilled artisans, those that created things for the love and process of doing so rather than for the money. However, now that the majority of us consider ourselves professionals, the word 'amateur' has become a bit of an insult, used to describe shoddy performance. We are Alex Hirst and Lizzie Penny, and we are amateurs. We do what we do for the love of the task. Our purpose is to create a happier, more fulfilled society through a world of work without bias. When we are passionate about what we do, we feel more empowered, we have more belief in our abilities, we are more creative and innovative, more motivated and our job satisfaction and performance increase.[13] :high_five:

Finding a sense of purpose in the work you do may feel like an impossible task for some, but the world of work is changing and making it easier for everyone. The B Corp movement is spearheading a wholesale shift from working for profit alone to working for purpose and profit. Research has shown organisations with purpose outperform others – a recent study by Accenture showed companies with better environmental, social and governance ratings generated returns 2.6 times better than those with lower ratings in this area.[14] One of the reasons for this is because their workers are more connected to each other and to the business. This change of emphasis is representative of a wider mindset change. Though it still underpins the vast majority of work, money is not the only motivation for us as it may have been for previous generations. We derive a greater sense of fulfilment by making a meaningful contribution and having a positive impact on the world.

Workstyle gives us the opportunity to choose to work with companies which share our values and on projects which connect to our own sense of purpose – wherever they may be in the world.

2. JOURNEY – Staying on course when life changes :smiling_poo:

Life changes and every life is different. The workstyle stories in this book are great examples of this, but everyone has their own story and their own journey to navigate. Our need to adapt to change is a constant within all of our lives, whether it's moving house, falling ill, new caring

responsibilities or simply getting older. Workstyle gives us a new opportunity to focus on this ourselves and to evolve our work alongside what's happening in our lives. Workstyle protects your ability to stay true to your purpose when life throws you curveballs and also affords you the capacity to adjust your purpose as you go through the phases of your life.

During those phases of change, our priorities are brought into focus – the more acute the change, the sharper the focus becomes. Life-changing events that have negative consequences can also bring hugely positive responses in return. Alex often says that reaching burnout was what forced him to change his life to focus on more purposeful work. Workstyle, change and purpose are interconnected. Workstyle enables us to adapt and respond to whatever life throws at us, consciously adjusting the when and where of our work to stay on the path of our purpose. A stronger purpose in turn makes us more resilient to change. Studies show that a sense of purpose protects us against stressful life events and makes us less likely to hit rock bottom.[15]

3. LEGACY – Working towards your eulogy :smiling_face_with_halo:

'What gets you out of bed in the morning?' Alex's dad would ask at a time in his teenage life when he couldn't think of an answer beyond the type of breakfast he'd ideally surface for at around 11 a.m. (anything that involved bacon, by the way). Of course, he was trying to understand what really excited Alex and what he was motivated to achieve. Alex spent the next two decades searching for an answer, and everything he did during that time took him towards it, step by incremental step.

Finding purpose through our work often means reflecting on why we work at all. For the vast majority of us it is to earn income and fund our lifestyle, but over and above that many people are conditioned to think of success in a specific way, be it job title, salary or some other modern-day equivalent of working your way to the corner office in the 1980s. But status doesn't necessarily benefit wellbeing. And beyond a certain point, income has little impact on happiness or improved human experience.[16] Feeling engaged in our work and connected to what we do is something for everyone to aspire to, but also something that is felt only by a small minority currently – just 15 per cent of people say they are truly engaged at work.[17]

When you are free to work with autonomy, you are free to work towards the things that matter to you – not necessarily towards a promotion or a pay rise. Your new definition of success is how your output contributes to your purpose, not whether you are climbing the metaphorical ladder of job titles. When you understand your purpose, you can choose to work with companies that will contribute towards it. This is key to a happier, more fulfilling career and a legacy you will be proud to leave behind.

Starting with why, in the context of our lives, is a big question, which we can begin to answer for ourselves when thinking about our legacy. For the first half of our lives, we both worked hard to improve our CVs. This was a conscious effort in furthering our 'success'. But this is what needs to change. We are conditioned to think of success as being promoted or earning the most, but when Lizzie was diagnosed with cancer, job title and salary were far from her mind – instead she reflected on what she had achieved in life, what legacy she might leave and whether the world would be a better place because of her time here.

Workstyle helps you live for your eulogy, not for your CV. A eulogy reflects on the type of person you were, the things that mattered to you, the journey you travelled and the way you made people feel. This is therefore a great place to start when thinking about your life's meaning, the impact you want to have on people and the planet, and therefore where you want to focus your attention and energy in your whole life, across work and everything else.

As strange as it may sound, try writing the eulogy for yourself that you would most want to be written about you. It might just give you some clues about the person you want to be remembered for being and highlight the path you need to take in the future or the changes you might need to make right now in order to live that life. We rarely make the time for such inward reflection, but it is always time well spent.

Geek box: How purposeful work can positively impact an individual's wellbeing

By Professor Joseph G. Grzywacz, Norejane Hendrickson Professor, Florida State University

Understanding the wellbeing implications of work is akin to understanding the brilliance of a well-crafted diamond (Longley et al., 2018).[18] Two elements of diamonds make them brilliant. The first is their dense atomic structure which slows the speed of light through the mineral. The second is facets or cuts imposed on that diamond by a craftsman to force that slowed light to twist and recoil in a manner revealing the full array of colours in white light. Work, like raw diamonds, has a dense 'atomic structure'. Although rarely considered, any given work has physical features, like air quality, equipment or tools, and possible exposure to agents. Work is also socially diverse in the types of relationships people create through it, the regularity of positive and negative interpersonal interactions, and the societal value placed on occupations (such as a police officer or doctor versus a check-out clerk or nanny). Finally, our work is often packed with diverse psychological meaning, mental tasks or responsibilities, and psychological responses like pleasure or stress. Completing the comparison with a diamond, the facets imposed on a specific job to enable or deny occupants' ability to have a purpose in their work will produce variation in the array of 'colours of white light', which metaphorically represents the distinct domains of employee wellbeing.

A rich array of social science thinking over the last 150 years points to purpose in work – individuals' belief that their occupational effort serves a greater valued good (Steger and Dik, 2010)[19] – as an essential ingredient for individual and community wellbeing. Durkheim's classic sociological treatise on suicide (Durkheim, 1897)[20] argued that fragmentation of workers and workflow produced anomie, or the breakdown of social norms and values, because workers could no longer see the greater good of their labour. Early industrial and organisational psychologists argued that working towards a purpose was a central employee motivation essential for job satisfaction (Hackman and Oldham, 1976;[21] Jahoda, 1980[22]) and that work creates an identity for individuals that serves as a litmus test for a purposeful life and subsequent wellbeing. The entire field of positive organisational scholarship emphasises virtues of positivity in the workplace (Cameron and Spreitzer, 2012),[23] and there are volumes of research extolling the benefits of 'meaningful' and 'purposeful' work (Dik et al., 2013;[24] Oades et al., 2017[25]).

Despite the rich thinking, there has been surprisingly little research on the role of purposeful work in employee wellbeing. There is evidence that meaningful work may promote better mental health (Allan et al., 2018),[26] including fewer depressive symptoms (Dich et al., 2019[27]). Research focusing specifically on purposeful work is corroborated by a broader literature organised around Person–Environment Fit Theory (Edwards and Cooper, 1990[28]). Mainly, Person–Environment Fit Theory argues that worker wellbeing results from a good 'fit' between a worker's values and those underlying the products, interactions or consequences associated with their work (Yang et al., 2008[29]).

There is a broader literature indicating that a sense of purpose in life produces multiple health outcomes. Adults with a high purpose in life experience less mortality, fewer sleep problems and a lower risk of depression (Kim et al., 2022).[30] Several studies of adulthood and ageing link purpose in life with better memory (Dewitte et al., 2021)[31] and better physical health during midlife (Willroth et al., 2021).[32] Likewise, purpose in life is associated with better physical function among older adults (Kim et al., 2017)[33] and reduced risk of Alzheimer's disease and mild cognitive impairment (Boyle et al., 2010).[34] As

Jahoda (1980)[35] argues, work and employment play a critical role in shaping individual identity; consequently, the profound and multidimensional benefits of purpose in life are likely given power and shape by purposeful work.

Working in our own workstyle helps us to focus on the purpose of our work, the output we're producing and the impact we're having. As it turns out, when we're doing something we're engaged in and passionate about, it's never easier for us to bounce out of bed. :tigger:

So instead of thinking about work and life as a trade-off, we should think about how in fact they complement each other. We should strive to view work as an integral part of life's purpose, not something separate. Whether we call this a 'work–life circle' or 'work–life integration', or something that smells less of corporate :smiling_pile_of_poo: – perhaps we just call all of this 'life' – the point is that, for those who can, we need to reduce the distance between what we do in our lives and what we do for work. This way, we can make sure our work is as true to our values and delivering against our purpose as much as anything in our personal life would. As we learn to embrace the opportunities presented to us through workstyle, we see a far greater choice to work on things that align with our sense of purpose and our values, taking fulfilling work with us at every step of life's journey, no matter how things may change along the way. This is the power of workstyle.

Chapter summary

- Purpose is critical to wellbeing – people who feel a strong sense of purpose are happier, more resilient and healthier. But traditional approaches to work make it more difficult to live a fulfilling, meaningful life.

- There is a growing awareness of the importance of purpose in the work we do – people are craving work that gives them a sense of purpose. We have found workstyle facilitates us being true to our sense of purpose in three ways:

  o **CHOICE:** working together in a workstyle way opens up our opportunities to work with organisations worldwide and choose work that aligns with our purpose, rather than being limited to those that can be reached within an hour or so's commute.

  o **JOURNEY:** whatever the change in our lives, workstyle enables us to stay true to our sense of purpose during those changes – our direction can remain the same if we want it to.

  o **LEGACY:** workstyle allows us to prioritise the things in life (including work) that will ultimately lead to the legacy we want to leave.

- Individualised work through workstyle can enable us all to pursue our own sense of purpose more easily, without the imposed limitations of location and time.

From the mouth of a workstyler: 'I joined the workstyle revolution because... I wanted to be defined by purpose, not a job title.' Qiulae, Auckland, New Zealand

Fact to remember: Eighty-seven per cent of Brits said they are yearning for a purposeful job and looking for more fulfilment through their work.[36]

And finally... Alex and Lizzie are amateurs, as you can probably tell by the words in this book. :heart:

Play your part in the workstyle revolution

Reflect

☐ Reflect on what is important to you in life. Why do you do what you do for work? Think beyond making money or paying the bills. Though these are, of course, fundamental, try to explore why you like your work and what you get from it. Think about the things you want to do, not the things you do because you feel you should.

☐ Now think big. What would you do if you had complete freedom? Imagine money, time and responsibilities don't exist and you have the ability to do the one thing or work for the one organisation that makes you feel happiest and most fulfilled.

☐ Next consider what makes you angry about the world. What would you change if you could? What causes do you feel most aligned to? Does this give you insight into what might be the most meaningful work you could do?

Act

☐ Write the eulogy for yourself that you would most want to be written about you. What insights does it give you into your purpose?

☐ Identify the key themes that run through the answers to your reflections. How can you use these to create more meaning in your work? For example, if you have realised that you love caring for others, how can you bring more of that into your work? These may be small changes you can make to feel more fulfilled or bigger changes to your role or responsibilities at work.

☐ Watch Simon Sinek's TED Talk 'Start with Why' on how great leaders inspire action.

Inspire

☐ If your employer or working group doesn't have a clear, stated purpose, raise this with your co-workers and ask for it to be defined. Show others at your work the statistics in this chapter so they understand how a strong sense of Simon Sinek's TED Talk 'Start with Why'[37] purpose can help support the wellbeing of everyone in the organisation.

☐ Tell others what your purpose is so that they understand the path you are on and can help you along the way.

☐ Ask others about their purpose and explain why this is so important for their wellbeing.

TEN

Workstyle helps you be well: LEARNING

Workstyle story: Ursula Capell

Multipotentialite, mum, creative, coach, explorer, self-reflector, cancer survivor

I'm a creative person with a lifelong desire for learning and exploring, but a few years ago I was far from living the life I wanted: I was working in the broadcasting sector in a job that didn't stretch me, in a culture I hated, while missing my son growing up.

I got up at 5.30 a.m., used the walk to the train station as my HIIT training, caught the 6.36 train to London, opened my laptop and began working. I spent four hours a day commuting. It was the same thing, day in, day out, week in, week out. There was no space for creativity to flow and no sparks of inspiration for innovative thinking. I felt dejected and uninspired. I was out of ideas and lacking in joy for life.

In 2003 I stepped away from the corporate world, setting up a facilitation business while also training as a coach, hypnotherapist, neurolinguistic programming (NLP) practitioner and reflexologist. But three years later I found myself ensconced once more in a creative agency. It felt like nothing had changed and again I was living to work. It took more than 10 years before circumstance became the catalyst I needed to quit the corporate world, for good this time.

Of course, I didn't sail off into the sunset; life isn't that kind. I had several obstacles to navigate along the way, including a devastating cancer diagnosis. But this was the wake-up call I needed to do all the things I'd been putting off and reprioritise my life. By the end of 2018 I'd finished my cancer treatment, sold my house, moved to a new town, become a workstyler, separated from my now ex-husband and enrolled in and completed my co-active coaching training.

I'm always developing my professional coaching skills further and I have just completed a master's degree in Applied Positive Psychology and Coaching Psychology, with a research dissertation on 'everyday creativity' (which I am planning to publish soon).

I'm passionate about learning in all its forms. Academic learning feels scary and is sometimes a big stretch, but I feel a huge sense of accomplishment after completing every assignment. For my self-development I love saying yes to trying new things, from coaching and self-reflection to learning to play the drums.

As a multipotentialite with a broad portfolio of work and learning, I have work that benefits from my coaching and vice versa. It's a fabulous cross-fertilisation. I find my best ideas come to me when I'm not trapped at my desk – inspiration can strike at any time: walking the dogs around the field, drumming or doing the washing-up.

I want to keep learning until my time is up. Learning makes me feel alive, thrilled, and helps me move on from my insecurities – I am always a work in progress.

Today I don't have a commute. Instead I use that time for reflection, and my weekends are spent with my beautiful son, George, and my fabulous partner, Mike. The life I was searching for is finally under way. For me, workstyle is about being able to choose what work you want to do, when you want to do it, and fitting it around living, loving and continuing to learn.

The growth opportunity

It won't surprise you to hear the first thing we think everyone should learn is how to work in a workstyle way. :blushing_smile: Seriously, though, regardless of how you work, one thing that is universally agreed upon is that learning, both in[1] and outside of work[2] and at any age,[3] is important to our wellbeing. Ursula's drumming as well as her master's degree have both improved hers.

According to LinkedIn's 2019 Workforce Learning Report, 94 per cent of employees say that they would stay at a company longer if it simply invested in helping them learn.[4] The same report found this feeling to be particularly strong among younger workers, with roughly a quarter of those born between 1981 and 2012 saying that learning is the number-one thing that makes them happy at work. Over and above this, 27 per cent of this same age group say the number-one reason they'd leave their job is because they did not have the opportunity to learn and grow.[5]

But this isn't just something that's important for younger workers – a report by the UK Department for Business, Innovation and Skills found evidence that informal learning was also associated with higher wellbeing for older adults (those aged 50–69).[6] The promotion of lifelong learning among this group can also significantly contribute to community wellbeing and social capital. Research suggests that the more active learning older adults engage in, the less they drain family and community resources and the more they are able to contribute to community wellbeing through their life experience and expertise.[7] This is crucial given our ageing population. The benefits are most pronounced when taking part in creative learning pursuits and hobbies[8] – the exact things workstyle provides time and capacity for, but traditional working structures might not.

Those traditional working structures are limiting our ability to learn and grow. Within the 9-to-5 and in large companies there is often support, but learning and development is still for the most part limited to what the organisation values as learning, compared with how we might truly want to grow and explore ourselves in ways that seem to fall outside of our job. We're not saying that it should be the organisation's job to fund every form of training or experience but that we should challenge the way we think about learning. Learning is fundamental to wellbeing, improving self-confidence, boosting self-esteem and helping us connect with others.[9] It's part of human evolution, but too frequently people leave their learning and growth in the hands of organisations, or don't make it a priority.

There are three ways we have found that workstyle benefits our learning and believe it could benefit others', too:

1. **PERSPECTIVE** – Growing through diverse perspectives and experiences.

2. **BESPOKE** – Accessing resources in your own way.

3. **OWNERSHIP** – Being accountable for your own development.

1. PERSPECTIVE – Growing through diverse perspectives and experiences :shuffle_tracks_button:

Learning a new language, skill or art that makes more complete use of both sides of the brain may really help us in our approach to work, our ability to connect with others, or our energy levels. But the way we typically think about learning relegates this priority to an evening or weekend class and makes it compete against everything else we have to juggle in life: our chores, health, fitness, families, friends, sleep, holidays, hobbies, travel and downtime. Did we miss anything?

Take scuba diving. Workstyler Kerry argues her training as a diving instructor helps her to stay calm under pressure with a client or when working to a tight deadline on her project management work, and that for real pinch points she uses the same strategies that she teaches to those learning to cope when they're running out of oxygen 30 metres below sea level and knowing they can't come up too fast without getting the bends. All her years of diving have improved her non-verbal communication skills, made her a more inclusive leader and helped her to be more self-aware, and therefore a better collaborator, too. :reef_with_brightly_coloured_fish:

Looking at our more functional exchange of knowledge, we learn from the people we work with. When employees want to learn a new skill, studies show that more than half (55 per cent) don't go straight to their official 'learning and development' department but instead ask a colleague.[10] Many companies believe that this is the reason why we need offices – to enable us to learn from one another. However, what we have noticed over the past eight years of testing workstyle is that the opposite is true. By sticking to the office-based 9-to-5 system we can *only* learn from the people who are physically there. By removing that limitation, we free ourselves to learn from people all over the world on all manner of subjects whom we trust, in a private, algorithm-free environment. From building client relationships to building Lego with our children, from project management hacks to cleaning hacks, and from industry news to football news, people can learn from one another online through trusted, vetted communities like Hoxby in a way that previously wasn't possible.

Whether it is working in a different environment which might trigger new ideas or boost our creativity or socialising with a broader variety of people (rather than colleagues who were all recruited because they largely fit the same mould), these experiences can help us to become richer, more rounded human beings.

The interactions we have, the company we keep and the things we do all build up to create a rich tapestry of experience which is at least equally, if not more, valuable to our learning than the traditional linear progression model of the job-for-life career mentality whereby learning is largely confined to the knowledge that is required to do the job, often delivered through a full day of training sitting in a room with windows that don't open listening to someone talk through PowerPoint slides or watching an 80s' video on a sticky VCR. :yawn: We have found that workstyle gives the opportunity for an entirely different type of learning, broad in scope and inspiring in ways we hadn't imagined.

2. BESPOKE – Accessing resources in your own way :phone_ beside_saucepan:

When we have the freedom to choose when and where we work, we can prioritise the learning that is important to us. Instead of the commute, or time wasted working to other people's schedules, we spend our time as we choose, including furthering our own learning, whether through trying new things, absorbing new information or more formal types of learning.

Workstylers approach their personal development knowing that we each learn in very different ways. Just as work should be individualised, learning, too, is a very personal choice[11] that each of us does in a different way, whether it's watching 15-minute TED talks, or going to an event to be surrounded by people, or one-on-one tutoring. Whether or not you believe in grouping different 'learning styles' such as the VARK framework (visual, aural, read/write and kinesthetic)[12] – and many don't[13] – isn't the point here. The point is that each person is an individual, and new methods of learning are popping up all the time so that we can teach ourselves in whatever way we feel most motivated to learn at that particular time – and with workstyle we are able to fit this into our days when we have the inclination and energy to do so. One thing that researchers do agree upon is that teaching something once and assuming a person will remember it isn't an effective way to learn. If new information isn't used, we forget 75 per cent of it in just six days[14] – you will likely have forgotten this statistic by the time you finish this book if you don't tell someone about it sharpish! An approach of little-and-often learning built around your workstyle and quickly put into practice leads to the greatest retention of knowledge.[15]

As you have probably gathered, we both love a TED Talk. We are fascinated by new ideas and emerging thinking spurs us towards our own reimagination of what is possible in life. But not all of our learning needs to be on subjects as deep as that and not all things are best learned through videos, despite 51 per cent of YouTube users saying they rely on the video service to figure out how to do new things.[16] Alex recently taught himself how to remove and install a kitchen, complete with sink, dishwasher, oven, fridge freezer, hob and extractor, using YouTube videos as well as through reading forum discussions and taking advice from friends over the phone. It wasn't a fast process, but it was possible. His experience supports what we believed already – that knowledge is more accessible than ever before and we each access it to fill the gaps in our understanding through our own preferred sources based on our individual learning styles, personal networks and existing knowledge.

3. OWNERSHIP – Being accountable for your own development :sponge:

As with so many of the changes to our world, technology means we are now empowered to decide more about our lives for ourselves, and our learning is increasingly falling into the same school of thought. :blackboard:

We have found taking control of when and where we work results in us making much more conscious choices about the work we do and why we do it. It means we take ownership for deciding it for ourselves where in the past we may have expected that to be dictated to us by our employer. Workstylers take on much more accountability for themselves and that extends to our learning. In particular, the remote and asynchronous approach to work that workstyle promotes means we must be more purposeful in enabling and designing our own learning.

Twenty-two per cent of learning and development professionals say they struggle to understand what skills to build or courses to recommend for their employees,[17] and 21 per cent find it difficult to identify skills gaps. So it's not surprising (though it is disappointing) that only 12 per cent of employees say they have been able to apply new skills learned through their organisations to their jobs.[18] Workstyle moves the onus away from the organisation and empowers individuals to be accountable for their own learning.

This independent approach to learning leads to better results. When we are able to take accountability for and set our own objectives, we are likely to set harder goals and achieve more.[19] :certificate: When teachers are given greater freedom over, and accountability for, the curriculum, they perform better,[20] and when students are given greater responsibility over tasks, they experience greater motivation for learning.[21] Self-directed learning leads to greater absorption of knowledge compared with traditional teaching methods.[22] We are also empowered to apply learning to real-life situations, deciding to improve our skills in the moment rather than relying on an organisation's 'learning and development' schedule.

We are taking the time to find things out for ourselves because we want to and because we can, even when this isn't part of a linear qualification but is instead in bite-size areas that we're curious about at that particular time. :explorer:

Geek box: How being accountable for our own individualised learning benefits our wellbeing

By Helen Tupper, CEO of Amazing If and co-author of The Squiggly Career *and* You Coach You

Careers today are full of change. The idea of a predictable, ladder-like career is no longer our reality. Today we can all expect to have five different types of career (McCrindle, n.d.),[23] and the World Economic Forum estimates that 50 per cent of the skills that we have right now won't be relevant by 2025 (World Economic Forum, 2020).[24]

In our increasingly 'squiggly' careers there is no one-size-fits-all version of success, and we're having to continually unlearn, learn and relearn the skills we need to do our best work. This ever-changing context increases the need for people to take ownership for their development rather than relying on their employer or manager to do so. The good news is that, with the right skills and support, we can increase the amount of control we all have over a future that feels uncertain – this alone benefits our wellbeing.

We can start by thinking about **values**, the things that motivate and drive us. Research suggests when we feel that we're living out our personal values we have a greater sense of wellbeing and we are more engaged in our work (Roberts et al., 2009).[25] Understanding our values helps us to make braver decisions, build better relationships and find more satisfaction in our day-to-day endeavours.

When you understand what makes you 'you', you can then focus on what you want to do. This is where **strengths** come in. Focusing on strengths benefits us and the organisations we work for. Strengths-focused development has been shown to lead to a 10–19 per cent increase in sales and a 9–15 per cent increase in employee engagement (Rigoni and Asplund, 2016).[26] By understanding what we want to be known for and when we are at our best, we can make strengths-focused development part of everyday conversations and take accountability for building on our strengths ourselves.

However, increased self-awareness has to be matched with **action**, and a lack of self-belief is a significant issue that holds people back. For many, the pandemic has negatively affected their career confidence, women in particular. LinkedIn's 2020 Workforce Confidence Index showed that women were 67 per cent less confident in their ability to progress their career in the next six months (Stuart-Turner, 2020).[27] Ensuring squiggly careers lead to opportunities for everyone means that we need to address this gap in self-belief. Organisations can start to close the gap by creating the conditions for psychological safety in the working structures they adopt, such as workstyle. But it is up to individuals to upskill ourselves and to turn the limiting beliefs that hold us back into limitless beliefs that help us move forward. Research proves that improved self-esteem is positively correlated with better life satisfaction and enhanced wellbeing.[28]

Taking ownership for our own development doesn't mean operating in isolation. Building a support network around your career has been shown to lead to higher salary and career satisfaction (Wolff and Moser, 2009)[29] as well as a greater likelihood of promotions (Wolff and Moser, 2010).[30]

Squiggly careers are rapidly becoming the new normal. The number of people considering a career change is increasing (from 53 per cent in July 2020 to 60 per cent in April 2021 (Aviva, 2021)[31]), and one in four adults are now considering a personalised portfolio career, an increase of 6 per cent compared with pre-pandemic (SME, 2022).[32]

When we have awareness of our values and strengths, the confidence to take action and the people around us who help us be our best, we can leave the career ladder behind and develop the adaptable, resilient careers we need to ensure our own wellbeing in the future.

Workstyle enables us to have more control over our work, and learning is a huge part of our wellbeing. With the freedom to access learning within our own workstyles, and through diverse experiences and interactions with others, we are empowered to grow under our own steam and in the direction of our own choosing. Like a sunflower that knows to face the sun, we become accountable for shaping our learning path into one which we enjoy and that motivates us. This is part of what enables us to be uniquely valuable and to grow into the people we aspire to be, for the good of our wellbeing. A mathematician might tell you that this is growth to the power of workstyle.

Chapter summary

- Having more control over when and where you work also gives more control over what and how you learn – both through the work you do and in addition to it. In our experience there are three ways learning can be facilitated by workstyle:

  o **PERSPECTIVE:** Working as part of a workstyle workforce creates a newfound ability to learn from anyone, anywhere in the world. Exposure to such diverse perspectives and experiences can give us much greater understanding and help us grow.

  o **BESPOKE:** Being able to access learning materials, content and classes within your own schedule and in the way that suits you best increases how much you can learn and the breadth of topics you can cover.

  o **OWNERSHIP:** With workstyle, you become more accountable for your own learning. This responsibility brings a great opportunity to tailor your knowledge in the ways that are best for you.

- Individualised working through workstyle increases the opportunity to learn more new things, from more new people, for yourself.

From the mouth of a workstyler: 'I joined the workstyle revolution because... I don't want to wait until I'm retired to do all the things I want to do. I love the fact every day is a challenge, either being understood in Spanish, seeking out new opportunities, delivering work in a new field, or nipping off to Benirrás Beach to hone my paddle boarding skills.' Melissa, Ibiza, Spain

Fact to remember: Only 12 per cent of employees say they have been able to apply new skills learned through their organisations to their jobs.[33]

And finally... Why not encourage your employer to fund your PADI qualification to improve your project management skills? :wetsuit:

Play your part in the workstyle revolution

Reflect

☐ Consider your experience. What transferable skills do you have?

☐ What learning are you already doing that you might not view as 'learning'? For example, cooking new recipes, shadowing a colleague at work or improving organisational or creative skills through a hobby.

☐ Consider the diversity of your community and those you learn from. Do they have a similar background, skill set and experience to you or are you learning from the diversity of their experiences and perspectives?

☐ Think back and compare your experience of mandated learning versus learning that you have chosen to do yourself. Which do you feel was more successful and why?

Act

☐ Explore the learning opportunities you have access to through your work. Are these different for different teams? Are there learning opportunities that you haven't considered previously where you could learn valuable new skills?

☐ Find a group, club or community where you can learn from different people, actively seeking to build relationships with people who aren't like you.

☐ Plan what you would like your development to be over the next 12 months. Set up ways to hold yourself to account for doing this (we find setting deadlines or having a workstyle buddy really helps).

Inspire

☐ Set up opportunities for group learning within your organisation where everyone can learn together and from each other. This could be a book club, virtual craft courses or masterclasses in anything that excites and interests people.

☐ Next time you have a challenge, find a co-worker or someone in your community who you know has a different background and perspective from yours. Ask them how they would tackle it. Encourage others at work to do the same.

ELEVEN

Workstyle helps you be well: CONNECTION

Workstyle story: Katy Kurn

Extrovert, entrepreneur, copywriter, single mum and free spirit

As a single parent, I'd always craved more quality time with my daughter. I didn't want to miss any more parents' evenings or sports days, but I still wanted and needed a successful career. I craved a life that enabled me to find the freedom to work when I chose, whether that was in the middle of the night or first thing in the morning, and I wanted to choose the types of projects I worked on. I decided to make the move into freelancing and fully embraced being part of the workstyle revolution.

As an extrovert, meeting new people and integrating into teams in person had never been an issue for me. But moving into the unknown world of working remotely with seasoned freelancers who were at the top of their game suddenly felt quite daunting. Could I create meaningful working relationships remotely? Would we be able to build trust and really get to know each other over video calls? Then I met Vix, and after a very short time I knew the answer to both those questions was a resounding yes.

I first met Vix when I worked with her on a project to curate other freelancers for client projects, and she immediately put me at ease.

Right from our first video call Vix took the time to get to know the real me. She asked questions about my life, my interests and how I felt about being a new freelancer. Vix seemed to have a sixth sense about things I might be fretting about, and answered questions before I'd even plucked up the courage to ask them. The more we worked together, the more we started to forge a real friendship. Our video calls were filled with laughter, and we always started with the question 'What's new with you?' We put effort into keeping in touch outside of project meetings, and we became genuinely invested in each other's lives. What started as a strong working relationship built on mutual trust, respect and collaboration evolved into a really beautiful friendship.

In 2019 Vix gave me the greatest friendship gift I could ask for. She asked me to be her maid of honour at her wedding. In the two years we had worked together, we had only ever met in person once. Yet here we were planning bridesmaid outfits, chatting menu options and sending each other very excitable voice notes about the big day!

My friendship with Vix has provided me with strength through my hardest times, someone to celebrate with in the good times, and is one of the most important relationships in my life. When I chose freelancing and to be part of the workstyle revolution, I knew I would be finding the freedom to work the way I wanted. But what I didn't realise at the time was that it would also give me the opportunity to meet one of the closest friends I've ever had. Vix may live hundreds of miles away, but she feels as close to me as if she lived right next door. We have a truly unbreakable, sister-like bond and a friendship that I know will last a lifetime.

The relationships opportunity

The need to connect with others is part of human nature. We are social animals, and quite simply we need to feel connected with each other in order to survive. One theory, known as the 'brain opioid theory of social attachment' (catchy) to those in the know, suggests that social interactions result in positive emotions because endorphins bind to opioid receptors in the brain.[1] Yep, maybe friends actually are better than drugs. :face_with_spiral_eyes: So yes, it's important, but not just for your mental health but for your physical health as well. Across 148 studies it was found that those people with stronger social connections were an unbelievable 50 per cent more likely to live longer than those with weaker social relationships.[2] :cheers:

When thinking about connection, people often assume it is about coming together in person. It is certainly true that meeting in person is good for our ability to build relationships, but building connection is more about relating to one another and the sense of feeling understood. This happens through the conversations we have, not simply by being in each other's company, as Katy's story shows. The assumption that presence builds connections can mean that we become less conscious about the connections we are making, preferring instead to assume that connections will come to us if we hang around each other enough. In fact, the opposite can be true. Research has found that those living in urban and industrial areas have higher rates of loneliness, with 8.3 per cent of respondents reporting they often or always felt lonely in comparison with only 5.7 per cent in countryside regions.[3]

The truth is that, in traditional working models, people spend much of their working days at a computer or in meetings and very little time talking to the people around them about anything that isn't work. This isn't an environment for connection; in fact it is contributing to a loneliness epidemic faced by millions of people who, despite being surrounded by people, feel isolated.[4] More than half of Brits say they suffer from loneliness in the workplace.[5] Even within the awful context of the Covid-19 pandemic, 73 per cent of remote workers said they'd had an improved work–life balance and enjoyed more time connecting with their family, children, partners and pets because of working remotely.[6] Outside of work, workstyle affords us the time and energy to prioritise the people that matter most. While in our work, workstyle enables us to be purposeful about connecting rather than relying on the serendipity of an office environment.

The amount of time we spend working in a digital environment can mean we don't spend as much time meeting people in real life, but that doesn't mean we aren't creating deep connections. Social media platforms have taught us how to build connections online. Text messaging on mobile phones was used for the first time on 3 December 1992, and we've been texting ever since – teaching us the basic art of maintaining connection without being in the same place or speaking at the same time. U dnt even need 2 spk 2 ne1, gr8 eh? ;o) Lol.

It's important to recognise that what we say to people will build or break our connections, whether those conversations are held online, offline, synchronously or asynchronously. While the medium is important, it's the message that ultimately matters.

Much of the way we connect happens without us really thinking about it. Like everything associated with workstyle, this important aspect of our wellbeing is only brought into our conscious thinking when we think about ourselves and the things in life that we want our work to fit around. When we start to fit our work around our lives, we think about the people who are close to us and how we can use our time to improve those relationships. When we think about working from anywhere at any time and conducting our work online, we begin to realise that we can connect with a global network of people on all manner of subjects – technology can connect us with anyone, anywhere, but we need to recognise its importance to our wellbeing and, for many, move it up the priority list.

We have found that workstyle enables us to build positive connections for the good of our wellbeing because it allows us to focus on three things:

1. **TOGETHER** – Bonding with people who need you (and whom you need).

2. **WORLDWIDE** – Uniting with people anywhere.

3. **OPT-IN** – Co-operating through asynchronous working.

1. TOGETHER – Bonding with people who need you (and whom you need) :tube_of_glue:

When we think about what we want our work to fit around, it is very often the people in our lives. When work fits around life, we can prioritise making time for the people we love most, strengthening the deep bonds we have that anchor our wellbeing. Those bonds may well be created by meeting in person, so this is something that work needs to fit around. For many of us, our primary relationships come through family. Our parents, partners and children are the people we spend the majority of our lives with, and along with perhaps a handful of close friends, they are the people we ultimately feel closest to both in good times and during tougher periods. For others of us, friends are the family we choose. They're the people we call when we're looking to celebrate some great news, who help us through troubled times when life throws tragedy our way, or those who can simply lift us up and make us laugh. :face_with_tears_of_joy:

But too often work gets in the way of allowing us to spend quality time together or makes it challenging to build, maintain and enjoy connection with people who are important to us. This can be through physical distance, for example when work has people travelling to an office or to meet clients or join meetings, or through a lack of time left in our busy lives, or simply because of not having any energy left to meet and connect with others when the working day is over.

One Monday morning, some years ago, a friend of Lizzie's called her in tears because she was having a miscarriage. Lizzie had the autonomy to down tools, knowing she was on top of her work and was able to spend a couple of hours supporting her friend and making sure she was OK: hugs and tea aplenty. Though there is no real way to help in these circumstances, simply being there to listen and give support can be the most profound connection in a time of need, something that traditional work wouldn't have allowed for at 10 o'clock on a Monday.

Workstylers Punam and Kerry describe a project which grew bigger than expected and changed to a much tighter deadline as 'one of those classic moments where work threatened to encroach on life'. But in spite of living on opposite sides of the world, they worked together so Punam could still enjoy the family time she had planned to fit her work around and Kerry – who was particularly passionate about the project, enjoys working weekends and also freely admits she loves working to a crazy tight deadline every now and then – could step in. There are countless stories like this. Workstyle doesn't just afford you the autonomy to choose when and where you work; it liberates you to fit work around life and put the people that matter to you first through being part of a supportive community of workstylers who can help each other without anyone needing to compromise their lives. Working in a workstyle way can have a positive effect on wellbeing far beyond the workstyler themselves.

If people are working and commuting for 12 hours a day, they're likely to miss a huge number of important small things. It might be seeing their child taking their first steps, listening to the heartache of a best friend, or being there for a partner who has just lost a family member. Individually, they might be relatively minor issues and seemingly unimportant, but taken together these day-to-day interactions add up to our whole lives.

Our relationship with work defines the type of worker we are. Whether we are dependable, loyal, reliable. But our relationship with work also defines whether we are a dependable, loyal, reliable, parent or partner, too. Whether we're a fun, giving, spontaneous or courageous friend or family member. Traditional work encourages us to live for traditional measures of success, to get along with our colleagues insofar as it's productive for us to do so, and then to leave work at work and build 'real connection' with others, outside of work. We don't think this is enough to lead a happy, fulfilling life. To do so we need to pay attention to how we interact with others, how we spend our time and what we choose to prioritise. Through focusing on these we can make the right choices with our time to build deep connections and focus on the relationships that have the most meaning in our lives. :smiling_face_with_open_arms:

2. WORLDWIDE – Uniting with people anywhere :planet_earth:

Beyond those closest to us, we have our wider friends and family, a group that is often shaped by the people we meet through our work. Given the importance of work in our lives, we can find ourselves building relationships which can last for a lifetime. Lizzie's colleagues from her early career are still some of her closest friends, even more than a decade after they stopped working together and in spite of many of them living in other parts of the world. :cheerleader: Work is a great potential opportunity for connection, but there are two key issues which might be holding people back from fully taking advantage of it.

First, some work behaviours can impact people's ability to build relationships. When they are encouraged to see work as a competitive environment, when they're on the lookout for the next promotion or they see others standing in the way of their progress, they're liable to look out for themselves more than others. They don't take time out to get to know each other personally. They spend more time thinking about how they can get their project funded or how they can beat their numbers than showing empathy for what's going on in someone else's life or building enduring relationships and deep connections with others.

Second, when people are a different person at work to who they are in their personal lives, they keep others at arm's length. They don't allow people to see who they really are and don't let themselves be honest and vulnerable. They keep co-workers as part of their 'professional network' but would baulk at the idea of following them on Instagram or inviting them round for a barbeque. They're their colleagues rather than someone they might rely on as a friend. In most traditional businesses only a select few make that leap. With most colleagues connection is little more than the depth of a business conversation.

Through workstyle things are different because work fits around life and everyone is open about their lives. We plan our own time and can fit socialising and connection in when it suits us. We can make a conscious choice about where our priorities lie and how we would like to connect with people. This desire to connect with our wider friendship group or family can help us to make choices about our workstyle, ensuring that work fits around connecting with them in the way we'd most like to.

Connection can feel easier to achieve within walking distance of home, but not all connection needs to be in person. Workstyle opens up a world of opportunities to meet new people, and it is often much easier to join a community online than finding, travelling to and getting accepted into one in person. This is supported by research conducted by McKenna et al., which showed that individuals who suffer from social anxiety, shyness or a lack of social skills said they felt that they could express their 'true selves' better online, and as a result were able to form close and meaningful relationships with people they met that way.[7]

Workstylers across more than 39 countries come together at Hoxby using online tools to connect with one another on all manner of things – from company performance and project discussions to TV programmes, gardening tips, home renovations, environmental issues and everything in between. These workstylers unite behind areas of common interest. There is a channel called 'The Watercooler', which is full of funny gifs, spectacular #ViewFromMyDesk photos and, of course, lots of cat and dog pictures. It replaces the kind of watercooler chats you might have experienced in an office with stories from diverse people all over the world that can be accessed at any time, rather than only in real time. There is no risk of missing out on a joke or hearing that 'you had to be there', reducing the likelihood of in-groups and out-groups forming. Hoxbies can access the conversation when it suits them, as a boost when they feel their energy dip, or as a welcome distraction at a time of their choosing. This is the complete opposite of people turning up unannounced at your desk and wanting a chat just when you're in the middle of a big piece of work. No need for competitively loitering around a quiet room at the office hoping it becomes free so you can sneak in to get some actual work done. :detective: Building work relationships on your terms enables you to get closer to more people and build deeper bonds, in the way that best suits you.

The digital environment is creating new ways for us to connect, for the good of our wellbeing. It means we don't always have to be face to face to have a laugh, or a cry, or a chat. We can enrich our lives by connecting with people from around the world once we realise that, online or offline, what matters is who we connect with and how openly we communicate.

3. OPT-IN – Co-operating through asynchronous working
:out_of_office:

Hoxby has delivered more than 1,500 client projects for businesses large and small, with workstylers connecting and enjoying working together around the world, without meeting in real life. We use Slack, Threadit and occasional Google Meets to connect. There will be some people reading this book who find it impossible to imagine how you can build deep bonds and collaborate brilliantly with people online, but Katy's workstyle story about her deep friendship with Vix shows the power of these relationships. And we feel it ourselves – we can count on one hand how many times the authors of this book have been together in real life in the last year and yet we are the closest of friends who know more about each other than almost anyone else.

Meet-ups have their place, but through workstyle you question when you need to be physically together and when you can build these connections remotely. At Hoxby, we meet clients in person, and we get together once a year for the sole purpose of having fun and getting to know each other more deeply. It's about building relationships and sharing good times for those who can make it, but never about excluding those who can't be there in person from a work conversation or from having their say in decision making. Work can be done from anywhere at any time, and it's more inclusive to do it asynchronously and online, so we focus on having fun when we're together. :champagne: :beers: :dancing_parrot:

We have been surprised to find that working remotely and connecting through Slack conversations in fact allows us to connect *more* deeply with others despite, in the vast majority of cases, never meeting in real life. We have found that engaging in a digital-first way provides an initial feeling of anonymity that helps alleviate social fears and breaks down the barriers to authentic communication. Conversing asynchronously also means we're never put on the spot. We can really consider how best to support and connect with others and how we want to present ourselves. For example, Lizzie is going through the menopause after her cancer treatment and has connected with an incredible group of resilient and inspiring women who have been searingly honest about their own menopausal experiences in their asynchronous group conversations over Slack. It has been a revelation to understand what others are going through, as well as an incredible support network. They have shared experiences, tips, podcasts, books, jokes, articles, poems and programmes to watch, as well as many personal stories. We doubt many, or perhaps any, of them would have had the confidence to set up a face-to-face menopause group and certainly not to share the details they have if they had all worked in an office. :people_holding_hands:

You might be one of those people who doesn't feel that they have actually 'met' someone until they have stood next to them in real life. You might be inclined to use such phrases as 'great to e-meet you' or 'nice to meet you, albeit virtually'. If you are, then please stop. We need to get over the idea that meeting one another has to happen in person. It doesn't. In-person meet-ups do strengthen relationships, as Nienke explains in her geek box, but it doesn't mean online ones can't be exceptionally strong, too. We should be delighted to meet new people in whatever circumstances and bond with them digitally without assuming that we'll only invest in relationships with people we are likely to meet in the flesh.

Nienke highlights that laughter and singing trigger endorphins that are important bonding mechanisms. We feel sure dancing must have the same effect and have been testing this theory for the past eight years with silly Christmas videos (thanks to Cat working her lyrical magic), making others laugh (and perhaps cry with our atrocious singing) and building deep bonds by showing others we are willing to make fools of ourselves for us all to feel more connected. :happy:

With the freedom to connect asynchronously with people all over the world, unrestricted by location or time zone, we become empowered to build meaningful connections in other ways than face-to-face conversation. When you think about the many ways you build relationships with others – through video calls, social media posts, text messages, voice notes, phone calls, voicemails and even posted letters – it's easy to see that these are just forms through which connection takes place and it's important to find the right balance for you. What really matters is the depth and enjoyment of the connection itself, however it happens.

Geek box: Human connection and how we can build meaningful bonds without physical proximity

By Dr Nienke Alberts, Research Associate, University of Bristol

Primates build and maintain relationships through social grooming (Dunbar, 1991).[8] Social grooming, which involves picking through the fur of others, triggers the release of endorphins which activate regions of the brain associated with reward and reduce pain (Bzdok and Dunbar, 2020).[9] Grooming makes others feel good. Investing in relationships in this way is time-consuming, which means there is an upper limit of about 50 social relationships non-human primates can maintain (Lehmann et al., 2007;[10] Dunbar, 2012).[11] Like other primates, humans today still spend around 20 per cent of their waking hours on social activities (Dunbar, 1998).[12] Yet, despite being under the same time constraints as other primates, humans typically are able to maintain around 150 social connections (Gowlett et al., 2012;[13] Dunbar, 1993).[14] Over the past 6 million years, our ancestors found more efficient ways to invest in relationships. Early in human evolution, laughter (Dunbar, 2012;[15] Manninen et al., 2017;[16] Dunbar et al., 2012)[17] and singing (Weinstein et al., 2016;[18] Pearce et al., 2015,[19] 2016[20]) provided such bonding mechanisms, while, later, language evolved to allow us to make these connections (Dunbar, 2017,[21] 2004[22]). All these behaviours trigger the release of endorphins in the same way that social grooming does but in multiple partners simultaneously (Dunbar, 2012,[23] 2022[24]).

In today's world many of the connections we make are online, but insights from our evolutionary past can help us understand how we can build these connections. For example, in a study in which participants were asked to rate the quality of their interactions with friends via different communication modes, face to face and video calling were rated higher than phone or text-based communications, such as SMS, group chat and email (Vlahovic et al., 2012).[25] This is because seeing a face, whether on or offline, allows us to read each other's non-verbal signals, which offers so much additional information about another person's emotional expressions, intentions and mental state (Sutcliffe et al., 2012)[26] and can increase the strength of the connection between individuals. The importance of reading faces in interactions can, for example, be seen in the morphology of our eyes. Other animals have very dark eyes compared with humans because the majority of the visible eye is taken up by the iris. The human eye is unique in that it shows a much larger portion of the white sclera on either side of the iris (Emery, 2000;[27] Kobayashi and Kohshima, 2001[28]), which makes it easier to see where an individual's attention is focused. The sclera of the human eye is an adaptation to allow us to communicate more easily through gaze (Kobayashi and Kohshima, 2001)[29] and is crucial in making a connection.

While language evolved as a bonding mechanism for humans, we still use the older mechanisms for making connections, too. For example, we still enjoy going to the hairdresser's for grooming. Generally, interactions that involve laughter, be it real or symbolic through emojis, help people feel closer (Vlahovic et al., 2012).[30]

Now, some of the connections we have are purely online. While such connections are theoretically not as close as connections with people that we also meet in person, there is huge value in such relationships. 'Weak ties' play an important role in accessing new information (Granovetter, 1973).[31] Such online-only connections are generally based around a niche interest which provides the link between an individual's online and offline worlds (Ploderer, 2008[32]). People join such online communities for support and to share information (Ploderer, 2008; Colineau and Paris, 2010[33]) that they would not have access to through their offline connections.

Thus, to make a deep connection online, show the whites of your eyes, use emojis (or wordmojis!) or connect over something niche.

Rachel, our Finance Director at Hoxby for more than two years, is someone we have never met in person (yep, you read it right – *never*) and yet it is one of the most productive and enjoyable relationships we have ever known. Having always worked in a traditional way, and in spite of some trepidation about how it would work in practice, she embraced asynchronous communication and threw herself into the workstyle way of working. We have come to know her innermost thoughts as well as her profit and loss predictions and we love working with her. We're not the only ones – workstylers are enjoying the same connections the world over. These are relationships fuelled by the power of workstyle.

Chapter summary

- The way we build connections is changing and although meeting in person theoretically builds the deepest connections, we can also build strong bonds without physical proximity. There are three ways in which workstyle helps build connection:

    o **TOGETHER:** With control over when and where you work, you can strengthen the ties with those closest to you by being available for them and making time to be there for the important moments in day-to-day life.

    o **WORLDWIDE:** Digital-first working enables you to connect with people anywhere, on any topic. This means you can start a conversation with a person or group in order to offer or gain support in a niche area such as the effects of going through the menopause.

    o **OPT-IN:** Whether it takes the form of a written message or short video, asynchronous communication enables you to start more conversations with new people and to access them at a time that suits you.

- Individualised work through workstyle allows each of us to work in the way that is best for us, but it can also drive new and deeper connections inside and outside work.

- **From the mouth of a workstyler:** 'I joined the workstyle revolution because... Hoxby feels like home. There's professionalism, leadership and learning, but with the corporate politics stripped away. I have never met any Hoxbies in real life, and yet we laugh together, work together and are changing the world together.' Victor, Rayleigh, UK

- **Fact to remember:** People with stronger social connections are 50 per cent more likely to survive.[34]

- **And finally...** The 160-character limit is now largely irrelevant because of the introduction of smartphones and wifi that also ushered in an era of instant messaging to replac 0/160.

Play your part in the workstyle revolution

Reflect

❒ Consider who is impacted by your workstyle and how.

❒ Reflect on the important occasions involving your friends and family over the last year – milestone birthdays, someone getting engaged or dealing with sad news. Were you there? What about the smaller but equally important moments – family dinners, forgotten PE kits or routine appointments? Could you make time, particularly in among your work, to ensure those most important to you felt supported and loved when they needed you?

❒ Is there an area of your life in which you feel you are lacking support or need greater connection? Maybe you have an unusual interest, are dealing with a difficult medical situation or are a carer living far from friends and family?

Act

❒ Create a list of the most important people in your life. How could you build a deeper connection with these people without relying on face-to-face conversation? Have a coffee with someone on a video call (and see the whites of their eyes!).

❒ Find an online community where you can make new connections and get support.

❒ Start an asynchronous conversation with that friend you never seem to find time to connect with. Send them a Threadit video with an update on your life to get the ball rolling.

Inspire

❒ Wherever you are in your workstyle journey, join the workstyle revolution at WorkstyleRevolution.com, share your story, support others and connect with fellow workstylers.

☐ Suggest that something which would normally be done in person is done remotely to include people who may otherwise be excluded. Get creative with office events – could work drinks be held virtually to include the parents that have to leave early for school pickup or those who work from home?

TWELVE

Workstyle helps you be well: BODY

Workstyle story: Anneli Lort

Northerner in the south of England, horse lover, author, copywriter and brand communications specialist, person with epilepsy

My first real experience of a regimented life was at boarding school. Everything we did – waking up, showering, eating – was dictated by the sound of a bell. At university I found a little more freedom, but immediately after graduating I was back in the world of regimented routine – in this case, the 9-to-5 of a PR agency. I found it stifling. It didn't suit me.

Perhaps surprisingly, routine itself wasn't my issue. I quite like a routine, but it needs to be *my* routine. The best solution for me was to move away from the office and become a freelancer, but it took more than frustration with an imposed schedule for me to take this daunting step.

Ultimately, the trigger for me to take charge of my workstyle came from my epilepsy. Epilepsy is a very personal illness and brings with it a great deal of anxiety, particularly when it's poorly controlled, as mine was when I worked in London.

That anxiety is magnified by travelling on the London Underground. Because the Tube is already a tense and pressured environment, the stress of using it can be amplified by a disability or chronic illness. I found it difficult to cope with these negative emotions ramping up every morning on the journey into the office, only to have to put in a full day of work afterwards. Then one day, after around five years of in-office agency life, the worst actually happened – I had an epileptic episode on the Tube.

It changed everything.

My immediate reaction was 'That's it. I'm done.' I would never commute to work on the Tube again. But the sting in the tail of epilepsy is that, after an episode, your driving licence is revoked for a year. To continue working in the office, I would have had no other option but to travel on public transport.

So I went home, wrote a resignation letter, and I never looked back. I was lucky in that I won a contract on my second day of freelancing, although the anxiety about bringing in future income was still there. But it was worth it.

My life now runs to my own rhythm. There's no typical day, but I'm a lark so I generally wake up at 5.30 a.m. and walk the dogs before heading to the stables to sort out the horses. By the time most people arrive at their office, I'll have done around two to three hours' work. Some days I can sit at the computer and work all day. On other days I might take a break at lunchtime and go for a ride or rest in the afternoon – when I tend to feel tired – and work again in the evening. When I'm riding, it forces me to be in the moment: it's great therapy. I'm as flexible as possible with my clients, but the ultimate governor of my workstyle is my mental and physical wellbeing.

I've now been freelancing for 25 years, and I don't regret a moment of it. The imposter syndrome and fear of failing to get work never quite go away but are more than compensated for by the fact that I get to run my life, my way. I've lost out on some jobs because of my 'inflexibility', as I insist on working from home, but it's completely worth it.

And the epilepsy? I've not had an episode for 15 years.

The physical health opportunity

Anneli's story shows the unseen challenges that traditional working can present and how workstyle can play a critical role in everyone's physical health. Since we have started working in our own workstyle, we've both become exercise fans. As it turns out, exercise is not only great for the body; it boosts productivity by 21 per cent and motivation by 41 per cent.[1] Win-win.

Maintaining a healthy body is critical for all of us and yet there are now six times more people in the Western world who are clinically overweight or obese than there are people living in food poverty,[2] and one in three men and one in two women are not active enough for good health.[3] The way the vast majority of people currently work isn't working out. :weight_lifter: Long before the coronavirus pandemic there was a global pandemic of physical inactivity.[4] How we use our bodies and what we put into them are the most important factors in determining how physically healthy we are.

We have found there are three ways that workstyle has really helped improve our physical health:

1. **EAT WELL** – Recognising there is more to life than sandwiches.

2. **EXERCISE** – Making time to regularly burn calories.

3. **STAND UP** – Working beyond sitting at a desk.

1. EAT WELL – Recognising there is more to life than sandwiches :dressing_on_the_side:

As well as shaping to a large extent how we use our bodies, which we'll come to shortly, for many people work unwittingly determines what they put into their bodies. As the bustling sandwich shops and takeaway outlets which line the streets of office districts demonstrate, time is often in too short supply for workers to make careful decisions about what they eat. People find their time is spent hopping between trains, calls and meetings, at the expense of considering the nutritional content of what they consume. Instead, millions of people end up grabbing food on the go from one of the sandwich shops within close proximity of the office and eating lunch 'al desko', in a meeting or on the move.

We can thank a card-loving duke for this – the Earl of Sandwich – who didn't want to leave his card game to eat and revolutionised our expectations around dining for ever.[5] :bread_beef_bread: That was in

1762, but many years later the sandwich concept enabled workers to extend their desk-tied hours and established its place in traditional working culture forevermore. As we told the shocked alien in Chapter 7, today nearly 3 billion sandwiches are sold in the UK every year[6] and, while undoubtedly convenient, they often contain high levels of sugar, fat and salt, which are no good for our health – some are even unhealthier than having a burger for your lunch.[7] :astonished_face:

Workstyle means taking the time for things that are important to us and gives us the opportunity for more mindful eating, which means we eat more healthily and are less likely to overeat,[8] and which also improves our mental health.[9] Workstylers also often work from home where we have access to our own kitchens and can make time to prepare ourselves healthier, preservative-free meals. We can also try different places to eat that take us out of the house, to meet people or even spend a few hours working while we're there.

2. EXERCISE – Making time to regularly burn calories
:red_face:

Nearly half of workers say they are unable to fit exercise into their daily schedules due to work,[10] and this is translating into a national crisis: 63 per cent of Brits are obese.[11]

It is possible to keep physically fit while having a demanding traditional job but it means making sacrifices in other areas of people's lives which they don't always want to make. So while individuals should, of course, take some responsibility for the epidemic of obesity, we should also consider the role the dominant current working system is playing in making this harder for people to rectify. For the majority of people, their jobs mean that they don't have enough time to fit exercise into their daily routines[12] despite their best intentions. Perhaps this is why 80 per cent of gym memberships last less than five months.[13] :money_with_wings: The system that makes us log on or clock in by 9 a.m. and keeps us tied to our desks until the early evening means barely half of us have time to fit any physical activity into the day.[14] Too often exercise is the thing people have to sacrifice when an urgent project comes in or because they're dealing with a burgeoning inbox. And the idea of going for a swim, run or cycle mid-afternoon sounds like they're taking time off, when in reality the hidden cost of not doing it is so much greater. The prioritisation of work over physical health is literally taking years off people's working and non-working lives.[15]

While we make a distinction in our five areas of wellbeing between the impact of work on our body and our mind, our physical and mental health are in reality deeply connected. If we're too busy to exercise or we're spending all day sitting at a desk, we're more likely to be stressed out, have difficulty sleeping and be more at risk of anxiety, depression and even Alzheimer's disease.[16] While there are multiple contributory factors, studies show that work-related stress also doubles the risk of heart disease.[17] NHS research shows that 150 minutes of exercise per week can equate to a 31 per cent lower risk of depression. Some people find it almost impossible to make time for this during a working week. With a workstyle of your choosing, you put these important elements first and fit work around them. Lizzie's swimming three times a week and Alex's weekly five-a-side football game are as important for their mental health as they are for their physical health.

The obvious benefits of workstyle are that we can exercise more often, eat more healthily and get more sleep because we can choose to do these things at a time that best suits our schedule rather than squeezing them around an inflexible timetable set by an employer or dictated by synchronous meetings.

However, what is interesting is that simply allowing flexible working hours doesn't have the same effect. A study conducted in 2010 by Durham University concluded that 'flexitime' had no positive impact on physical health, whereas interventions that 'increased worker control and choice' did lead to positive effects on tiredness, sleep quality, alertness and blood pressure, as well as mental health.[18] :red_heart:

Sometimes it's fun to exercise 'together' even if we're apart. The Hoxby community has collective exercise challenges to motivate workstylers to stay physically active. Between us we aim to circumnavigate the globe each year in our World365 initiative which not only brings us a great sense of satisfaction but also improves our productivity, physical health and mental health. That's 6,371 km of exercising together each year – running, walking, cycling, rowing and swimming. :virtual_relay:

3. STAND UP – Working beyond sitting at a desk :chair_ without_coat:

The traditional way of working has forced people to adopt behaviours that are not adapted to human origins and are not good for them. Nine and a half hours is the average time working-age adults spend sitting down each day,[19] even though our species has evolved to stand up, run and rest.

With traditional work, many in professional jobs are largely inactive. Although a comfy desk-based office job might seem comparatively appealing to working in the depths of a coal mine, it is in fact causing us similar levels of real, long-term, unforeseen harm. Coal miners in northern England in the 1920s on average lived for six years less than the average male at the time;[20] some studies today suggest that sitting can quicken the ageing process by around eight years.[21]

Sitting for too long slows our metabolism, which affects our body's ability to regulate blood sugar, blood pressure and break down body fat.[22] It increases our risk of chronic health problems, such as heart disease, diabetes and lung, uterine and colon cancers – even just sitting for four hours a day puts us at 'medium risk'[23] and more than eight hours at very high risk of an early death. Being sedentary has a similar impact on our physical health as smoking – and yet we don't (yet) have the public health awareness, campaigns, laws and regulations to help us address it. So it's up to us to address this unhealthy aspect of work ourselves.

What's more, when people head to the office, their desks aren't designed appropriately for them as they are typically designed for a 6-ft 2-in male.[24] To us this seems absurd – our friends certainly aren't *averagely* 6 ft 2 in tall. :face_palm: It excludes almost everyone apart from workstyler Kieron, who just so happens to be exactly this height. Nice one, Kieron.

People who spend excessive time at their desks might also be interested to know physical inactivity costs the global economy $67.5 billion each year.[25] You would think this would be a strong enough incentive for organisations to give their workers the freedom to shape their own work environment.

The workstylers at Hoxby try to inspire each other by getting out and about and sharing photos of the '#ViewFromMyDesk', working from different places and sometimes exercising in the process. We even encourage the occasional collective dance break. More dancing, less sitting! :mirrorball: :worm:

Workstyle opens up the full range of possibilities for when and where we work – we do some of our best thinking during exercise, get a fresh perspective while taking a walk or take our portable desk to the nearest tree so we can work outside. :work_from_tree:

Geek box: The damage that sitting at work can do to your body

By Jonathan Smith, chartered physiotherapist and Corporate Wellness Director, MLH Physio

Human advancement has taken us from being mobile upright hunter-gatherers 80,000 years ago to static upright manual workers some 300 years ago thanks to the industrial revolution. This change in working activities brought with it increased physical ill health and a high mortality rate due to the unsafe working practices and lack of health and safety regulation. Our working environments today have changed again, this time even more rapidly, as over the past 50 years many of us have become sedentary and immobile desk workers. The speed of such a dynamic change has not allowed for natural evolutionary adaptations to occur and we are now paying the price with our health and wellbeing.

With most workplaces still favouring static seated desks (Zerguine et al., 2021),[26] there is an increased risk of muscle and joint pain. One study found 80 per cent of office desk workers have had musculoskeletal pain during their working lives. This was predominantly found to be pain in the lower back (69 per cent), the neck (64 per cent), the upper back (46 per cent) and the shoulder (44 per cent) (Chadwani et al., 2019).[27] These areas are more likely to be affected as the front side of our bodies is bent forward, causing those muscles to flex and become tight, while the back muscles become lengthened and subsequently weak, causing the increased strain, stiffness and pain over time in the highlighted areas.

The duration of time spent sitting, the quality of the seat and correct set-up of the desk and chair are underlying factors that can be easily modified to reduce the risk of pain (Chadwani et al., 2019).[28] It has become increasingly easy to choose the posture you adopt and there is a plethora of alternative seating ideas, from ergonomic kneeling chairs to the more radical ideas of treadmill desks and cycle chairs. The most adopted dynamic piece of furniture is the standing desk. Most standing desks now have motorised capability to vary the height, giving the user the freedom to choose between different postures. Limiting time spent in one posture is hugely beneficial in combatting the effects on the musculoskeletal and vascular systems when compared to long-term sustained postures (Bodker et al., 2021).[29]

Although disorders of the musculoskeletal system are the most commonly associated danger of prolonged sitting, there are many other areas that can be affected. The more sedentary a life we lead, the fewer calories we burn and the more likely we are to gain weight and become obese. The risk of weight gain due to being seated at work is less than being seated for leisure but is still apparent (Saidi et al., 2013),[30] so a sedentary working environment coupled with a lower than average amount of recommended exercise is a real cause for concern for developing severe health issues. This can only be exacerbated by the pain caused by muscle and joint stiffness which may lead to further avoidance or reluctance to move and even in severe cases lead to fear of movement.

There are notable links with excessive sitting and a host of medical issues such as diabetes, high cholesterol leading to heart disease (Wilmot et al., 2012)[31] and certain types of cancer (van Uffelen et al., 2010).[32] Inactivity contributes to 6 per cent of all deaths per year worldwide.[33]

The combination of a static seated desk and a strict 9-to-5 time frame does not easily allow for flexibility to exercise to the advised level of at least 150 minutes per week (Department of Health, 2019).[34] Prioritising time for exercise is more easily achieved with autonomy over when and where you work, and finding ways to work other than in a sedentary position would help us all to live longer, healthier lives.

So traditional working is actually killing us,[35] and yet we already know that, if we can work in the right way – the workstyle way – and each stay in work for more years beyond traditional retirement age, this can actually help us to live longer.[36] We could eat better, exercise regularly and work in a way that is better for us physically. We could all lead happier, healthier lives. Such is the power of workstyle.

Chapter summary

- Traditional working hours that are spent sitting at a desk are rendering our bodies inactive and unhealthy. Our species hasn't evolved so that it can sit down all day every day. Workstyle helps our physical wellbeing in three ways:

  o **EAT WELL:** We can make better decisions about what we put into our bodies when we have more control over when and where we work. We can make more healthy meals at home or go to a place we want to buy lunch rather than defaulting to the nearest option.

  o **EXERCISE:** Having your own workstyle means you can fit your work around the exercise that you most enjoy or best suits you. Being part of a workstyle community can also provide the encouragement you need to do it.

  o **STAND UP:** Individualised work gives you more choice to avoid the health hazards caused by sitting at a desk all day. This might be standing while you work or even working while you exercise. Anyone for a walk and talk?

- Individualising work through workstyle allows us to look after our bodies and to tailor our choices to be optimally healthy.

💬 **From the mouth of a workstyler:** 'I joined the workstyle revolution because... I wanted to prioritise my health, avoid the commute and city air. I wouldn't have thought being able to have my own desk set-up at home would make a big difference, but now I'm such a fan of my standing desk that I tell anyone who cares to listen! It's better for my back, my mood and working standing up gives me energy.' Anna, Southampton, UK

⚙ **Fact to remember:** The average working adult spends nine and a half hours sitting down each day.[37]

And finally... Lizzie and Alex have both deprioritised exercise in the past because of work – sometimes for years on end. :embarassed_faces: We both play our (very small) part in the Hoxby World365 challenge to collectively exercise our way around the world each year. We consider ourselves responsible for the short stretch of the M4 motorway between our houses as our leg of the trip. :out_of_breath:

Play your part in the workstyle revolution

Reflect

☐ Take a moment to consider how much you exercise and whether you would do more if you had a workstyle that meant you could work around it. Would you like to go for a jog at sunrise, feeling like you have the world to yourself, swim when the pool is empty mid-morning, or hit the gym when it is busiest so you get the buzz of being surrounded by other people?

☐ What are your unhealthy influences? Are you sitting for too long each day or eating the wrong foods? What changes could you make in these areas to improve your health?

☐ What would you eat for lunch each day if you had more time?

☐ Consider where you might work if you had to work without sitting down.

Act

☐ Get yourself a standing or portable desk (or request one from your work).

☐ Book yourself in for an exercise class during your normal working day and see what happens to your work. Do you feel energised? Are you more productive?

☐ Go for a walk next time you talk to someone on the phone.

☐ Eat all your meals away from your desk for a week. How does it impact your wellbeing?

Inspire

☐ Connect a group of people and share in the challenge (and enjoyment) of exercise. Set a goal to collectively walk, cycle, swim, row or run a certain number of miles, or do 1,000 push-ups if that's more your thing. Pick a charity to raise money for or a common purpose to help you reach your goal.

☐ Speak to your company or working group about the importance of not sitting for too long and share inspiration from this chapter about ideas for how to work differently.

PART 3

WORKSTYLE STEP-CHANGES YOUR PRODUCTIVITY

THIRTEEN

What is productivity?

It may feel intuitive that having a workstyle of our own choosing is better for our wellbeing, but what's perhaps more surprising is how much better it is for our productivity. While it may feel like fitting our work around our lives would mean we get less done, the opposite is actually true – having this autonomy can in fact transform our productivity,[1] something we saw echoed in our research.

There is a perplexing paradox when we look at the productivity statistics of the industrialised economies[2] (which we often do :wink:). Despite some pretty eye-popping technological breakthroughs (video calling, online messaging services, collaboration tools, virtual reality headsets...) we're still about as productive as we were in 2007.[3] And this continues a trend over the last half a century which has seen productivity growth in the West decline dramatically since the 1970s,[4,5] as illustrated by the chart overleaf.

Economists have pondered this for decades and blamed almost everything from here to the moon for the decline – the fat-cat bonus culture,[6] a 'rentier' economy,[7] bad management practices,[8] national debt,[9] an ageing population[10] and cheap labour immigration,[11] to name just a few. :perplexed:

UK PRODUCTIVITY GROWTH OVER TIME

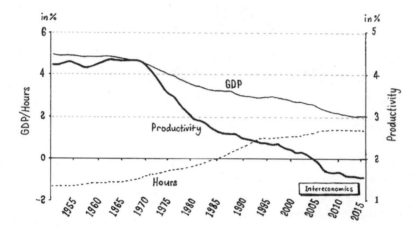

We think there is a single, simple explanation that sums it up: that our predominant system of work hasn't evolved to keep up with the pace of technological breakthroughs. We're in good company with the likes of American academic Robert Solow, who has spent much of his life advocating this same theory.[12] He famously said that you can see the computer age everywhere except in the productivity statistics.[13] We couldn't agree more, and we believe industrial-era norms and legacy cultural working practices have been holding us back from being as productive as we could be.

In conversation with: Sir Bobby O

[The lights come up on Lizzie and Alex standing chatting at a high table, drinking tea and working productively from a nameless café that looks a lot like the one from hit sitcom Friends.]

[Enter Sir Bobby O, stage left. A man with a commanding presence but with kindly eyes and dressed as though he's just walked off the front of a bottle of famous whisky.]

[Audience cheers.]

SBO: A good day to you, Mr Hirst and Ms Penny. *[He doffs his cap.]* How are your merry selves this day?

Alex: Ah, Sir Bobby, welcome to the 21st century. We are indeed merry but we're feeling frustrated. As a business owner yourself, you'll appreciate how frustrating it is to witness the very limited productivity gains that have been made in recent years and, in fact, decades.

SBO: Why so? With so many people in the world now receiving an education and the almost global adoption of my… *[He turns to the audience and in a booming voice proclaims]* …eight hours' labour, eight hours' recreation and eight hours' rest… *[He turns back to Lizzie and Alex]*, productivity should surely be through the liggering?

Alex: The what now… ? *[He looks to Lizzie, confused.]*

SBO: The liggering - how are your master thatchers supporting the crest o' the roof if not with liggering?

Lizzie: Ah, gotcha. Sadly not. I'm afraid that the world has changed a lot since your time. We're no longer a manufacturing economy for a start; we're now a service-based one. And we've made some discoveries, too - for example, some people work brilliantly in the morning whereas others have a different circadian rhythm that means they work better late into the night.

SBO: *[murmurs]* Actually that does explain why Clarence down in the loom fixers' team was never at his most fulsome in the morning time... *[He stands even more upright and puts his hand to his chin in pensive reflection.]*

Alex: Also, huge groups of people are judged on the amount of time they spend sitting at a desk, not on the work they actually do. Some people get into their shared place of work early simply to put their coat on the back of their chair, to be seen to be there, even if they are in fact on a cold walk to a nearby café for a coffee. *[He shivers at the thought.]* I bet they didn't do that in your factories.

SBO: *[outraged]* They most certainly did not!

Lizzie: And whole groups of the workforce still work in fixed shift patterns, including many of our most important workers - those in the police or in healthcare. Plus we now have 'open plan' offices where actually everyone gets less done... *[tails off]* To be honest, it feels like we've made giant leaps forward in technology but the way we work hasn't in any way kept pace with the change happening in the world.

SBO: You coxcombs! Do you not know a B from the foot of a bull? It is clear and simple – it is your responsibility to rectify this problem. You must muse and reflect on a new approach to work, galvanise support and henceforth transform society through its adoption. *[He throws down his handkerchief.]* Don't dither, there is nothing of greater importance than this. Stop spinning a yarn and get on with it! There is a world to be changed: for this productivity problem of yours, and also to happen upon a solution that can simultaneously promote wellbeing and happiness to the highest possible level.

[SBO exits with gusto stage left. Lizzie and Alex exchange a knowing glance, then hurriedly set about changing the world of work to be fit for the digital age. Lights fade.]

Productivity as it relates to workstyle

In Chapter 6 we shared our study that showed the link between workstyle (autonomy), wellbeing and productivity. The results from this study imply wholesale improvements to autonomy at work can bring about wholesale improvements to our productivity, and further confirm the extensive literature that supports the link between autonomy (workstyle) and productivity. As we highlighted, autonomy has huge benefits for productivity[14] and engagement,[15] while stress,[16] turnover[17] and exhaustion[18] are decreased. Workstyle provides a new opportunity to improve individual productivity in a way not seen before. The very essence of workstyle is that it allows work to be tailored for each of us and allows us each to be at our personal productive best (Alex after a bacon sandwich, Lizzie after tidying the kitchen) while also looking after our wellbeing. :rocket_taking_off:

Economists may argue that if autonomy boosted productivity in this way, then competition should mean that, if one organisation didn't take advantage of new working practices, another would come along and do so, be more efficient, win their market share and so put the first one out of business. And to an extent this has happened. We know that organisations which look after the wellbeing of their employees tend to show better bottom-line results[19,20] and we are starting to see more and more businesses taking incremental steps to support wellbeing as a result.

However, it seems that there continue to be industries and domains where almost everyone is stuck in the same way of thinking, having not yet capitalised on the opportunity we first saw in 2014. Eight years is a long time not to spot this source of competitive advantage, but there are many examples of seemingly obvious – in hindsight – innovations which took a surprisingly long time to be discovered. We endured suitcases which didn't have wheels for nearly 80 years, for instance. :free_wheeling: It is possible that the entrenched way people have been working has acted as a natural handbrake on the innovation in work that otherwise would have created faster productivity growth.

Workwear
I like
inside

FLEXIBLE WORKING

WORKSTYLE

Large-scale studies have shown that non-traditional working structures can be more productive, especially when the workers have the autonomy to choose how they work,[21] and even in the worst conceivable circumstances – during the coronavirus pandemic, when new ways of working were thrust upon thousands of people, 94 per cent of 800 employers noted that productivity was the same as, or higher than, it was before the pandemic.[22]

Over the next five short chapters we're going to focus on where we've seen real improvements in our own productivity through working in a workstyle way. The Alex and Lizzie workstyle approach to productivity, tried and tested at Hoxby, begins here and with it, as you might expect, our fourth hand gesture. :five_fingers:

These are the five ways we have found we are able to be more productive when working in a workstyle way:

ENERGY – Managing our own momentum.

CLARITY – Doing the right things, at the right times.

MASTERY – Becoming great at the things we are passionate about.

TRUST – Feeling accountable and co-operating with others.

ENVIRONMENT – Finding optimal places to work.

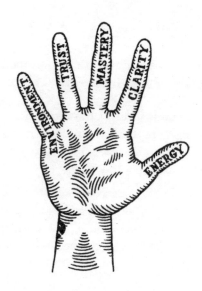

FOURTEEN

Workstyle step-changes your productivity: ENERGY

Workstyle story: Auws Al-Gaboury

Entrepreneur, video producer, individualist, hobbyist boulderer, professional night owl

You know those dark, cold winter mornings, the type where the ground is actually frozen and you see every breath leaving your body as it ventures into the air? Well, those mornings have been my nemesis for as long as I can remember. In fact, all types of mornings – any that involve the majority of the world (in the same time zone) waking up 'bright and early' to start a new day.

Leaving the cocoon of my bed to face the world outside is bad enough, but then having to function and be productive, too? No thank you. Everything about the pressure to perform in the morning just feels wrong to me. My body and mind just don't want to conform.

At school and then studying film and TV at university, I wasn't alone in my rebellion as many of my morning classes were full of fellow zombie-students. Once released into the 'real' world, however, and forced to pay a premium for everything including rent, I had to take a job that required me to show up and be one of those 'bright and early' people every morning. Keeping my productivity levels high for long consecutive days was like torture. It became a lonely struggle and a battle against the accepted working system that my humble body clock was never going to win.

I felt constantly fatigued and semi-functional in a system built on 'one-size-fits-all'. The late nights which have always been my optimum time for output and when I'm most highly charged and energised had become too high a price to pay for the dread of the early alarm the next day. I started to feel like the 'Monster' energy drink I was becoming reliant on. (*Other energy drinks are available.)

I was also beginning to tire of asking myself the same question on repeat: when will I bite the bullet and start a business of my own in which I can dictate when, where and how I work?

One day, out of sheer desperation to change the track-on-repeat in my head, I put down my energy drink and picked up my phone. I called two good friends to propose an idea that has since grown into the production company I am so proud now to call my own.

Living the last few years as part of the workstyle revolution has given me the freedom to unlock my productivity, realise my night-owl potential and create some of my best work. Not to mention the unintentional perks for my many clients in the US. I often get concerned notes checking I'm not overworked when I respond to their early evening messages at 2 a.m. Fortunately, my clients know already that our vision as a company is results driven and that it's not about physically showing up at set times every day. It turns out that 'one-size-fits-all' doesn't, in fact, fit all at all!

The momentum opportunity

Like the many talents each person has acquired in their lives, long or short, and the unique experiences we have each lived through, productivity is an individual thing. You may have elements in common with others but no two people will be exactly the same. Being told when and where to work assumes we're all going to react in the same way to the same environment and be as productive as each other. As Auws points out, this one-size-fits-all system of work is not suited to everyone and, for many people, doesn't fit well at all in terms of making the best use of our energy.

Unfortunately, many of the characteristics of work currently, from shift work to working in an office, are without an appreciation for our uniqueness. Jobs are defined by organisations based on what they need, and although in many cases every effort is made to find a great match between employees and those needs, they very often require some sort of adjustment or compromise by the worker.

Workstyle not only frees us from the unspoken need to 'fit in' that we explored as part of wellbeing, it also frees us from needing to fit the time and schedule of the other people we work with. We have found over the past eight years that we can therefore direct our energy into being the best, most productive versions of ourselves rather than fighting our natural selves in order to fit a traditional schedule, as Auws spent a long time doing. :monster:

In order to do this well, we need to be better at understanding our energy and where it comes from. For example, it may surprise the more extrovert among you to learn that introverts are not people who are shy, retiring loners – they aren't even a group. Introversion and extroversion represent opposite ends of a spectrum of where a personality type gets its energy from.[1] For more introverted personalities, their energy comes from within themselves, whereas more extrovert personalities draw their energy from external sources such as other people. Understanding who we are for ourselves rather than perhaps how others may have labelled us can be important in maximising our energy and planning our workstyles to bring out our most productive selves.

We have found that, when our lifestyle and workstyle are more equally within our control, we can get the most out of our energy in all aspects of our lives and in doing so increase our work productivity in three ways:

1. **TEMPO** – Finding the right rhythm.

2. **BUZZ** – Maximising energy.

3. **PRIORITISATION** – Channelling enthusiasm where it's most needed.

1. TEMPO – Finding the right rhythm :metronome:

We have found that achieving the most productive use of our time requires that we understand our personal rhythm. Our natural energy ebbs and flows over a 24-hour period, and there's a scientific reason for this that helps to explain why. All of us have a master time clock that resides in a portion of the brain called the suprachiasmatic nucleus (not quite Mary Poppins :umbrella:) and it reacts to light entering the eye.[2] It uses this information to send neural signals that regulate body temperature, which for each of us fluctuates about one degree every 24 hours. It is the circadian rhythm of our body temperature that determines whether we're a late-working 'night owl' like Auws or an early-rising 'lark' like Anneli (see Chapter 12). The body temperature of a metaphorical lark rises quickly, achieving peak temperature early in the day, and then plateaus, while the metaphorical owl's temperature rises slowly during the day and peaks at night.

It's easy to see how an industrial 9-to-5 system has been benefitting the larks for more than two centuries, and as Chris Barnes has shown in his research, there is an opportunity to be more inclusive of the night owls in our midst by enabling them to work later in the day when they may be at their most naturally productive.[3]

Mandating work hours be the same for everyone doesn't take into account our individual circadian rhythms. Understanding these can help us to design a workstyle that maximises our productivity by fitting work around our individual ebbs and flows of energy over the course of a day, which may also change for each of us based on our individual circumstances or life stages.

Whatever our rhythm, getting enough sleep is critical for us all. When Sir Bobby O advocated each person having eight hours' rest, he was right – we all need 7–9 hours of sleep to recharge our batteries,[4] and not getting enough sleep has a negative effect on our productivity. One study of more than 4,000 workers in the US found 'significantly worse productivity, performance, and safety outcomes' among those who slept less, and estimated a $1,967 loss in productivity per worker due to poor sleep.[5]

It was this statistic that made Alex commit to getting eight hours' sleep each night, which meant a 'no work after 10 p.m.' rule was written into his workstyle, given Olivia and Tate tend to wake him up any time after 6 a.m. No $1,967 lost productivity from Alex then (Lizzie breathes a sigh of relief).

Recent history has seen many people wake to the sound of an alarm, mandated by the time they need to start work, and so they have managed their sleep on the basis of knowing when they will wake up. It has long been the thing they compromise first – they work longer, eat later and don't give themselves any more sleeping hours to recover. :beep_beep_beep_beep:

Planning your workstyle means understanding when you like to sleep and ensuring you get the right amount of sleep at the right time for your body to guarantee you have the most productive day (for those who can – we know that for many people, such as those with chronic illness or pain, or women going through the menopause, getting enough sleep is easier said than done).

Over and above our own rhythms, predefined hours of work still reinforce a culture where people are expected to be present rather than productive. This expectation of presence means people haven't learned that it's perfectly OK to take a nap in the afternoon and perhaps pick up things later in the evening. Instead they are forced to work at times when they're less productive, not because it best suits their bodies but simply because that is the way it has always been done. In fact, not only is napping OK but it is also hugely beneficial. Research shows that a 20–30-minute midday nap is more effective at improving work outcomes than caffeine or even sleeping more at night.[6]

2. BUZZ – Maximising energy :electrified:

In a completely informal analysis of just about every leaving speech we have ever heard, the phrase 'I'll miss the people' won hands down, yet research shows that the most common reason for resignation is not to leave a company but to leave a boss.[7] We have found that who we work with has a massive impact on the energy we feel towards our work day to day, and this affects our productivity.

Having the autonomy to decide when and where you work gives you much greater freedom to surround yourself (virtually or physically) with people who you enjoy being with both inside and outside work, particularly if you're a more extrovert personality. Whether co-working with friends who aren't actually your colleagues or working with colleagues who are more like friends, greater control over the people around you can give your energy a much-needed boost. :person_punching_air: Researchers Emily Heaphy and Jane Dutton found positive social interactions at work bolster your physiological resourcefulness[8] (you say physiological resourcefulness, we say energy :tomato_tomato:), supporting what we have heard anecdotally through our workstyle working.

There are some people in life who give you energy and some that take it away, and who these are will be different for each person – Oprah Winfrey famously referred to them as 'radiators and drains'.[9] For the most part, it is easy to identify who the radiators are in our lives – they give us energy whereas the drains tend to use ours up. :weary_face:

We have found it's important to consider *why* some people are radiators and some are drains for us. Constructive challenge is not a bad thing and doesn't have to be a drain – in fact, at Hoxby it's one of the behaviours we specifically encourage in order to facilitate collective intelligence (more on that in Chapter 22) and improve productivity. We've found that what determines the impact on your energy is more often the way in which a message is delivered or feedback is given. Workstylers take time to think about the way they construct asynchronous written or video messages in order to ensure positive energy for the reader or viewer, even when the message is one of constructive challenge. For example, one of Lizzie's favourite things is people highlighting that something is wrong and at the same time proposing an idea that would address the problem. It is one of the many reasons we love working with the Hoxbies. They are a hugely diverse group in terms of experience, ethnicity, location, environment, age and many other factors, but because all of their energy is being directed towards the same goal, this enables constructive challenge. The workstyle opportunity is to surround ourselves with people who are different but who we can still get great energy from.

Negative energy is all too common in traditional work. According to a recent Gallup report, 51 per cent of employees are disengaged in the workplace, while 13 per cent are actively disengaged.[10] Actively disengaged means feeling miserable at work and spreading negativity to colleagues.

And perhaps unsurprisingly these energy levels also translate into an organisation's performance. If people are unmotivated and lacking drive, they are less productive than if they were passionate and meaningfully engaged on a day-to-day basis. Low levels of engagement have been linked with higher absenteeism, higher employee turnover, lower-quality production, lower customer service scores and lower sales in a range of organisations.[11] Another Gallup report on employee engagement shows that companies with a highly engaged workforce have 21 per cent higher profitability.[12] They also have 17 per cent higher productivity than companies with a disengaged workforce,[13] so it's important for every organisation to get this right.

Given autonomy is a central theme of this book, it's also interesting to contrast these statistics with those of the self-employed, who are more likely to be working in a way that is more akin to workstyle – 84 per cent of whom say they are very satisfied at work.[14] For us this happiness translates into positive energy and productivity; the more that we feel we are in control of the work we do, the more we will be motivated to throw our energy into it.

3. PRIORITISATION – Channelling enthusiasm where it's most needed :air_traffic_control:

Before workstyle, when we both had traditional jobs, we remember that feeling we got when we would have something in our personal life to take care of but couldn't because at the same time we also had to be at work. Like getting your car fixed when you have a day full of meetings. Those conflicts exist because most people live with two lists of things to do (whether written down or in their minds) that compete for prioritisation. Unfortunately, in traditional working structures, one list has the person's attention for most of the day and the other one has to make do with whatever time they have left.

Remaining productive while life throws curveballs your way may feel almost impossible within a rigid system of work. For a long time, people have worked under an assumption that life is something that can be lived either side of our working hours. This puts huge limitations on our ability to be productive overall, even without navigating unexpected factors such as a cancer diagnosis, needing to care for a parent, moving house or having a sick child suddenly home from school, that present themselves over the course of life. In fact, the multitasking inherent in fitting life around work can lead to up to a 40 per cent reduction in productivity.[15]

It is worth remembering at this point that the traditional way of working was built on the assumption that housewives would cover the domestic responsibilities of the household. Today, though, three-quarters of families with one or two children have both parents in employment, which leaves considerably less time for juggling the priorities of life and work.[16] Times have most certainly changed.

We have found that having the autonomy to decide our individual workstyles has meant we can prioritise our list of things to do across both our working and non-working lives. We can accommodate medical appointments, be available for school plays, visit family members and do a load of washing alongside finishing the presentation we are working on or analysing the latest performance update. By giving ourselves the same autonomy to manage our working time as our non-working time, we have found we are able to get a load more done. :washing_machine: Alex went all-out for his kids' Halloween party this year, and Lizzie was fully prepared for Christmas earlier than ever. :life_goals: Putting energy where it's needed allows us to maximise how we spend our time and keeps us accountable for what needs to be delivered across all aspects of our lives. We have personally found that this level of autonomy to be productive with our non-working time in order to get on top of what needs doing outside of work makes us more energised and focused with our working time, which can then be spent free from distractions of life outside work or trying to ignore the nagging 'life to-do list' at the back of our mind. :laser_focus:

It also means we can experiment and gradually identify the most efficient ways of working for us personally. Taking regular breaks can also boost our productivity by giving us time to recover from the demands work places on us.[17] This may be to make lunch, to fold the aforementioned washing, or to go for a walk and get some fresh air (clocking up those 150 minutes of exercise we each need a week). Research has found that this type of active rest, where you are resting by engaging in non-work activities, is one of the best types of rest for restoring energy. Active rest leads to significantly higher levels of recovery between work periods[18] and therefore improves overall productivity and efficiency.

Studies into the subject of autonomy and productivity have found that those with more autonomy are more efficient through being able to choose their optimal working conditions,[19] save time and energy by reducing commuting time[20,21] and are forced to communicate more effectively.[22] We have experienced these three things first-hand. Not only does workstyle allow us to schedule our work in such a way as to be most productive, it also allows us to unschedule the things that make us less productive. Choosing what we don't do, as well as what we do, has been really important to improving our productivity through workstyle. This means less time spent commuting alongside thousands of others to get to shared offices. Less time on synchronous phone calls and video calls. Less time doing work that we don't enjoy or doesn't have an impact on the world or that doesn't align with our values. To be effective with our prioritisation, we have to become adept at saying 'no'.

Working asynchronously increases our available time each day because it individualises work for each of us to do tasks when we're at our most efficient or when it suits us. For everyone who is used to working synchronously, this is an adjustment. Even we, the inventors of workstyle, have taken some time to really understand the potential of being able to work across any of the 24 hours of the day, or any of the seven days of the week. Deciding for ourselves that we want to go swimming when the pool isn't crowded or get a mid-morning haircut helps us manage our lives in ways which improve our productivity across both life and work. At Hoxby, the #ViewFromMyHairdresser hashtag has been popular for years – great wifi while waiting for highlights to take can be such a productive time if we allow ourselves to use it that way. But we're all individuals, of course, and this won't be right for everyone – Alex, for example, rarely has time to get much done at the hairdresser's. :balding: We can only reach this energy efficiency if we stop feeling guilty for not working at a particular time of the day. A study by North Carolina

State University shows that it is in a company's best interest to give people autonomy to take microbreaks when they are needed as it helps them to effectively manage their energy and engage in their work throughout the day.[23] The Pomodoro technique is also a good example of this – taking a five-minute break to recharge for every 25 minutes you work.[24]

The freedom of workstyle, then, means we can enjoy Christmas shopping when we're not hassled by crowds and wrap gifts when we're not surrounded by the recipients. Catching up on the latest episode of a gripping police drama while doing the ironing at 10.30 a.m. on a Monday doesn't mean you aren't deeply passionate about your career; it just means you have really reflected on what you want your workstyle to be (thanks for the inspiration, workstyler Liz, living your best workstyle life!).

Too many people find it perfectly acceptable to check their work emails in bed but wouldn't dream of a trip to the supermarket at 11 o'clock on a Thursday. Breaking free of entrenched beliefs about work and when we should be directing our energy towards it isn't easy, but it is possible and we have found there are huge productivity gains to be made if we can. Through workstyle, we can show everyone that they could be surfing while the swell is awesome, like workstylers Mariza and Ben do in Costa Vicentina in Portugal and Holywell Bay

in the UK, respectively, and then working when it's not. Each person's reasons for working their own way may be different, but the important thing is that we encourage one another to start making the right decisions to be efficient with our energy, to maximise our productivity when we're working, as well as when we're not, and begin enjoying the transformative impact it can have for each of us.

Geek box: Rhythms, energy and the benefits of autonomy at work

By *Dr. John P. Trougakos, Professor of Management, University of Toronto*

The energy employees have on any given day is an important factor in their job performance (Beal et al., 2005).[25] Moreover, this energy is limited and depletes with sustained use (Trougakos et al., 2008).[26] Consequently, people have a limited capacity to be effective and perform at their optimal levels. As energy depletes across the day, working effectively and productively requires more effort and energy compared with performance episodes earlier in the day. Autonomy has long been recognised as a critical determinant of employee energy impacting motivation, wellbeing and performance (Deci and Ryan, 2000).[27] Below I outline three critical ways autonomy can impact employee energy and productivity.

At a basic level, autonomy is an essential psychological need (Deci and Ryan, 2014)[28] that enhances people's intrinsic motivation. Intrinsic motivation represents the extent to which someone does something for inherent desire and satisfaction rather than external factors (Ryan and Deci, 2008).[29] Higher autonomy means that people find tasks more engaging and enjoyable to do. Consequently, this requires less psychological energy expenditure. When employees lack autonomy, the effort, and thus energy, required to engage in their work is substantially higher than when they work autonomously. Moreover, even when energy is depleted, people with greater autonomy are able to persist and perform at work more effectively (Gagne and Deci, 2005)[30] and are hence more productive. As a result, autonomy also serves as a type of buffer or counter to energy drain (Trougakos et al., 2014).[31]

Second, working autonomously means that people have a say in what they work on, how they work on it and when they work on it. This means that they can schedule work when they feel most engaged and motivated. This can prevent people from feeling overwhelmed as they can plan their work in a manner that best suits their personal way of working, allowing them to be maximally effective and efficient. Additionally, different people work more effectively at different times of the day. Research on circadian rhythms highlights that people have natural energy cycles that fluctuate throughout the day (Horne et al., 1980),[32] with energy levels peaking and dipping at different times for different people (for example typical rhythms, early risers and night owls). Furthermore, people experience energy fluctuation between days for a variety of reasons, including sleep, illness, nutrient consumption and overall life demands. Considering that everyone's energy patterns during days vary, and individuals' energy fluctuates between days, autonomy allows workers the opportunity to schedule tasks at times and do them in ways that provide opportunities to maximise their productivity and effectiveness.

Third, further contributing to work productivity, autonomy also facilitates people being able to work in ways that allow them to balance their life and thus avoid other negative consequences. For example, people who have greater work autonomy also have lower levels of work–family conflict (Senecal et al., 2001).[33] In addition, having greater autonomy means that workers have a greater opportunity to set up their work day to facilitate healthy lifestyle choices such as exercise, engagement in hobbies and positive social experiences. Lastly, higher autonomy is consistently linked to lower levels of burnout and better wellbeing in general (Ryan and Deci, 2017).[34] Taken as a whole, autonomy translates to happy and healthy workers who have higher levels of energy and are overall more effective and productive.

We have found that our energy levels rise and fall when we're working on different projects. Sometimes it's because we are working at the time of day at which our energy peaks, or working on things we are most passionate about and the time seems to disappear. Other times, we find ourselves wading through the treacle of tasks that we'd rather not be doing or become distracted by negative influences that make it hard for us to focus as the minutes tick by. Thankfully, our energy is something we can be mindful of when setting our workstyles. Paying attention to our body, our state of mind, the people around us and the work we're doing can help us use our energy wisely and ensure we spend each day soaring through the clouds high above the treacle river. There you will find the power of workstyle.

Chapter summary

- Working with autonomy gives you the opportunity to maximise your energy – directing it into the areas that matter, at the right time and alongside the right people. We've found workstyle helps us manage our energy in three ways:

  o **TEMPO:** We each have a different circadian rhythm which is individual to us and means working in the way that best suits us individually will make us more productive. Some people are at their best working in the evening (owls) whereas others are at their best first thing in the morning (larks), with many variations in between.

  o **BUZZ:** We have found that, like Oprah, some people give us energy (radiators) and others take it away (drains) and that through workstyle we have greater freedom to surround ourselves with more people who give us energy and with fewer people who don't.

  o **PRIORITISATION:** Working in a workstyle way also allows you to channel your energy where it is most needed, reflecting on your priorities and dividing your time (7 days a week, 24 hours a day) in the way that best suits you in order to maximise your energy and therefore your productivity.

- All these elements mean working in an individualised, workstyle way facilitates making the best use of your energy to be your most productive self.

  From the mouth of a workstyler: 'I joined the workstyle revolution because... I like to work when I feel inspired, not when someone else tells me to be.' Lui, Camiguin Island, Philippines

  Fact to remember: A 20–30-minute midday nap is more effective at improving work outcomes than caffeine or even sleeping more at night.[35]

  And finally... Do you have more radiators or drains in your home? Consider this question both literally and metaphorically. :thinking_face:

Play your part in the workstyle revolution

Reflect

☐ Try to observe when you feel you have the most energy on any given day. Are you a lark, a night owl or somewhere in between?

☐ Do you struggle to sleep at night or feel you could benefit from working differently to accommodate an afternoon nap?

☐ Think about the people in your life who give you energy and the people who drain your energy. How do you behave around them?

☐ Are you more of an introvert or an extrovert? Do you get energy from within yourself or from others?

☐ What are the things you struggle to juggle in your life? What are the things that constantly get postponed as you can't do them during the working day?

Act

☐ Keep a record of your energy levels – note down which times of day you feel most energised and when you feel most drained. How can you adapt your work schedule to capitalise on your peaks and troughs? Block out times in your calendar to prioritise active rest at the times you need it.

☐ If you're someone who gets energy from working in an office, consider ways you can recreate that buzz while working in a workstyle way, for example by using co-working spaces or cafés or perhaps listening to podcasts.

☐ Write a list of all the things that you need to do but haven't been able to fit in around work. Block out time in your calendar to get those things done.

☐ Experiment with the Pomodoro Technique to see how it impacts your productivity.

☐ Watch Chris Barnes' TED talk on sleep and work.

Inspire

☐ Share this chapter with your team at work to make the case for individualised working as a route to improving productivity in your organisation.

☐ Encourage others to think about their own natural energy by starting a group discussion about it.

FIFTEEN

Workstyle step-changes your productivity: CLARITY

Workstyle story: Sophia Lynch

Globetrotter, graphic designer, illustrator, night owl and honorary Berliner

Anyone who works in the fashion industry can tell you it's absolute chaos. The phrase 'dog eat dog' comes to mind, and this ingrained competition creates a world of overwork and unbearable office politics. It's exhausting.

In 2013 I became a part of this industry, fresh-faced and eager to work in fashion. I'd completed a design degree in my home city of Sydney, Australia, majoring in textiles and graphic design, before moving to Berlin, full of freedom and creative energy. The plan was to stay for six months. That was six years ago, and I'm still here.

In the Berlin fashion scene I could apply my skills to the pattern on a sofa or the floral design of a dress (I draw a lot of florals). I enjoyed my work, but eventually the industry got to me. Excitement about my work had been replaced by frustration at yet another time-wasting meeting about the communal dishwasher, and I couldn't understand how we were supposed to be more productive in a bustling office than in the peace of our own homes.

Working in a 9-to-5 job since university, I realised early on the importance of having a passion for what you do. And this wasn't what it felt like. Fuelled by never-ending deadlines, I was nearing burnout and I knew it. So, I turned to freelancing. But freelance life comes with its own stresses, and it's very easy to continue to overwork in order to prove to yourself that you're 'doing it' – a trap that I fell into. I felt like I was on a hamster wheel, saying yes to any work I could get my hands on, until I came across the idea of workstyle. For me, this was revolutionary, but in Berlin there were glimmers of workstyle everywhere. There are so many freelancers here who prioritise the little things in life like going for a stroll in the sunshine, making a long phone call or going for coffee with a friend, and it dawned on me that it was what I had been missing. That taking time away from work during the day could enhance my overall productivity.

So now, I have a workstyle of my own, starting work at around 10 a.m., having a long afternoon break and continuing from 9 p.m. late into the night when I'm most able to get into my flow (I'm a real night owl when it comes to creativity, something I've learned to embrace). I live most of the time in this incredible city, but make the most of mine and my partner's lifestyles by travelling often, spending a few weeks each year in the Canary Islands to escape the dark Berlin winter. I've also emerged from my pigeonhole of textile design to offer branding, art working and animation. The variety of projects I'm able to work on does amazing things for my productivity.

The best part is, I didn't have to give up fashion, I just had to make it work for me. Setting up my own online digital print studio allowed me to cut out all of the things I don't enjoy, while maintaining a balance of illustration and graphic design which I love. I still get a kick out of walking past someone wearing one of my prints.

I can now say that I love what I do every single day and can take advantage of any work or travel opportunities that come my way. That's not to say I don't question my decision occasionally when I watch people back home 'climbing the career ladder', but right now as I pack my bags for a trip to Sicily, realising all I need is a laptop, iPad and good wifi, I feel so lucky to have this level of freedom in my life.

The brainpower opportunity

A common characteristic of the traditional way of working is meetings. Meetings about everything from strategy and planning to communal dishwashers. Meeting, even, about meetings. In our previous working lives we have been in meetings many times thinking to ourselves, 'I don't need to be here.' We often hear our friends complaining that they are in back-to-back meetings in their traditional jobs, finding their only time to do actual productive work is in the evening or early morning and their only time to think is on the commute. Too much of the time they are actually working is out of their control, largely because of synchronous behaviour that takes away the opportunity to schedule work in their own way. It forces everyone to conform to an inefficient way of working, which prevents clarity of thought and makes it much harder for them to find their productive utopia.

Research in the US found that 65 per cent of senior managers said meetings keep them from completing their work and that 64 per cent said meetings come at the expense of deep thinking.[1] Not great for productivity then. Poorly organised meetings are estimated to have cost the US economy $399 billion in 2019.[2] Working in a traditional way becomes about finding time rather than creating time to work in the way that best suits you to be productive.

Sophia's story illustrates that sometimes it's the cultural norms of traditional work that stop you from working in a way that gives you the best clarity and, as a consequence, productivity. Those extend to unrealistic deadlines and an expectation for work to be done 'ASAP' (as soon as possible) or by 'COP today' (close of play). :sick_in_mouth: This may force a volume of work to be done, but it doesn't enable considered work to be delivered with the headspace it needs. In fact, deadlines are cited as the primary reason for workplace stress,[3] which in turn reduces productivity.[4]

The autonomy of workstyle has enabled us to get the most out of our brains because we can individualise the way we use them. We have identified three ways that working in a workstyle manner can help us to improve our productivity through having greater clarity:

1. **GROOVE** – Getting in the zone.

2. **PRECISION** – Focusing on the right work at the right time.

3. **DAYDREAM** – Creating headspace for free thinking.

1. GROOVE – Getting in the zone :tripping_the_light_fantastic:

Aristotle once said there were four types of happiness in life, which related to learning, pleasure, recognition and money.[5] He suggested the desire to make money should play a part but perhaps not be the only part of our lives. Instead, he suggested a new word that we might use to think about how we spend our time (he liked inventing new words, too). Rather than being in work or in leisure, we should aim for what he called a state of *energeia*, which meant to be fully engaged in who you are and whatever you are doing.[6] More recently, psychologist Mihaly Csikszentmihalyi proposed a similar concept which he called 'flow'.[7] Also known as 'being in the zone', this is the psychological state in which we're fully immersed in an activity with a feeling of energised focus, full involvement and enjoyment in the act of doing something. His research on other cultures and how to achieve happiness found that those who made both their work and everyday 'chore' activities into as close to flow activities as possible experienced greater productivity and greater satisfaction from their work than those who didn't.[8]

Where workstyle is at its best, and specifically most productive, is where we can each create the best holistic work experience in order to experience flow.

A good starting point is to understand yourself as deeply as possible. More extrovert personalities like Lizzie might enjoy working alongside others, in person or, in Lizzie's case, remotely, fuelled by the energy of their colleagues, while more introverted personalities like Alex might prefer working by themselves, though they may still connect profoundly with others online to build relationships and get energy.

When we have a good idea of who we are and how we like to work, we can look at the type of work we actually do and how we can maximise our time spent in a flow state. Whether it's mostly communicating with others, preparing artwork files or calculating tax returns, there will be certain elements of our work that we just know we will be able to plough through once we are in the zone. Getting into that zone can be tricky, but it is much easier if we have control over the way we work – in a specific place, with certain lighting or a favourite playlist – whatever you want it to be. :headphones: When you have the autonomy of workstyle, you can create the perfect conditions to get into your flow. If you need convincing any further, a ten-year McKinsey study on flow and productivity found that the sample group were five times more productive during flow.[9]

2. PRECISION – Focusing on the right work at the right time
:microscope:

When people bounce between their inboxes, meetings, group chat notifications and office small talk, they confuse being busy with being productive. They are jumping around from task to task to such an extent that their attention is only fit for 'shallow work', as it is described by Cal Newport who coined the term in his book *Deep Work: Rules for focused success in a distracted world*[10] to describe the 'non-cognitively demanding, logistical-style tasks, often performed while distracted'. They can reply to an email or move boxes around on a slide, but these efforts tend not to create value in the world and are easy to replicate, as opposed to 'deep work', described by Cal as 'professional activity performed in a state of distraction-free concentration that pushes your cognitive capabilities to their limit'. This is also the time when people do things that have the most value for their organisations. Where people solve problems or produce quality content which has the most impact, or where they learn and improve their skills.

Whether it's open-plan offices, technology devices or a shift change of other staff, there may be many distractions from spending more time on high-quality, meaningful work. People bring some of this on themselves as their brains are increasingly hacked by the short-term dopamine hit from receiving a message or a notification.[11] It's easy to switch out of deep work mode and into shallow tasks like responding to emails or ticking off little tasks on our to-do list, but it's much harder to move in the other direction.

We can all think of times we've spent doing deep work. Deep work almost hurts the brain sometimes, and we each have our own times and places to do it optimally (not if you're feeling tempted to make a 'music for concentrating' playlist like workstyler Fran!). Having the autonomy to choose when and where we work through workstyle enables us to eliminate distractions and to create the conditions for focus to do deep work, in whichever way suits us best.

We have found that the autonomy of workstyle enables us to focus on deep work in the mornings but then switch to shallow work in the afternoon or evenings. This ensures we get the best of our brains, applied to the tasks of most importance, which makes us more productive overall – particularly when shallow work is allocated a dedicated time window during an episode of the latest Netflix binge: we like to spend an hour on it on select evenings to prepare for a morning of unadulterated deep work.

3. DAYDREAM – Creating headspace for free thinking
:away_with_the_fairies:

Optimal working will be different for each of us, and this includes finding our own way to create headspace to do our best, most productive work. But not all of the value in the deep work we do comes from conscious effort and dedicated thinking time. Sometimes it is only when we switch our conscious brain off that we allow our unconscious brain the freedom to wander and make the connections that we really need to find. So, to use more of our available brainpower, we need to stop trying to use it and allow ourselves headspace in our days for menial tasks or distractions that take us away from thinking about our work. Rest, daydreaming and staring into space are traditionally seen as non-productive 'downtime'. It goes against our ingrained beliefs which presuppose that you have to be 'doing' something to be productive. But research shows that daydreaming heightens creativity,[12] and engaging in an unrelated task while we ruminate makes us more likely to find a solution to a challenging problem.[13]

Very much anchored in negative language and associated feelings, the idea of doing 'chores' doesn't sound particularly appealing to anyone, but, much like work, this is because of the relationship we have with chores. For example, Lizzie's workstyle specifically refers to time spent folding laundry as a great source of satisfaction – time that allows the brain to wander while she is organising her home, which also makes her more productive during work time. Some people may see it as unusual to have folding laundry as an integral part of your work day, but reflecting on the way we personally work best, which will be different for each of us, will ultimately be what makes each of us our most productive selves. :organised_piles_of_washing:

Alex is the same with washing-up. Having started his career as a pot-washer at a nearby Happy Eater restaurant :smiley_face_in_profile: he spent his early work life learning about how restaurants operated while building up a subconscious belief that washing-up was the work nobody really wanted to do – the bottom of the metaphorical ladder. During his progression to running bars and restaurants, Alex built a subconscious belief that washing pots at home wasn't a task to enjoy but to endure. Only recently has that relationship changed to a valuable moment for reflection that concurrently creates order, which, as someone who likes everything in its place, is important for his mental wellbeing as well as his ability to focus on work when the time comes.

It may not seem like it, but laundry folding and washing-up have similar benefits to showering. More than 70 per cent of us have our best, most creative ideas in the shower.[14] Psychologists have found the reason for this is that, when we're alone, in a non-judgemental environment, and we allow our mind to drift, we tune into our inner stream of consciousness and daydreams.[15] Working at home often creates the ideal conditions for time spent folding laundry, washing pots and showering, but going for a walk, taking the train or working in a new environment can also give our brain the stimulation it requires to make new connections and put things together in new ways. Creative agencies have long known that, if you want someone to come up with a brilliant, original idea, you can't have them chained to their desk all day, yet many of them do just that. One wonders

how many individuals sacrificed their creativity by being forced to conform to the traditional way of working and what the human and social cost has been of these lost ideas.

When we allow our minds to take a break from the external world before rejoining it later, we give ourselves the opportunities to make connections between the inner and outer worlds we inhabit, which, according to renowned creativity expert Scott Barry Kaufman, is where creativity lies.[16] We shouldn't be told, nor be telling ourselves, where to be (desk, at home or otherwise) and monitoring when we're not there. Instead, we need to create more headspace through workstyle to do our best, most productive work. :thought_shower:

Geek box: How brain function impacts creative thinking

By Dorian Minors, cognitive neuroscientist, University of Cambridge

At the core of creativity is the intuitive 'insight'. Not the kind of analytic insight that comes when figuring out how to navigate the subway or solving a difficult maths problem. Intuitive insight is the 'aha' or the 'eureka' moment – the kind of spontaneous insight that comes as if from nowhere. It often comes when least expected – in the shower or while out on a walk. Other times, it comes as if it were hidden somewhere outside our consciousness, like when we're struggling to understand something and a word or idea all of a sudden brings everything into focus. These features of the creative insight are a clue to its origins.

A crash course in neuroanatomy

Our brain is largely comprised of two kinds of cells: grey matter and white matter (Kandel et al., 2013).[17] **Grey matter** refers to our neurons, the basic signalling unit of the brain. Each neuron is connected to nearby neurons and passes electrical and chemical signals to these neighbours. These chains of interconnected signalling devices make up a complex series of 'pathways' for information about the world to travel along, and in this way neurons pass information about our perceptions to our muscles so that we can make the appropriate responses.

Some of these pathways are handed to us by evolution, but many more are developed by us over time. Certain combinations of inputs (sights, smells, familiar ways of moving our bodies) will develop neural pathways to combinations of output (habitual ways of responding to the world). In this way, our brain begins to create patterns that reflect the statistical structure of the world (Minors, 2021).[18] Regions of the brain that respond to things in the world – things we regularly sense – become linked to regions of the brain that tell us what can be done about those things – how to feel about them and how to respond to them.

White matter refers to the other kinds of brain cells – glial cells. White matter fits all around the neurons (the 'grey matter') and takes care of them – protecting them, repairing them and improving their performance. Importantly, the more you practise something – a particular pathway of input to output – the more white matter will grow around those pathways – all the better to support them in doing this thing that we do all the time. This is wonderful for speed and performance. But it means that these neurons, now surrounded by all this construction, can't change their connections very easily any more. It means these neurons are quicker at doing some things but much less good at doing others. The patterns in our brains become increasingly rigid.

How intuitive insight comes about

Many domains of psychology consider effective problem solving a case of putting together 'chunks' of information into the correct sequence, from the older information processing and gestalt approaches (Öllinger and Knoblich, 2009;[19] Simon and Newell, 1971[20]) to more recent computational theories (e.g. Duncan, 2013;[21] Friston et al., 2017[22]). First, we must recognise the food, then reach with the arm, then grasp with the hand, then put the hand to the mouth. Only then can we eat.

These 'chunks' of information and their sequences can be mapped to our neural patterns – brain regions that represent the information and the pathways which connect them (Graziano, 2016).[23] But because these patterns become increasingly rigid with time, we are most often drawn to the familiar sequences.

Intuitive insight occurs when we are able to move beyond these familiar patterns and discover new ones. In the brain, 'aha' moments are characterised by neural processes that are more diffuse – less associated with clear or typical patterns of behaviour or neural activity or more open to different possibilities and patterns than those more readily available to us (Kounios and Beeman, 2014).[24]

This is why intuitive insight feels so spontaneous. It is the unexpected combination of a pattern unfamiliar to the problem at hand, opening us up to the possibility of new 'chunks' of information and new sequences of combinations.

And so, to best harness creativity, take a break. Do something different and activate different pathways. There are many kinds of intuitive insight, but the key to all is change (Klein and Jarosz, 2011).[25]

We have found that our work has benefited hugely from tailoring our workstyles to suit the different types of work that we do. Whether it's turning up the music to get into our groove or saying 'no' so we can get deep into our flow, we are taking ownership for our work through our workstyle. So let's take it. Hang out that wash load and let your daydreams answer your problems! Therein lies the power of workstyle.

Chapter summary

- Having control over your workstyle allows you to define how and when you will deliver the different aspects of your work. There are three ways workstyle working benefits productivity through improving our clarity:

  - **GROOVE:** With control over your workstyle, you are more likely to be able to create the conditions you need to get into the 'zone', achieve 'flow' (our most productive, deep work) and find your productive utopia.

  - **PRECISION:** Being productive is also about doing the right work at the right time. Deep work and shallow work, for example, require different conditions to optimise productivity, and having your own workstyle means you can do them at times that best suit you.

  - **DAYDREAM:** Creating headspace is important to productivity. Not all value from work comes from getting lots done. Sometimes detaching your brain is the best way to find creative solutions. Our workstyles can give us the time for that valuable detachment – whether it's in the shower, doing the laundry or washing-up, or going for a walk, so proactively factoring this in is central to finding clarity and therefore boosting productivity.

- Individualising work through workstyle allows each of us to consider how we work best as an individual, through deep work, shallow work and creating headspace to think subconsciously, giving us greater clarity and making us more productive.

  From the mouth of a workstyler: 'I joined the workstyle revolution because... I always do my best thinking when I'm picking up dog poop, which wasn't allowed in my office job.' Ella, Episkopi, Cyprus

  Fact to remember: More than 70 per cent of us have our best, most creative ideas in the shower.[26]

  And finally... Take off your clothes. Get in the shower. Stumble across an answer to that impossible problem at the back of your mind.

Play your part in the workstyle revolution

Reflect

☐ Reflect on the work you're doing and when might be the best time for each aspect of what you need to do. How much of your work is deep work and how much is shallow work?

☐ When is your best time for deep work and shallow work? How do you create headspace? What blocks you from doing the right work at the right time?

☐ Think back to when you have had your best ideas. Did they come when you were sitting in front of your laptop or when you were in the shower or walking to the bus stop?

Act

☐ Look again at your notes about your energy levels from Chapter 14 and note down when you are best able to tackle deep work and what the optimal times and settings are for you. Also observe the times when you feel less focused that are better suited to shallow work.

☐ Protect your ability to get in the flow by creating boundaries in your working day. Turn off notifications and use applications that block any distractions. Where you can, use automations in order to reduce the amount of time you spend on shallow work.

☐ Block out time in your diary to get headspace. Do things you usually wouldn't do during the working day – take a shower, do the washing-up, get some fresh air, let your mind wander and create space for subconscious thinking.

☐ Read *Flow* by Mihaly Csikszentmihalyi and *Deep Work* by Cal Newport to understand more about these concepts.

Inspire

☐ Suggest that your team or those you work with block out time for headspace each week. Ask people to share their experience – what did they discover when they let their mind wander at different times of day? Did anyone come up with great creative solutions to problems?

SIXTEEN

Workstyle step-changes your productivity: MASTERY

Workstyle story: Sam Robinson

Father, marketeer, blogger and young widower

In June 2019 my wife Lauren was diagnosed with cancer for the second time. Incurable cancer. She was 30 years old. Our daughter Molly was just two, so it's fair to say that our lives were turned upside down and inside out. How could this be happening?

Let me rewind a little... I'd been happily working 12-hour days in marketing for more than 10 years, progressing my corporate career, but now things needed to change – and quickly. When Lauren was first diagnosed with breast cancer in 2017, I wanted to be around to attend all her appointments. Prioritising my family was what mattered most. Happily, I found a job working for a company which offered me the flexibility I needed, enabling me to be there for Lauren (and Molly) when it counted. It became clear that judging someone on their output made far more sense than counting the number of hours they worked.

Lauren approached her diagnosis with an attitude that left me awestruck. She had chemotherapy, then radiotherapy and did everything she could to keep herself well. Unfortunately, it wasn't enough, and in 2019 the terminal diagnosis shattered the shared future that we both longed for. My employer continued to be supportive, which helped manage my recurring thought that every day in the office meant a day less with Lauren and Molly – precious, scarce time as a family. Fast-forward a few months and I was made redundant from my leisure-industry job due to Covid-19, which in hindsight was a blessing. A month later Lauren died.

It's impossible to describe how it feels when you lose someone so closely stitched into the fabric of your life. It's like a bomb has gone off and you are left to pick the shrapnel out of every aspect of your life and piece things back together again.

My sole focus then (and now) was being there for my young daughter Molly. The first few weeks were a bit of a blur, but before long I had to start thinking about earning in order to pay the mortgage and put food on the table – it's as simple as that. Molly had already lost 50 per cent of her parent availability, so I had one clear objective in mind: provide what I needed financially and still be able to pick my daughter up from school every day. I could only see one way forward, and so I set up my own marketing consultancy and joined the workstyle revolution.

My current workstyle is 9 a.m. to 3 p.m. while Molly is at school and some evenings when she is in bed. As we approach the anniversary of Lauren's death, I'm always more reflective – I'm doing everything I can to make it work – and so far I'm doing OK. I've had to completely evolve my workstyle to fit my new life circumstances, and I'm thankful that I can. Life is incredibly busy, and I'm proud of what I'm achieving with my work, but more importantly as a dad to Molly. She's a remarkable little girl, also trying to understand what's going on in her life. She thinks about Lauren all the time and asks me questions like, 'Will Mummy have snacks where she is?', 'Has Mummy got friends in the clouds?' and 'If Mummy can talk to other people in heaven, why can't she talk to me?' Consider for a moment how you explain all this to a four-year-old when you are coping with your own grief. I know that Lauren would be really proud of us both, making the best of the circumstances we are in.

Workstyle is enabling me to piece the fragments of our lives back together, inching forwards one day at a time, and for that I will be forever grateful.

The devotion opportunity

Sam's story is heartbreaking, but among the tragedy is also a story that can give us hope. Hope that no matter how low we might find ourselves during the journey of life, we can adapt and move forward one day at a time. Changing our priorities is part of managing our workstyle and our motivation, and it doesn't have to mean letting go of the career we have built.

Over the course of our careers we each seek to get better at the work we do – to hopefully one day reach a point where we feel confident enough to say we've mastered it. Along that journey, and whatever the ups and downs, we try to find the time to hone our skills and also to maintain our motivation while navigating the things that inevitably happen in our personal lives.

Research that proved the relationship between personal mastery and productivity has emphasised the role empowerment could play in improving mastery.[1] This is consistent with what we have anecdotally found through our workstyle experience – that even in the worst of circumstances we can be more productive because workstyle allows us to have control over how we nurture and grow our skills. Mastery can improve productivity by 100 per cent or more when it is directed towards a goal or a problem,[2] so with the right motivation our pursuit of mastery can be revolutionary for our productivity.

We have found that workstyle improves our productivity through mastery in three ways:

1. **TIME** – Perfecting the art of practice.

2. **DEDICATION** – Committing to the things you're passionate about.

3. **ADAPTABILITY** – Continuing to improve in the face of change.

1. TIME – Perfecting the art of practice :decade_wall_planner:

Mastery is all about getting better at something – building deep knowledge or skill in a particular area. Research by Ericsson et al.

in Germany published in 1993 showed for the first time that, rather than natural talent, time spent deliberately practising is what matters most in order to achieve mastery.[3] Their original research pointed to ten years of practice, and Malcolm Gladwell then popularised their concept by picking 10,000 hours as the magic number for mastery in his book *Outliers*[4] (though not without attracting controversy and frustration from the authors of the original research for his oversimplification of their findings! :awkward_face:).

Given we know that time practising something is the proven route to mastery, it makes sense that being able to deliberately make time for that practice and prioritising it over other things is fundamental to achieving the level of skill needed to claim you have mastered something. Unlike the one in three people who say that they have only 42 minutes per day for things they enjoy,[5] we have found that workstyle enables us to divide our time in a way that fits with our priorities and gives us more time to learn a new skill or hone an existing one within our week. This control over our mastery schedule also means we can build in the time needed to rest. Ericsson and his fellow researchers point out that effortful activity such as practice can be sustained only for a limited time before causing exhaustion. So in order to build up to mastery, we must also be able to plan effective recovery periods.

Since starting Hoxby we have learned a whole new skill set of virtual leadership that we've since grouped into a few key areas, including authenticity, experimentation, technology and communication. For example, we use short videos to connect with individuals or groups within Hoxby and beyond. Before we record a video, we have a

conversation about the key messages we want to cover, the tone we want to project and how to make it engaging. We used to take half an hour for this conversation before each video and then proceed to record 15 takes before, wearily, we arrived at one we were vaguely happy with. But over time and with practice we have learned to do this much more quickly, knowing how to focus each video on three central points to keep it concise and being more comfortable with our creative tools for engagement, as well as now having our own style and high energy for consistency. Feel free to check out our early Workstyle Freestyle videos to see how much we've improved since then! :embarrassed_face:

The downside of having the freedom to decide how to use our time and access to all the resources we need is that it does then require us to make difficult choices we perhaps wouldn't otherwise have had to make about what skills we want to learn. We have a newfound power to choose and with that power comes newfound responsibility (thanks, Peter Parker :spider:). But when we strike on the thing that excites us, we have the power to make the time available to develop our skills to achieve mastery.

2. DEDICATION – Committing to the things you're passionate about :all_in:

Coming back to the 1993 research by Ericsson and his team one more time, another one of their caveats was that practice in itself is not inherently motivating and so it can be difficult to maintain momentum. Workstyle solves this in two ways (we'll come to the second in the next section). First, the freedom and autonomy to choose to practise things you are deeply passionate about, or fascinated by, means you can align these with your purpose and thereby create your own intrinsic motivation (motivation that comes from within you).

Stepping out of the traditional work mindset of job titles or fixed working hours and adopting a workstyle approach encourages us to view ourselves as people spanning both work and everything else in our lives, encompassing the various transferable skills and unique traits that we bring to the world. :one_of_a_kind: Doing this has helped us to question more broadly where we want to achieve mastery and then begin to practise these skills for ourselves. When we started out on our workstyle journey, we had a clear vision of what we wanted to achieve in terms of a more inclusive world of work, but working in a workstyle way over the years has fuelled a fascination for us in digital-first collaboration between diverse teams, and our ability to master this through our day-to-day work in this area of personal passion means we are doing so with more rapid progress than others.

That dedication to building mastery increases productivity is also supported by self-determination theory showing that the intrinsic motivation that leads to better-quality learning thrives when we are able to work autonomously.[6] Workstyle working at Hoxby has consistently scored highly for both of these in our longitudinal study, showing that workstyle increases our capacity for mastery. Pop back to Annika's geek box in Chapter 6 to read more on this theory if you haven't already.

Workstyle also has the advantage of giving us the opportunity to explore new things to see if we like them, develop our understanding of them and gradually build up a clearer picture of what it is we want to do more of and what we can happily do less of, too. A 'side hustle' may become more than a bit of work on the side when we aren't restricted to fixed working hours or from a specific location, and portfolio careers emerge trying new things and broadening our range of skills, the importance of which Ben explains in his geek box below. With the autonomy to decide when and where we work, we have much greater control over the variety of working avenues we can explore and the skills we choose to dedicate ourselves to. We can make more efficient use of our time, prioritise our personal pursuit of mastery and channel that towards a goal in order to improve our productivity.

3. ADAPTABILITY – Continuing to improve in the face of change :camper_van:

The second way in which workstyle solves the motivational challenges that get in the way of mastery is that it enables us to adapt to changing circumstances so that we can develop our skills with enough consistency to see results and build momentum through extrinsic motivation.

Take workstyler Josh, for example, an Australian who lived in the UK when he was working on the first draft of the illustrations for this book. He decided he wanted to see more of the world, first in Europe, then in Central America. When he did the final illustrations Josh was in Mexico, with the ocean lapping his toes and a margarita by his side (while we were in overcast Britain, with a touch of drizzle) – we're sure you'll agree they look all the better for it. Communicating via Threadit and collaborating on Google Slides, we could work seamlessly together. Respect the workstyle. :work_packed_in_suitcase:

We talked in Chapter 9 about how workstyle enables us to keep doing the things we love or are passionate about when times change, to keep working towards the same goals but change when or where we do it. We have found the same applies for mastery – whatever life throws at you, you can continue the route to mastery. For many workstylers, their life changes but, rather than change what they do, they can continue to build on the skills or knowledge they already have and fit it around their new life, like Sam or Josh.

This greatly helps our productivity because we can build our mastery over time, through practice and iterative improvement. This is made possible through the individualised learning that we explored in Chapter 10. The better we get, the more we can attract further work that helps us to perpetually hone our skills, to make progress and be motivated to continue the path to mastery. :virtuous_circle:

Geek box: Why variety, or range, is critical for mastery in a complex world, inspired by the brilliant research of David Epstein[7]

By Ben Foulkes, business psychologist and 'The School of Life' faculty

The common insult 'Jack of all trades' has been misconstrued since 1592 when it was first directed at a young poet who had been helping out in a wide variety of jobs in a theatre company, from copying scripts to trying his hand at bit-part acting. The full version of the phrase was actually 'a jack of all trades is a master of none, but oftentimes better than a master of one' (Epstein, 2019),[8] and the poet in question was William Shakespeare. It turns out that, rather than being an exception to the rule, many of the greatest masters in history, from Edison with his invention of the light bulb to Newton and his theory of gravity, have evolved from experimentation in a wide range of fields rather than early specialisation in just one (Rose and Ogas, 2018).[9]

Today the world of work is often described as volatile, unpredictable, complex and ambiguous (Bennett and Lemoine, 2014),[10] characteristics which create a 'wicked learning environment' where information may be missing, delayed or inaccurate, making our experiences difficult to learn from (Hogarth et al., 2015).[11] In order to achieve mastery in such a world, rather than specialising in a narrow field where we get more efficient with experience in solving narrow problems, we are more likely to achieve better long-term outcomes by experimenting in practice, sampling many different areas and learning to make connections between them (Epstein, 2019).[12]

There are two key benefits to developing our adaptability and engaging in sampling and experimentation in our careers. First, it increases the chance of us finding what psychologists call 'match quality', the degree of fit we find between the work we do and who we are (Jackson, 2013).[13] Not only are we statistically unlikely to hit upon the best use of our talents in the first thing we turn our hand to, but it turns out that even things that we think are fixed about ourselves, such as our core values, preferences and even our personalities, can change throughout our lifetime (Srivastava et al., 2003).[14] We all have 'multiple possible selves' (Ronfeldt and Grossman, 2008),[15] so learning to adapt and experiment with different activities, social groups, contexts, jobs, careers and then reflecting and adjusting our personal narratives can increase our motivation to continue and improve our fulfilment and quality of life (Ibarra, 2005).[16]

Second, this type of mastery is more likely to lead to breakthroughs in intractable problems, as we benefit from bringing an 'outsider view' to the problem (Tversky and Koehler, 1994).[17] Problem solvers have a tendency to employ familiar methods even if better ones are available (Luchins, 1942),[18] known as the Einstellung effect, and to look upon an object as having only the one known function, when in fact it may have others, an instinct known as 'functional fixedness' (Duncker and Lees, 1945).[19] Perhaps the best-known example of this is in the candle problem, where participants are given a candle, a box of tacks and a book of matches and told to attach the candle to the wall such that wax doesn't drip on the table below. Solvers typically try to either melt the candle to the wall or use the tacks to attach it to the wall directly, neither of which works. When the problem is presented with the tacks outside of their box, solvers are more likely to view the empty box as a potential candle holder and to solve the problem by tacking the box to the wall and placing the candle inside.

So, Epstein argues, rather than 'pick and stick' to one industry or function (Epstein, 2019),[20] we should approach our careers and projects rather like Michelangelo approached a block of marble, willing to learn and adjust as we go, and even to abandon a previous goal and change direction entirely should the need arise. The result of doing so is that we're more likely to truly excel in our field in the long run and solve intractable, wicked problems to boot.

Life changes for better or worse, but along the way we are continually learning and treading our path to mastery within the areas that interest us. Through workstyle we are able to create the much-needed time and resources required for practice in the pursuit of our own proficiency. We can try our hand at different things more easily and make informed decisions about what we want to dedicate our working lives to. As life's winds of change seek to throw us off course, we can adapt, change aspects of our workstyle to fit work around our lives and stay motivated as we bravely tread the path we have chosen. We need not break stride, but continue to improve and to make ever-more productive use of time along the way. In always moving forward, we discover the power of workstyle.

Chapter summary

- Control over when and where you work gives you a greater opportunity to get better at the things you're passionate about or that you are highly skilled at. We have found that workstyle improves our productivity through mastery in three ways:

  - **TIME:** Workstyle enables us to make time for our priorities, including improving our skills towards a goal. Such time to focus on the things we are passionate about can enable us to gain the required hours of dedicated practice to develop mastery. Workstyle also enables us to access a greater variety of the resources needed to learn and build sufficient rest time into our schedule.

  - **DEDICATION:** By exploring things that excite us and being able to try, fail and learn from them, we can identify and commit to improving things that align with our sense of purpose. Through this intrinsic motivation we become more productive, dedicating ourselves to the things we are most excited by.

  - **ADAPTABILITY:** Whatever changes in your circumstances, workstyle means you can practise with enough consistency to see results and you can continue on your path to mastery.

- We have found that individualised work, through workstyle, has enabled us to develop our skills, building our confidence and motivation and in turn transforming our productivity.

From the mouth of a workstyler: 'I joined the workstyle revolution because... I wanted to be the best mum to my kids, have time to develop as an artist, and build my skills as a business director and project manager through my work. Working in this way has been amazing. I feel supported, valued and enjoy every minute I commit to work.' Punam, Kent, UK

Fact to remember: Ten years of dedicated practice is what research has shown you need to achieve mastery.[21]

And finally... We've been mastering virtual leadership for eight years. Still two years to get good at it, then. :green_morph_suit: :clapper_board:

Play your part in the workstyle revolution

Reflect

☐ What do you want to get really good at? This might be something you already do or something entirely new, and it could be inside or outside work.

☐ Are there things that you know would improve your productivity if only you had the time to get better at them? Consider how working in a workstyle way could help.

☐ Reflect on the things that might derail you from your path to mastery – how can you adapt your workstyle to create more time and protect consistent practice?

Act

☐ Choose three things you would like to master. Plan what you need to do to get good at them over the next week, month or year. For example, you might set aside a dedicated hour each week, attending a course or joining a group.

☐ Become a master workstyler! If you don't already have one, create a document to lay out your workstyle. Remember your workstyle should change and adapt over time. Decide when to reflect and review it (we suggest at least every three months) and block out time to do this.

☐ Watch our early Workstyle Freestyle videos at WorkstyleRevolution. com to see how much we've improved!

☐ Read *Outliers* by Malcolm Gladwell to understand the factors that contribute to mastery.

Inspire

☐ Identify within your organisation or working group where traditional working structures and norms might be blocking people's pursuit of mastery. Are people enabled and empowered to learn and grow? What can you do to build and support a culture that encourages the pursuit of mastery?

☐ Speak to friends and colleagues to understand what they want to get good at. Can you approach your goals collectively? Connect people with similar interests and goals.

SEVENTEEN

Workstyle step-changes your productivity: TRUST

Workstyle story: Laura Derryman-Warren

Finance consultant with one husband, one dog, two nose rings and a rainbow of hair colours

I never really fitted in at school. It was only when I left to do my A levels at a further education college with more freedom that I could feel myself blossom. Then came the world of work: payroll, accounts and tax, all things I am good at. But with them came a corporate ethic that demanded total submission to unspoken rules and codes of conformity where trust to deliver your work didn't come into the equation.

For me it came to a head when I arrived at work one Monday, having got a nose stud over the weekend, and my boss sternly asked: 'Who gave you permission to do that?' I was shocked. Who did I need permission from? I was a grown woman, able to make my own decisions. But this workplace was like something out of a Dickens novel. For seven and a half hours every day, I belonged to the company. Any sign of my life outside of work, the real me, had to be hidden away: no passions, no personal phone calls, no personal style, no personality. And certainly no freedom or trust to do things my way.

Like so many others I know, I left the real me at home and got on with the job. And I was good at it: the invoices I raised and chased were always paid on time, my client relationships were excellent, and I was top of the leaderboard for recovering outstanding monies.

But you know what my line manager said in my next appraisal? 'Your signature: it's too loud, too flamboyant.' I laughed! I couldn't help it. She just stared at my nose ring. 'We think you are very good at what you do,' she said. 'But you won't be any good at doing anything more.'

I stopped laughing. How did she know I had nothing more to give? She simply replied, 'How are you going to change our perception of you?'

In other words, lose your personality – lose the nose ring, lose the blue hair and lose any character from the way you write your name.

I wasn't prepared to do that. I wasn't prepared to do the mind-crushing commute, only to work in a soul-crushing environment. My husband had got a big promotion not long before that gave us some financial security. So I left.

Soon after, I heard about the workstyle revolution and, blue hair and all, decided to give it a go. I felt like I was bringing nothing but two nose rings and a dog under the desk. But those things were important to me, and fellow workstylers recognised strengths that had never been valued in my corporate life and I was trusted to deliver like never before. Rather than focus on what I looked like, I was able to focus on the task, getting it done on my terms and in my way. My personality and sense of humour were embraced. I go on a lovely long dog walk every day when it suits me. And I have never missed a deadline. True, I never missed one in the old job either, but that was through fear of failure rather than the pleasure of fulfilment. Living the workstyle life means even tricky things never feel like work. I am trusted and I am appreciated.

In the last five years I've changed my hair more than ten times – fringe, half-head shave, green, undercut, black, blue, bob, pink, red, whole-head shave, bright purple... – and felt nothing but love and support from other workstylers to express who I am.

The teamwork opportunity

Trusting one another means believing in each other to reliably deliver what we have said we will. Not tightly regulating every moment of their day, nor attempting to control elements of their personality that are irrelevant to the output for which they are responsible as Laura so painfully experienced.

When we aren't working in the same place or at the same time as other people, the comfort some people crave of visibly being able to see that someone is working is removed. This gives them one of two options: a) perpetuate presenteeism by installing some sort of surveillance equipment on their computer to see what work others are doing, :panopticon: or b) trust that they will get their work done and measure their contribution by the quality of their output rather than by their visible busyness. :collaboration:

Somewhat unbelievably, significant advances have been made in the technology that can monitor your every keystroke and report your productivity to your bosses. We think it's outrageous and misses a much greater opportunity to build a positive, supportive work environment built on a culture of trust, which research shows is a better driver of productivity than any of the command-and-control approaches that have been adopted by a startling number of companies over the last few years.[1] The micromanagement implicit in command-and-control ways of working increases the pressure felt by workers and makes them less likely to succeed in their tasks,[2] reducing their productivity.

Some of this stems from the misinterpretation of an office-based management style. 'Management by walking around', as it was promoted by management consultants Tom Peters and Robert Waterman,[3] was largely misunderstood by middle managers. Whereas the term was originally used to describe how managers in the best-performing organisations would frequently be on the front line – meeting customers and staff on the shop floor, in the factory or in shops – it was taken by others to mean that they needed to keep an eye on their teams in the office. Aware that they were being closely monitored and performance was based on these observations, presenteeism proliferated across the corporate world, to the point where in a survey by the CIPD, more than eight in ten office workers report experiencing it in 2018,[4] despite research suggesting it can cut productivity by a third or more[5] and cost organisations billions of dollars per year.[6]

This, combined with cultural norms at many organisations, means many people still consider the number of hours at their desks as a marker of a productive day at work. The pressure of needing to be available and online costs UK businesses up to £26 billion a year[7] and that's not just for those who work in the office. With more remote working, digital presenteeism is on the rise, too.[8] More people are now sending an email late at night to prove their dedication, or moving the mouse on their computer periodically to keep the green dot live next to their name. So, despite its origins in the office environment, the issue of presenteeism is psychological and attitudinal and thankfully therefore treatable.

There are still a shocking number of organisations that are stuck in the mindset that you have to be present to be productive, and it speaks volumes for the lack of trust that exists in the relationship between employees and their employers. We know hours spent working don't equate to productivity. If we look at the most 'productive' economies in the world, they are not the ones where people work the longest hours,[9] and studies have shown that in fact working fewer hours leads to greater productivity. [10]

Trust is the opposite of presenteeism. It is based on empowerment, and we have found it creates greater accountability and co-operation. Trust is the cornerstone of any relationship, whether it be with your family, friends, colleagues, pets – you name it. The quality of our relationships, the success of our teams, and ultimately our productivity can all be distilled down to the extent to which we trust one another. :workmate_falling_backwards: The evidence supports this, too: compared with people at low-trust companies, people at high-trust companies report 74 per cent less stress, 106 per cent more energy at work, 76 per cent more engagement, 29 per cent more satisfaction with their lives, 40 per cent less burnout and, crucially, 50 per cent higher productivity.[11]

In the early days of Hoxby, Lizzie was sitting next to a man at a conference who was intrigued by this way of working and the vision we had for workstyle. He loved the concept but simply couldn't get past the idea that we would be able to have an organisation where we couldn't see anyone actually working and had never met those we were counting on to deliver work. Lizzie has a vivid memory of his furrowed brow and confused face as he asked, 'But how can you possibly *trust* these people you've never met?' Since then we've worked with 2,500 amazing workstylers to deliver more than 1,500 projects for charities, companies and organisations around the world, and the answer we would be able to give him now is not just based on theory but grounded in having seen first-hand how incredible it is when teams are trusted. We, and those who we have the privilege of working with, have found that autonomy has increased our productivity because of the trust-based way we work together. And in response to the concerns of the man at the conference (who we very much hope is reading this book), we would argue that there are three ways in which we have seen this workstyle-enabled trust translate into productivity:

1. **EMPOWERMENT** – Feeling free to deliver work your way.

2. **ACCOUNTABILITY** – Doing what you say you will.

3. **CO-OPERATION** – Working together in new ways.

1. EMPOWERMENT – Feeling free to deliver work your way
:shackles_off:

Workstyle is a great leveller. It gives everyone the same level of autonomy. In our experience the success of workstyle relies on each person assuming that their colleagues and co-workers can be trusted to deliver and that their intent is positive. We have found it almost always is, perhaps because people are selected to join the workstyle working community at Hoxby based on aligning with our shared vision for change, or maybe because for the most part humans simply can be trusted. We're all doing our best and deserve to have one another's 'swift trust', whereby a group or team assumes trust initially and later verifies and adjusts trust beliefs accordingly.[12] By trusting others in this way, it is reasonable for us to expect to be trusted in the same way, too – this concept of reciprocity underpins workstyle working. We have found empowerment, autonomy and working towards a shared vision to be an unbelievably powerful combination in enabling this.

When we're working with people around the world that in all likelihood we will never meet in person, it becomes a mandatory requirement to trust early and this is thankfully a skill that digital technologies are enabling us to become better at. You may not have realised it but in recent years you have become much more trusting of your fellow human beings. The sharing economy is a booming example of our newfound swift trust in action – who would have thought we would be booking a room at one another's houses or hopping in and out of each other's cars, but innovations such as Airbnb and Uber have supported us all in learning to trust one another by providing a framework to do so, and they have made the process of arranging a taxi or an overnight stay considerably faster as a result. Workstyle is no different.

The visibility of such platforms and the transparency of customer reviews give us confidence to trust people we have never met to come into our homes and undertake repairs through TaskRabbit or to deliver our food through Deliveroo. Much has changed in the way we live and work, and almost all of it has changed our perception of how to trust one another.

If we can trust a stranger to host us safely in their home, then we feel sure we can extend the same levels of trust to our colleagues. We have found this mutual exchange of trust to be liberating, and it means we and the teams we are part of work more quickly, more productively and with a greater sense of positivity. Workstylers all trust one another to get the work done, and we know we are each trusted to deliver the output we have signed up to. We share in the belief that we should all uphold our own workstyle, and this benefits our working relationship by deepening the trust between us not only through what we deliver but through the way we deliver it. :win_win:

2. ACCOUNTABILITY – Doing what you say you will :word_ of_honour:

For workstylers, we are interested in one another's workstyles because it helps us to understand each other better. We support, we reassure, we don't judge, and we understand that each of us has our own reason for wanting or needing to work in a workstyle way. If we can trust each other, the actual workstyle that each of us has becomes irrelevant. We access our work on our own terms and have no interest in what time messages were sent and no interest in when ours will be read. We trust one another and free ourselves from the burden of presenteeism to focus on our individual and collective productivity. But with this enlightened way of working comes a responsibility that we are each keenly aware of – the model works when we each take individual accountability for playing our part in the overall output. Because workstylers are determined to make this way of working the norm, we're accountable not only for our work but also to one another for making sure this way of working produces great output. It's no coincidence that one of the values at Hoxby is #PlayYourPart.

When trusted to be accountable for our work output rather than judged on the hours that we work or the place that we go, it is incumbent on each of us to deliver that work on time, to the standard we have agreed. This reduces the inefficient back and forth of traditional hierarchies and enables decision making to happen more freely while empowering us to be productive in our own way.

We have found that, within workstyle, accountability and autonomy go hand in glove. Accountability is the 'Ant' to autonomy's 'Dec' – they are inextricably linked. When creating the conditions for autonomy, it is only through accountability that this way of working can be sustained. We can have the freedom to choose when and where we work because we remain accountable for what we deliver. :psyche:

Luckily, research shows that when true autonomy is enabled by trust, it promotes high levels of experienced responsibility[13] (where an individual feels personally accountable and responsible for the results of the work they do). In fact, as you may remember from Chapter 6, we found in our own research that workstyle and the resultant autonomy and trust cause such high levels of accountability that

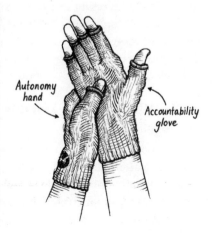

Autonomy hand

Accountability glove

it can prevent people from respecting their workstyles. Hoxbies feel so personally responsible for their own work, and they believe so strongly that others on the team feel the same way, that they are likely to go above and beyond to deliver outstanding quality and will not rest until they feel satisfied with their work. So rather than a lack of accountability working this way, there is actually such increased self-accountability that it may be a problem. This is something we are constantly on the lookout for at Hoxby – to ensure we support the team in respecting their boundaries.

Just as we are more trusting of others, we are also becoming more accountable. Think about how much of what used to be done by other people we now do for ourselves. You only have to look at how much of the process of banking or of travelling we now administer for ourselves from wherever we are to see how our autonomy can make us more productive. :two_clicks: We are able to book our own accommodation, on the basis of as much research as we want to undertake. We are willing to take on the responsibility for that decision, knowing that we understand our likes and dislikes better than a travel agent might and that it makes a more productive use of our time to do it ourselves.

Moreover, when we are experiencing it, on the plane or in the hotel, we understand that the experience is the result of our own decision making, for better or worse, which improves our ability to do it next time. We are investing in ourselves, our own understanding of what works and doesn't work, our likes and dislikes, which over time is making us more effective at the process of booking holidays. It sadly doesn't make us more effective at waking up in the middle of the night to catch a flight, as 'deep-sleeping Alex' can confirm. :zzz: :panic_face:

3. CO-OPERATION – Working together in new ways :apart_but_together:

The empowerment and accountability of workstyle relies on open and transparent communication. This level of trust enables people to work together across different parts of the organisation as well as across time zones, languages and cultures. Research shows that trust is a key ingredient in effective teamwork.[14]

As we discussed in Chapter 4 and as Kit's geek box shows, technology has made this co-operation possible in new ways that have yet to truly translate into the productivity statistics. It was as long ago as 1957 that Robert Solow found that around 80 per cent of productivity (growth in output per worker if you want the technical term) was attributable in some way to technical progress.[15] This highlights the importance not only of technology itself but of how we shape our organisations around it in the way we deliver work in achieving gains in productivity. We have found that workstyle provides great leaps forward for us in the efficiency of how we collaborate with others. By working in digital-first, asynchronous ways, we avoid meetings, communicate more effectively and work in small groups, increasing the opportunity for collaboration. Our co-operation is also boosted by the implicit trust we place in each other to further our cause and work towards the greater good: the success of workstyle itself depends on collaboration. We are interdependent within the workstyle team – we co-operate in new ways, finding those with 'mesh workstyles' to complement each other when setting up projects and stepping in to cover others to accommodate last-minute changes to workstyle. We collaborate in the way the work gets done as much as in the work itself.

Solow also found that new working models are more productive as they are based on new technology,[16] and this is perpetuated since technology itself is always evolving and improving. This underpins everything that we have found – Hoxby started operating only when the right technology was available for the workstyle model to work, and it's therefore no wonder that long-established organisations have to work harder and invest more to adopt new technologies and ways of working to reap the same benefits.

At a more practical level it is intuitive that co-operating in an asynchronous way is more productive. In 2017, 71 per cent of executives said meetings are unproductive and inefficient,[17] and yet nothing is changing – the number of meetings is actually increasing, just as they have been for the past 50 years.[18] Working in a workstyle way removes meetings that *feel* like co-operation, instead replacing them with more productive, efficient and individualised forms of *actual* co-operation within the team. The holy grail is blending productive solo working with the energy, alignment and collaboration of co-operation, and we believe workstyle is just that. We save our chats in 'The Watercooler' channel at Hoxby for when we personally need a break and a laugh, but only when it suits us, on our terms. :pets: :recipes: :trivia:

Co-operating in this way does take good planning, great communication, clear and standardised central tools, and lots of trust. Setting up a new working model that suits every individual isn't easy but we are hopeful that, for all the reasons laid out in this book, it will become increasingly commonplace through workstyle. The demand for autonomous working is being driven by the improvements we are seeing every day to personal wellbeing and productivity at work – it does work and it will become commonplace. 'The juice is worth the squeeze', as Alex would say. :orange:

Geek box: Trust and breaking new ground in human co-operation

By Dr Kit Opie, Lecturer in Evolutionary Anthropology, University of Bristol

Co-operation takes place across the natural world but is a very fragile entity, easily undermined by cheats. Cheats are those that take the benefits of co-operation while evading the costs. The only way to avoid being exploited by cheats is to build trust through frequent interaction of individuals who know each other over a long period of time. Primates build trust by grooming each other in a reciprocal way, and those individuals can then count on support in other circumstances such as disputes over food or mates (Trivers, 1971).[19] Trust built in this way is necessarily one to one and rarely allows co-operation to go further than between two individuals.

The great divide between humans and other primates is due to the evolution of language in our species. Language allows co-operation to take place between numbers of individuals because trust can be built across a group. Furthermore, language allows for the policing of cheats through reputation, which in turn is based on what Robin Dunbar calls 'gossip' (Dunbar, 1998).[20] Language enables networked co-operation and provides a means for testing the levels of trust that individuals can place in each other. For 95 per cent of our time as a species on this planet, society was based around networked co-operation and trust, and was largely egalitarian.

Writing changed everything. This new information technology first invented in Mesopotamia (southern Iraq) 5,000 years ago enabled the emergence of the first states (Goody, 1986).[21] The organising principle of these early states was a strict hierarchy, largely based on the literacy of a tiny minority of society. Early states enabled a huge increase in production and wealth based on the organised work of the majority within those societies, many of whom were slaves (Lévi-Strauss, 2011).[22] Coercion rather than trust was the way that large numbers of people were engaged in productive work, which benefited the states enormously.

The invention of the alphabet allowed for writing to spread across the world and for literacy to be accessible to a slightly larger section of society. But it was the invention of another information technology, printing, that changed the basis of trust and co-operation in society to a great extent (McLuhan et al., 2011).[23] A large increase in literacy led to the breakup of the Christian Church, an enormous expansion in science and, ultimately, the emergence of democracy across many societies. However, despite a major shift from agricultural labour to manufacturing, the nature of work and its organising principles changed little. Even the huge expansion in white-collar work still depended on a hierarchy where supervisors were able to see their workers at all times and ensure that productivity was maintained. Trust hardly entered the equation.

It took a further invention in information technology, computers, to completely change the nature of co-operation again. Unlike writing, computer technology enabled mass access from the start, so that now nearly 5 billion people (60 per cent of the world's population) have internet access just 30 years after the invention of the World Wide Web. Computing facilitated a new era of networked collaboration. However, trust remains the basis for this co-operation just as it did in the pre-literate societies of our ancestors. Reciprocity, reputation and new social norms based on trust are the only means to enable new ways of working that don't require hierarchies or presenteeism.

Trust remains hard to build but, just as for other primates, frequent interaction between individuals who get to know each other will provide the basis. Social activity can build trust in the same way that grooming does. Singing, dancing, sport and even eating together have been shown to build emotional closeness and trust within groups (Dunbar, 2018).[24] Rituals can also provide a fast route to building lasting trust across networks. In this way it will be possible for people to collaborate as never before. Across huge global networks, but in co-operative ways that our pre-literate ancestors knew well.

We are all individuals. The way we treat each other is the way we remember each other – we can decide whether to leave a lasting feeling of trust or not. We can install surveillance equipment and carry on assuming that we need to see each other to be working, or we can trust one another as we might hope to be trusted. Workstyle relies on our ability to do this swiftly, and the reciprocal nature of working this way builds trust between us as people, creating firm foundations for individual and collective productivity. We become more accountable for our work, and this foundation of trust in our relationship with work means we can co-operate with one another in new ways that could be transformative for our futures. Trust unlocks the power of workstyle.

Chapter summary

- Giving everyone the freedom to work when and where they choose means trusting people to do their work rather than relying on being able to see them. This can replace presenteeism and its associated toxic behaviours. We have found that using trust as a basis for collaboration improves productivity in three ways:

  o **EMPOWERMENT:** People are far more trusting than we used to be, to the extent that supermarkets let us scan our own shopping and strangers will host us in their homes. By applying the same level of trust between ourselves at work, we empower one another to deliver our best and be at our personally most productive.

  o **ACCOUNTABILITY:** With workstyle, accountability is the 'Ant' to autonomy's 'Dec' – they are inextricably linked. It is only through clear and respected accountability that working with complete autonomy can be sustained. Workstylers can have the freedom to choose when and where we work because we remain fully and unwaveringly accountable for what we deliver.

  o **CO-OPERATION:** Technology has exponentially increased the potential for collaboration, in large groups and across continents, but trust is fundamental to the co-operation of the people within those groups and a critical part of realising productivity gains.

- Individualised work relies on higher levels of trust to succeed – workstyle makes us feel more empowered, more accountable and enables new forms of co-operation.

From the mouth of a workstyler: 'I joined the workstyle revolution because... doing my best work to my own workstyle makes simple, solid sense. I want to do high-quality work but be free to choose when I do it. It's liberating to know that no one is expecting me to be sitting at a desk just because it's a certain time of day – I am trusted and my outputs are my measure of success.' David, Lisbon, Portugal

Fact to remember: People at high-trust companies report 50 per cent higher productivity.[25]

And finally... When Lizzie was at a conference, rather than listening to the keynote speaker, she was talking to the person next to her about workstyle. :motor_mouth:

Play your part in the workstyle revolution

Reflect

☐ Reflect on the extent to which you trust other people that you work with. If you had autonomy to choose when and where you work, would you trust your colleagues or co-workers with the same? Do you feel trusted to deliver by the people you work with? Does the level of trust you have affect your productivity?

☐ Do you feel a high level of responsibility for the work you are doing? If not, why not?

☐ If you feel that the type of work you do relies on being around the other people in your team, then reflect on this further. Why does it? What assumptions have you based this on? If you understood how to engage with your team in other ways to build trust, could some or all of your work be delivered in a workstyle way?

☐ What words would you use to characterise the way co-operation typically happens in your organisation and what steps could you take to move to more of a trust-based system?

Act

☐ Next time you brief a project or manage a team, emphasise trust and promote accountability by giving freedom in when and where the work is delivered.

☐ In your own work, assume accountability not just for the work you've been asked to do but for the greater success of the project.

☐ Talk about the benefits of a trust-based environment with your team at work and, inspired by this chapter, suggest ways in which they can empower each other.

Inspire

☐ Ask the people you work with what their workstyle is – when and where would they like to do their work? Can you help make that a reality?

☐ Collectively identify any gaps in the team's workstyles and consider solutions for these – for example, can two people cover the same responsibilities at different times? Share your experiment with the wider organisation.

EIGHTEEN

Workstyle step-changes your productivity: ENVIRONMENT

Workstyle story: Shigeri Takamatsu

Forest dweller, mother, beekeeper, luxury brand consultant and recovered workaholic

If you had looked at my shoe rack in my old life, all you would have found were high heels. These fitted the corporate life I led, bouncing between Tokyo, Munich and Paris. I prioritised building my career and was a self-confessed workaholic. So how did I end up living in a Czech forest with a shoe rack full of trainers and gardening boots?

After leading a highly stressful corporate career, I had the joy of meeting my husband, a forest ranger in Czechia. But a period as a 'single mother' in the week commuting to Paris for work as the main breadwinner followed, spending the equivalent of a whole month on the road, and a burnout. I'm pleased to say I now have the bi-cultural, trilingual, forest-dwelling family life I never knew I could, and I fit my work around it.

Moving to a Czech forest was gradual, and if I'm honest sometimes painful. But it has been revolutionary for me and my family.

Workstyle enabled me to exercise the freedom to live and work with more self-reliance. Storms, power cuts and water shortages – they all teach us that we can live with simplicity. Fewer intermediaries and less dependence on 'services' means more moments of appreciation.

In the natural world the movement of 'hours' or 'weeks' does not matter. I have learned to synchronise my working routine with the nature around me. It has taken six years and is no quick fix, but now I have a workstyle that allows me to follow the powerful rhythm of nature. I have learned to funnel this power to increase my effectiveness in all aspects of my life.

During winter nature is calm and quiet. I am focused on my clients and their projects. As spring starts to bring life back into the forest, I wind down any client projects. During this short season I allow nature to lead the tasks I am doing, like gardening and beekeeping. In the summer months I choose to only work on small projects with existing clients. I use this time to consider and plan the year to come. My daily routine is led by nature, as we harvest and preserve food – tomatoes, cucumbers, paprika, beans and herbs. Next year we will grow Japanese edamame, too. We also harvest from the walnut trees, cherry trees and apple trees in the garden. Raspberries, wild strawberries and mushrooms grow in the woods which we gather during our walks. Thankfully, we have a large freezer as our neighbours share venison, boar meat and eggs with us.

In autumn I start to dive into new projects with refreshed energy. Using nature's calendar ensures I am in tune with my own mindset and creates a dynamic with clients that is respectful of boundaries, which in turn boosts sustainability.

Besides the seasonal workstyle, I have designed my perfect work environment to yield productivity. For me that is an uninterrupted four hours of work, then jogging in the woods and family time. I still travel to cities every once in a while for reflection and inspiration.

Since connecting to nature, I have been better able to focus due to the calm and peace I have found. This allows me to work more productively and boost my positivity, both in my work and my family life.

Nature's rhythms have allowed me to step away from living by the clock and societal constraints. My workstyle fitting around a sympathetic natural world has ensured my mental health, my family unit and my independence remain firmly rooted in the ground.

The workspace opportunity

Until the beginning of the 18th century coffeehouses and people's homes were the predominant place where most administrative work was done. In the 1600s the East India Company traded cotton, silk, salt, spices, tea, opium and, much to its shame, slaves. Documents were handwritten and delivered by ship, so the arrival of a new ship in London would herald a barrage of paperwork to be dealt with. In 1729 it was decided that, in order to handle this more efficiently, a central place was needed to bring people together to review and process the huge volume of documents, and the company's headquarters, the first corporate office as we came to know it, were built on Leadenhall Street in London. :paper_mayhem:

Over the last 150 years technology has reshaped the office, with the telegraph, the telephone and then the typewriter all having an influence on its design. Alongside these technological influences, a number of trends and fads came and went as first cubicles then open-plan designs, corner offices and later 'collaboration spaces' and carefully curated objects to help provoke 'creative collisions' came into vogue. :ping_pong_table: Not content with treading on each other's toes on morning commuter trains, firms are now crafting their working spaces so that we might bump into each other for exactly the sort of interaction that might have happened quite naturally in a London coffeehouse in the 18th century.

Modern offices typically adopt an open-plan design which has been shown to impair memory and make people feel more sick, insecure and unmotivated as they worry about eavesdropping and spying colleagues.[1] :awkward_face: Open-plan office workers are more likely to suffer from higher blood pressure, be more stressed, act in a more hostile manner and have more arguments with their colleagues.[2] The ultimate outcome is lower productivity[3] (not to mention the negative impact on their mental health). A few multicoloured bean bags in the corner do little to counteract this cost to productivity.

In the three centuries people have been working in offices and cities our global population has increased from 0.8 billion to 8.0 billion.[4] :boom: We've built more offices and roads and added more routes to our train lines to meet the demand for workers' needs, but people are now getting in each other's way at every turn and overburdening our creaking infrastructure. :automobile: :automobile: :automobile:

We can solve an array of problems if we start to recognise that work isn't a place we go but a thing we do. The overcrowding of cities, unaffordable house prices and overburdened infrastructure can all be eased by allowing individuals to make their own choices about where they work and therefore live, and by giving as many people as possible the chance to choose their own workstyle. Working from home isn't for everyone, and we're not suggesting everyone should move to a Czech forest like Shigeri (though it does sound incredible). But being able to choose where we work should be universally available for those whose work isn't tied to a particular place. Some people might enjoy the solitude of a quiet corner at home. Others might just be grateful to save 10 hours a week standing on a crowded train, and maybe some of us can now live out our romantic dreams, travelling and living in new places while still being able to further our careers as we'd planned. Nomadic workstyler Victoria does this often, booking flights and travelling at a moment's notice and working from anywhere and everywhere. :working_from_beach:

This ability to choose where we work can lead to great progress for us as individuals and also for organisations. Working from home improved work satisfaction and lowered staff turnover as well as improving productivity, according to pre-pandemic research.[5] In fact, even when forced to work from home under some pretty extreme circumstances in 2020 during the coronavirus pandemic, most people were more productive than they had been in the office.[6] There are still many workers who contribute hugely to our society and economy who, because of what they do, simply can't choose where they work (or, at least, not for most of the time). But for those who can, we feel they should have the freedom to choose – not only for their wellbeing but also because it provides an opportunity to increase their productivity.

Over the past eight years we have found that being free to choose our work environment has improved our productivity. These are the three ways we have found it helps:

1. **PERSONALISATION** – Tailoring your space.

2. **DIGITISATION** – Controlling your technology so it doesn't control you.

3. **INSPIRATION** – Making the world your workspace.

1. PERSONALISATION – tailoring your space :banana_leaf_plant:

Offices are typically designed to be helpful for only certain types of work, and only certain types of people thrive in them. Open-plan offices and environments which people don't get to choose are particularly poor for productivity – workers are less collaborative[7] and come up with fewer new ideas, [8,9] make more errors and complete tasks more slowly. For people working in a traditional way, there is little chance to define how they choose to work in an office or to get into their own 'flow' because of the distractions of others dropping by their desks. All of these mean offices are having a negative impact on productivity.

Different types of work can also lend themselves to different places of work, and we all have differing preferences – it's a question of knowing ourselves and what conditions are needed to be at our best. The concentration of deep work might require a quiet spot whereas shallow work could be done on the bus or while watching the TV. We can choose to obsess about these details to create the perfect space for deep and shallow work, or we can choose not to; it's our choice, and that's what matters.

With the autonomy of workstyle, we can structure and shape our environment to suit each of us as individuals and the type of work we need to do. If that is something that requires deep work, thanks to Airbnb and sharing economy platforms we don't need to be a millionaire to go away for a week to a cabin in the woods to structure an important research project or perhaps to write a book (though, trust us, that takes more than just a week in a cabin :mind_blown:). Equally, we are free to choose whether we need to spend time meeting people face to face to build deep relationships, perhaps visiting customers or meeting potential clients to propose new ideas, or to do so virtually and save a huge amount of carbon in the process. If we spend a lot of time in front of a screen, then simply going for a walk mid-morning to clear our heads can help us get a fresh perspective.

Having settled on a country, region, town and some kind of temporary or permanent shelter to work from, we can focus more on our immediate physical work environment. Rather than be allocated a space or a desk, we can design something of our own, for our own needs. Craig Knight showed in a number of experiments that even something as simple as being able to pick the plants and decorations in our working environment causes us to make fewer mistakes and work more efficiently[10] and that workers who have autonomy over the layout of their workspace are happier, healthier and up to 32 per cent more productive.[11] Notwithstanding the limitations of our homes and co-working spaces, having the freedom to design our own workspace means we can all finally sit in a chair that is the right size for our bodies (whether you're Kieron-sized or Lizzie-sized), have the surroundings that suit us best as individuals, and if we are worried about the health implications of extensive sitting (as we ought to be after reading Chapter 12), we can have a set-up that enables us to work while standing up or on the move. :stretch_legs:

We can choose the most suitable technology for the work we do, from spreadsheets and presentations to editing photos and composing music. We all use technology differently and can decide which devices to use for which tasks. We might have a standing desk, a keyboard positioned at the right height for our arms, and a camera at eye level with the natural light behind it. We can, like Alex, choose plants that oxygenate the air (:jungle:) and, like Lizzie, adjust lighting to set the mood for the work we're doing (:cool_glow:). Tailoring our workspace in this way will help us to do our best, most productive work.

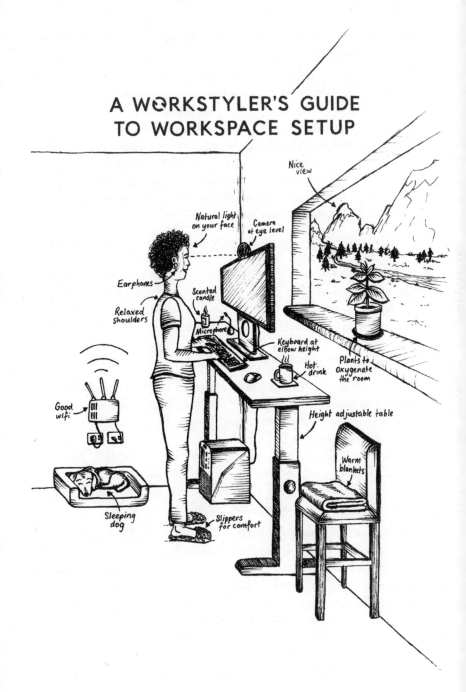

A WORKSTYLER'S GUIDE TO WORKSPACE SETUP

2. DIGITISATION – Controlling your technology so it doesn't control you :notifications_off:

As we discussed with Sir Bobby O in Chapter 13, we have experienced a technological revolution that has seen us move from a manufacturing economy to a service economy: 75 per cent of employment in Europe is now in services.[12] Google, Slack and many others have developed digital working methods that enable us to collaborate and work productively, and enjoyably, with one another wherever we are in the world. This revolution in working practices challenges the core assumption of industrial-age methods – physical presence is no longer the foundation for human collaboration.

With that release for work to happen anywhere at any time comes the reality that work happens on our technology devices and in the software we use. Software is our gateway to one another and increasingly the place where we spend our time working – work is wherever our devices are. And so taking control of our digital environment determines how successfully we can extract ourselves from the industrial-age, presence-first paradigm and puts the power of how we work more squarely into our own hands.

We have found controlling technology so it doesn't control us is a fundamental part of having a productive workstyle work environment. The average worker spends around 30 per cent of their time reading and answering emails and more than 60 per cent of their work week in electronic communication and internet searching.[13] This isn't conducive to doing deep work and means many workers end their working day wondering how much they've really achieved. There are huge productivity gains to be made here.[14]

Even seasoned workstylers are still learning and adapting to the constant stream of new technologies which all serve to help us work this way. It's important for us to stay on top of technology as it can help or hinder our ability to set boundaries and therefore respect our own workstyles. We can't overstate the importance of this to workstyle – we're sad to say we have known workstylers who have gone back to working in the traditional way specifically because they haven't managed their technology well enough to maintain working in a workstyle way. But for those of us who get it right, the rewards are laid out across the entirety of this book. As we enter the later years of our lives, we can look forward to working alongside the next generations who will be so proficient at working this way, we can't even begin to imagine. :intergenerational_workforce:

For anyone adopting digital-first working, there is a learning curve in picking up the functional skills to do it well and therefore be productive. Alex likens it to when his then four-year-old daughter was learning to ride a bike. She could already balance thanks to her balance bike practice, but the transition to pedals introduced a new challenge that she struggled to overcome at first. Despite her being able to pedal and balance, she didn't want Alex to let go of the saddle. The bike was daunting to her, and therefore in control of her state of mind. It wasn't until she changed the way she perceived the bike, as a friend (or unicorn in fact), as someone who would do what she asked it to, that she took control of it and rode away into the distance, leaving her dad in a crumpled heap on the floor. :sunset:

For many of us who download an app to our computer, tablet or phone, the idea of changing the settings can feel alien. Like a bicycle to a four-year-old, we are intimidated by technology and so we allow it to control us – gathering our personal data, serving us with adverts, pushing notifications to us and causing us stress. Once we are in control of our technology, the fear subsides, our confidence grows and we can really use it to our advantage.

We have found taking control of our technology means knowing which software we use for what purpose and why, making sure that we access it on our terms. It means adjusting the settings within those systems to suit our individual workstyles. For us it is turning our notifications off, managing our status updates, making certain apps available on certain devices or blocking them at certain times of the day, or even burying apps within our phones – whatever it takes to put the boundaries in place that we need to make our working technology work for us. Through this we have created fewer interruptions for ourselves, preserved specific times of the day for deep work, and made sure we have the right combination of technology for us to be happy, engaged and productive in a way neither of us have been before. Workstyle makes it possible to really love what you do.

Workstyle gives us confidence and control over our technology and enables us to design our work environment to fit around our life. We can tailor the way we work to bring out the best in our unique selves, and look after our wellbeing. And we can be productive in ways we never thought possible – through inspiration, creativity and sublime levels of efficiency (spot the productivity nerds!).

3. INSPIRATION – Making the world your workspace :hammock:

For many people, exploration and travel are adventures that they earmark for retirement. But Chapter 4 showed retirement is getting further away and may itself be retired altogether, so many of us want the inspiration of working from different places to specifically boost our productivity now rather than seeing it as something we do when work is done.

Historically people have made choices about where they live based on where they work, but when we can work from anywhere, where we choose to live becomes a much more liberating (but perhaps also difficult!) thing to decide. We might even decide to live somewhere for something as simple as how it makes us feel – if your happy place is by the sea, that could be your home. :shocked:

Talking of homes, Alex once did a video call from an Ikea showroom and nobody was any the wiser, with some actually admiring his stylish 'living room' setting. When great wifi is wherever you have phone reception, the only limitation of where you can work is your own imagination. Oh, and having a toilet nearby. :roll_of_paper: :blushing:

In a workstyle world, no longer are we restricted to just the 20 days of annual leave we were given in which to scratch off the different countries on our wall-mounted travel maps. We can be free of a fixed abode if we want to be. Digital nomads are paving the way for a broader adoption of global working, movement between countries and living without the traditional anchors of the past. Countries are capitalising on the trend, too, actively encouraging remote workers to their towns for the benefit of their otherwise restricted economies. To lure newcomers, the Italian towns of Santa Fiora in Tuscany and Rieti in Lazio will pay up to 50 per cent of the rent for anyone who decides to move and work remotely from there on a long-term basis.[15] :olive_grove_inspiration:

So, rather than limiting ourselves to living within a sensible commute from the office or close proximity to co-workers, within our means we have the freedom of the planet. Lizzie lives in Bristol, a vibrant city in the south-west of England, and Alex lives in a picturesque village in the middle of the great British countryside. We're like the town mouse and the country mouse – we each have our own preferences for our personal productivity and happiness, but still we can collaborate brilliantly as a team. There are examples like this from workstylers the world over.

New inventions are making changes of scenery for inspiration more accessible, too. Notadesk is a great example of this – it is in fact a desk, but it's portable and you can put it wherever you like: on a window, round a tree, on your lap. We both have one, and it means we can enjoy a call with the editor of this book from a tree in the British countryside whenever the weather is good enough to do so (rarely, then!). In fact, we have written this book from an arboretum, a hospital, a pub garden, on a train, at a hairdresser's, in a taxi, while doing weights in the gym and from bed (plus occasionally at a desk). :weightlifter:

Geek box: Why working in nature can boost your productivity

By Andreas De Smedt, inventor and CEO, Notadesk

I selected my first employer based on its respect towards its employees, the job content and the salary. But the advice that I would give anyone is to ask to see your physical desk (if there is one) before signing your contract. I believe it helps you to understand how much your future employer will value your work.

If I had done so, I would definitely have chosen to work somewhere else, but then perhaps I would never have started notadesk.com (every cloud has a silver lining). I struggled so much to focus in the open-plan office that I resigned, and it sparked the idea to design a flexible desk which could have helped me to regain focus if they were invented (or allowed) in my previous job.

I have found there are three ideal requirements for a healthy working environment. The first is nature. As a very active person, nature helps me to relax and have more patience, and it helps me to see things in perspective. Research has shown that hospital patients recover faster,[16] prisoners will be less likely to relapse[17] and even students will score better on tests if they have more interactions with nature.[18]

The positivity of being in nature is further supported by research proving that at least 120 minutes a week in nature can be associated with good health and wellbeing, and ideally up to 300 minutes per week.[19]

The second requirement is individuality. I truly believe that nobody knows better how you work best than you. And in addition, different tasks need different desks. It may be important for the impact of your voice and confidence levels to stand while talking. Hence professional singers seldomly sit, and call centre salespeople are advised to take calls standing for a 45 per cent increase in productivity compared with their seated counterparts.[20]

But most important is movement. The possibility to change your set-up throughout the day will help you to move. And that's exactly what your body is made for – sedentary life is the fourth deadliest risk factor in the world.[21] People who sit 10 hours a day have a 34 per cent higher risk of death compared with those who sit only one hour a day.[22]

Even making time for just half an hour outdoors and in nature can create a 45 per cent increase in productivity.[23] My dream for the workstyle age is that there are mobile workspaces available in public parks all over the world. Call me a dreamer, but it's how I work right now.

Freed from the limitations of cubicles and offices, we can now go about our work on devices wherever we choose, so we must evolve ourselves alongside technology and control our interactions with it if we are to thrive through this rapid evolution of work. Taking work with us wherever we go liberates us to choose our work environment, or to design one of our own and tailor it to our specific needs. We can stay at home, share a co-working space, work inside or work outside, at the beach or in the car. We can establish our own routines or we can throw routines out of the window and explore the world while we work. There is a whole world of options that we could explore if we chose to. Let your imagination run wild with the power of workstyle.

Chapter summary

- Advances in technology and connectivity mean many of us can now work from anywhere. This invites us to make conscious decisions about where we as individuals are at our most productive. There are three ways we have found choosing our environment boosts our productivity:

  - **PERSONALISATION:** Research has shown that tailoring the space that you work in to you and the nature of your work can improve your productivity by a third. Through workstyle you can set yourself up for optimum productivity.

  - **DIGITISATION:** Our digital devices and the software we use are increasingly the place we spend our time working, regardless of where those screens are located. So, taking control of your digital environment is equally as important as your physical one.

  - **INSPIRATION:** The freedom to decide where to work can inspire you to work from different places for different things. Whether that's within your home, somewhere nearby or a different country, your workstyle needn't be limited to one place, in fact it should positively embrace the freedoms at your disposal to find your happy place.

- Individualised work through workstyle means we can tailor our work environment to be the best fit for us and to suit the work that we do in order to improve our productivity.

From the mouth of a workstyler: 'I joined the workstyle revolution because... I detest the term "trailing spouse" – the workstyle revolution allows me to have my own career and sense of purpose, and my own colleagues so I can avoid feeling lonely, while working wherever I want, whenever I want, from Africa to the Maldives.' Kerry, Phuket, Thailand

Fact to remember: Workers who have autonomy over the layout of their workspace are not only happier and healthier but also up to 32 per cent more productive.[24]

And finally... If adding a plant to your workspace can increase your productivity by 15 per cent,[25] then how much more productive would you be if you added five plants to your workspace? Using those calculations, how productive would you be working from an arboretum? :maths_exam:

Play your part in the workstyle revolution

Reflect

❏ Reflect on your current workspace. Where do you spend most time when working? How does it make you feel mentally? How does it make you feel physically?

❏ Assume for a moment that your work could be done from anywhere. Where would you choose to work from? Where would you be at your most productive? Do you feel happiest looking at green rolling hills? Do you feel most energised surrounded by the hustle and bustle of a busy co-working space?

❏ Consider whether the technology you're using is helping or hindering you – could you take more control or change your technology or software in order to be more productive?

❏ Consider where you need to be able to access work – do you really need emails on your phone? Can you work to change bad habits and take more of a workstyle approach to setting boundaries with your work?

Act

❏ When you're next working, take a moment to really scrutinise your workspace. Is your screen at the right height? Does your posture feel supported? Are you getting enough daylight? Tailor your workspace to maximise your individual productivity. Buy a plant for your desk if you don't already have one (or a cactus if you're as bad as Lizzie at keeping greenery alive).

❏ Try working from new and different environments where you can meet people or experience fresh perspectives. Buy a laptop stand or whatever equipment will help you be most comfortable and productive in a variety of places.

☐ Interrogate your use of technology, building on your thinking in Chapter 15. Write down all of the applications, programs and platforms you use and the devices you use them on. What is the purpose of each and do they serve this purpose?

☐ Turn off all your notifications to avoid interruptions and take back control of your technology.

Inspire

☐ Run an experiment in your organisation – have one day where everyone works from a place of their choosing. Encourage each person to share a #ViewFromMyDesk to see the variety of places people choose to work.

☐ Start a competition with friends or coworkers to see who can work from the most unusual place. Create a group chat where you can share photographic proof and inspire each other to further the workstyle revolution.

PART 4

WORKSTYLE HAS A LASTING IMPACT ON SOCIETY

NINETEEN

How could workstyle impact society?

When we came up with the idea of workstyle, the thing that gave us the spine-tingling excitement and motivation to throw ourselves into it was the potential impact it could have on people's day-to-day lives and for society as a whole. Our exhilaration came from seeing how individualised work could fundamentally break down barriers to inclusion in a way never seen before. But we have come to believe the implications may be even more far-reaching than we first thought. We love what we do, and that's because it is all in pursuit of what we are about to share here, in this section. :heart:

We are convinced that a move to individualised, autonomous working will happen. Workstyle working *is* the future. If we come together, each contributing in our own way, including through the suggestions we've provided at the end of each chapter in this book, then we can accelerate this change and in doing so have a monumental impact on people and society.

To help us explain the impact that workstyle can have on society it is useful to consider the framework of the Human Development Approach. This is a way of looking at, and measuring, our progress as a society based on the freedoms and abilities afforded to each of us as individuals. It was created in the 1990s by economist Mahbub ul Haq[1] and is rooted in Nobel laureate Amartya Sen's thinking on human capabilities, specifically what we are able to 'be' (well fed, sheltered, healthy) and 'do' (work, education, leisure) as humans.[2,3]

There are three key aspects of the Human Development Approach:

1. **People:** In contrast to the school of thinking that economic success will inherently lead to greater wellbeing for all (and therefore measuring development in terms of only gross domestic product – GDP), the human development approach focuses on improving the lives of *individual people* directly.

2. **Opportunities:** The second aspect is all about creating greater freedom for people. This is enabled by education (knowledge), income (means), and good health and wellbeing. If these three things are fulfilled in a person's life, they will have the individual *opportunity* to progress.

3. **Choice:** Lastly, it is important for individuals to be able to create their own destiny rather than having it forced upon them. While others may be able to give them the opportunity to grow and develop, ultimately it is up to each one of us to *choose* the life we want to live.

Mass adoption of workstyle could positively impact society through each of these three aspects of the Human Development Approach – it is a system that enables each and every person to *live individual lives*, it is created to provide *universal access to opportunities*, and it is entirely built on having the *autonomy to choose* the path we each take in pursuit of the life we each want to live. In short, workstyle is good for human development.

An open letter to the world

To everyone, everywhere,

We write to you at a time when humankind and the planet we call home are under serious and imminent threat because of decisions we have collectively made.

We must wake up from our sleepwalking state of work that we know so well and realise that the world is moving faster than we are. Huge swathes of our society are being excluded from meaningful work, left out of a one-size-fits-all system they don't fit into. Trapped inside that same system of work, organisations are missing out on their rich and incredible talents and the diverse contribution they could bring. The people within these organisations are not representative of the diversity inherent in humankind because not everyone has an equal opportunity to take part in the workforce in a meaningful way.

This waste of human talent is also having a detrimental effect on our ability to work together, as a species. People are working in groups with others who look, think, talk and act the same rather than alongside a diverse mix of people whose collective brainpower could help us all to solve the challenges we face. When compared with other life on this planet, we humans are individually intelligent but collectively ignorant. Our population is booming, and yet our planet is deteriorating. We are creating problems faster than we are able to solve them. We must evolve more quickly, we must overcome our fear of change and be prepared to change ourselves in the pursuit of a better future. Our own existence is under threat. Not only do we collectively have the capability to solve these problems but it is also is incumbent on us to do so. We can only do this by coming together in new ways.

We know that an individualised system of work can improve wellbeing and productivity for each of us. We can also see how a newfound ability to bring together more of society's collective brainpower has the potential to resolve the threats we must address, by working together better. We believe that through workstyle we can address many of our problems and flourish as a society in a way not seen before.

We are doing all we can, but we cannot do it alone. If everyone could play their part – large or small – and recognise the potential of individualised working and how it can bring more diverse minds together, then the effects could be transformative. We ask you to start talking about the power of workstyle, and together we can create a revolution in working practices that will be better for individuals, better for organisations and, most importantly, better for society.

Yours hopefully,

The Workstylers

Society as it relates to workstyle

The more we have travelled along the workstyle path, the more we have come to believe that the opportunity for workstyle to improve the world is beyond anything we had initially imagined.

Workstyle can bring the scale of change needed to begin to resolve our many interconnected challenges as a society. Social inequity in all its guises was where we started this journey, but we now feel widespread adoption of workstyle could also start to help us to look differently at the many challenges in the world – persistent levels of poverty for millions of people, or the climate crisis, or more broadly how to achieve the United Nations' Sustainable Development Goals. But we also understand that this is just the very start of a sequence of many, many steps that will be needed to get there.

We have seen first-hand how workstyle can transform people's lives, and while we have shown throughout this book that workstyle can have a significant impact on wellbeing and productivity, its power can be far greater than this. Workstyle is an important, and necessary, part of driving the development of humankind in a way that will enable us all to fix the problems and seize the opportunities presented to us in this digital age.

We have three hypotheses that we are hoping to prove over time through our implementation of workstyle and that we'll explore in the following chapters to show just how profound we believe the impact of workstyle could be:

1. **HYPOTHESIS ONE: INCLUSION** – workstyle can fundamentally restructure work to design out bias and barriers to inclusion and thus transform equality, diversity and inclusion in a way that can never be achieved with traditional working structures.

2. **HYPOTHESIS TWO: ATTITUDES** – workstyle is an attitude as well as a new structural approach to work. It is a mindset of seeing people as individuals that can help us to overcome many forms of discrimination.

3. **HYPOTHESIS THREE: COLLECTIVE INTELLIGENCE** –
   If brought together in the right way, the fully diverse workforce
   that workstyle can create could enable humanity to find rich new
   solutions to even our most complex problems.

And yes, there's a hand gesture for this one too. :wink:

TWENTY

Workstyle has a lasting impact on society: INCLUSION

Workstyle story: Katerina Kontogergou-Gilbert

Carer to my son, mother, wife, communications and marketing consultant, food, wine and sun lover

Before kids, I lived out of a suitcase. I spent my days country hopping across the world, with an exciting executive career in marketing and advertising that allowed me to globetrot in style and at a fast pace. I'm originally from Athens, married to a Brit, and in my pre-mum life, jumping on a plane from London and landing in a meeting room in Barcelona, Paris or Cape Town (among other places) was just 'another day in the office'.

After my eldest son was born in 2005, I spent my maternity leave writing proposals and taking calls in between breastfeeding. Yes, I was driven. But this was also the societal expectation: achieve more as a woman, a stakeholder, a career-focused mother. It was the birth of my youngest son in 2009 that changed my life – and my career – for ever.

My second son was born prematurely at 27 weeks' gestation. He spent months in intensive care undergoing multiple surgeries, followed by a series of health scares. When he was finally released from hospital, we received devastating predictions for his future, and throughout the years multiple diagnoses emerged, including cerebral palsy, epilepsy and neurodiversity. Our lives had changed, and a 9-to-5 office-based career was no longer an option for me.

Overnight I went from focusing on my career to becoming a carer. We committed to give our son the best quality of life possible, and it was essential to find an alternative solution to traditional work so I could balance my roles as a mother, a career woman and, now, a carer. I may need to take time off to be in the hospital with my son or I may need to see a consultant to discuss his health and care plan, or be at home with him for his recovery after a surgery – and no office job can indefinitely accommodate that need.

Workstyle has allowed me to shape my work around my personal and family circumstances. As a carer you stop thinking on a self-centred level and switch to being a provider, a fighter and a supporter. And that is a life choice. It's exhausting and vulnerable and challenging and requires a deeper level of trust and transparency in all working collaborations I commit myself to.

My son's arrival has changed our lives for ever. He is progressing at his own pace and doing remarkably well considering the difficult start to his life. And although we had to find new ways of doing things, workstyle allows me to still be *me*. And that means being more than a carer, a wife or a mum. I get to work in different ways, I continue feeling fulfilled, mentally challenged, have fun, and feel appreciated in the virtual work environment.

No matter what challenges the future may bring, I'm optimistic that we will be able to rise to them. The reality is that my son will always need our support. That's why I have to work on my own terms. And this is why my workstyle is great for me. It enables me to choose when and where I work. It allows me to prioritise my children's school drop-off and pick-up times, to work Mondays to Thursdays remotely for five hours (which five changes on a regular basis) and keep Fridays free for me. And if something happens with my son, my schedule can be changed.

Workstyle has given me the freedom I need to work in the way that best suits me and empowered me to focus on my caring responsibilities, without compromising my career.

Katerina's story is just one of many, many workstyle stories that could have opened this chapter. Sadly, along with the others, it shows that, without workstyle, our prevailing working structures mean there are whole groups in society who are fundamentally excluded from participating in work. These include those living with physical disabilities or mental health challenges, carers, parents, older people, those who are neurodiverse or people living with chronic or terminal illness. Without stereotyping these groups, it is important to recognise that there are specific tranches of society that are fundamentally excluded from work and that for those individuals the widespread adoption of workstyle could be transformational. Many people in these groups simply cannot engage with work in the same way as others can so long as the default system of work is one based around the traditional structure of working 9-to-5, five days a week, in an office.

Through its individualisation of work, workstyle creates the inclusive conditions for each person to work in the way that best suits them, regardless of whether they define themselves within one of these 'excluded groups'. The best way to illustrate this is to explore each of these groups for whom widespread adoption of workstyle would give the most benefit. We have seen this first-hand and repeatedly hear it from the workstylers we have worked with, who between them cover all of these groups.

To understand the impact workstyle could have on society, it's important that the scale of the challenge at hand is better understood. In each of these excluded groups there is a 'gap' (in some cases a chasm) that could be closed through the collective adoption of workstyle. It is on all of our shoulders to close these gaps and in this chapter we will illustrate why this is so important.

In this chapter we are going to look at our first hypothesis for society:

1. **HYPOTHESIS ONE: INCLUSION** – Workstyle can fundamentally restructure work to design out bias and barriers to inclusion and thus transform equality, diversity and inclusion in a way that can never be achieved with traditional working structures.

The diagram gives an overview of the seven groups. Over the coming pages we will explore each in a little more detail, including looking at the size of the gap we need to close for each group.

THE WØRKSTYLER'S GUIDE TO EXCLUDED GROUPS

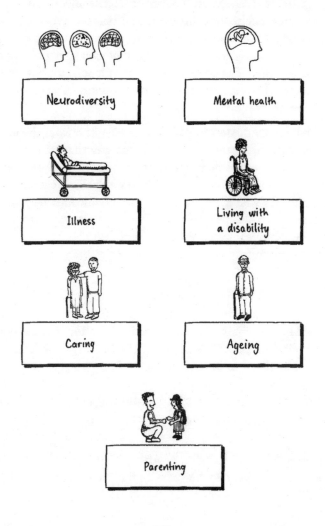

Living with a disability

Our ultimate goal is to create a world of work without bias – where we are all happy and fulfilled – and that cannot be done without changing things for the 15 per cent of the world's population who have a disability.[1]

There are more than 1 billion people globally living with disabilities,[2] whether that's a physical impairment, vision or hearing loss, or a short-term injury. In the UK there are 8.4 million disabled people of working age.[3] While some may not be able to work, there is a theoretical disability employment gap of around 29 per cent. For millions of people around the world, 'disability' is a barrier to work, not because of the intrinsic nature of the condition itself nor a lack of desire to work but because of the limitations created by our traditional working system, coupled with attitudes of employers.

The reason for this is traditional work environments often have built-in blockers, such as outdated attitudes and misperceptions, that the disabled workforce consistently face. In 2018, 24 per cent of UK employers said they would be less likely to hire a person with a disability and 66 per cent said that the cost of workplace adjustments would act as a barrier to recruiting people with disabilities.[4] :outraged: As shown by the many organisations that are now allowing significant numbers of employees to permanently work remotely, this was never a real cost, if only organisations had been visionary enough to see it. Rather than seeing accessibility as expensive modifications to improve office access, it's actually the removal of costs – like that of the swanky head office – which can create equal access to work for all and help to make entry into the workforce more accessible.

People with disabilities face discrimination in their non-working and working lives every day. For some, their disabilities are visible, for others they aren't, but living with a disability is often living with prejudice. Our society is, seemingly, decades behind where it needs to be in terms of positively valuing the contribution that people living with disabilities can bring. When it comes to employment, the picture is dismal – 82 per cent of people without disabilities work, but only 53 per cent of people with physical disabilities do.[5] Disabled people face

PHYSICAL DISABILITY

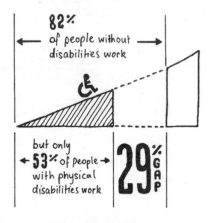

82% of people without disabilities work

but only **53%** of people with physical disabilities work

29% GAP

challenges getting jobs, retaining them and progressing in them. They also earn less than non-disabled workers – the disability pay gap is 18 per cent for men and an appalling 36 per cent for women.[6] :head_in_hands:

There is, evidentially, a misconception around what people with disabilities can contribute to work. And a worrying unfairness. A shocking 50 per cent of disabled people feel that, if they disclosed their impairment, they would be at risk of losing their job.[7] Worse still, according to research by the charity Scope, 32 per cent of people think disabled people are not as productive as non-disabled people some or most of the time.[8] Unbelievable.

Some concrete policies have theoretically helped; there's a legal imperative for workplaces to be accessible to their employees,[9] for example, and support schemes to help disabled people find jobs that suit them.[10] But there is a simpler solution: take the work to those living with disabilities rather than expecting them to come to where the work is. And make this the norm so they are not part of an out-group. Systemic change can enable organisations to work with people with disabilities – and give them the freedom to work when and where they want.

While constraints on when and where they work are felt by many people, the lack of options when it comes to location, technology and work norms such as regular meetings are felt much more acutely if you use a wheelchair, need to go to additional medical appointments, struggle with face-to-face engagement, or experience any of the other challenges that people living with disabilities might face.

Workstyle can, and will, transform access to work for people with disabilities by making it not only acceptable but *expected* that each individual is responsible for dictating when and where it best suits them to work. Over and above this, society needs us to create opportunities for those living with disabilities. We need awareness raised, expectations realised and transformation to happen. We can't think of a better way to achieve this than to see, in practice, people living with disabilities flourishing through workstyle work.

Inclusive working cultures have been proven to be one of the most effective approaches to supporting people with disabilities or health conditions at work.[11] And workstyle can take this one step further by giving complete control to individuals and ensuring we are all judged on our output.

 From the mouth of a workstyler: *'I joined the workstyle revolution because... living with a disability does add complexity to my working life. But, then again, it's no different from people who have young children and need flexibility around school pickups, or somebody who is caring for an elderly parent, or somebody who juggles other roles like being a magistrate or in the Territorial Army. Lots of organisations are flexible but with some caveats like a restriction on how often somebody can work from home, or that the technology is not as good as it could be (so people don't have the tools to do their job wherever they are). Companies that embrace workstyle working will be the organisations that flourish in the future.' Toby, London, UK*

Mental health

We are living through a time where the prevalence of mental health issues is at an all-time high. More than 15 per cent of people in the world have a mental health problem.[12] The terms 'mental health' and 'mental wellbeing' are increasingly in the common vernacular and public figures talk about their mental health struggles more openly than ever before. :loud_hailer: Though there still isn't proportionate funding for mental health services, attitudes are improving and in some parts of the world mental health is starting to be seen as just as important as physical health.

So we're making progress, we're moving in the right direction, it would seem. But for those whose ability to work has been affected by mental health problems, we're still operating in the dark ages. Just 43 per cent of people with mental health problems are in employment compared with 74 per cent of the general population[13] – that's a staggering 31 per cent of people being excluded from work. :appalled:

Part of the issue lies in the stigma that is still sometimes attached to mental health – 47 per cent of workers with a mental health issue feel discriminated against in the workplace.[14] And the *Thriving at Work Review* found that 300,000 people leave work each year in the UK due to a long-term mental health problem, often because of a lack of understanding around, or negative attitudes towards, their mental health.[15]

MENTAL
HEALTH

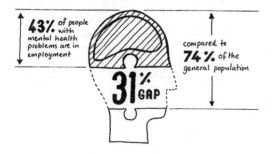

43% of people with mental health problems are in employment

compared to
74% of the general population

31% GAP

For those with existing mental health problems, our current working model and its rigidity excludes them from productive work on their terms and sometimes from working altogether. Though the 2010 Equalities Act gives employees a right to reasonable adjustments, the current legislation doesn't cover all people with a mental health problem.[16] It's not through lack of drive, passion or talent that members of this excluded group aren't working – as many as 90 per cent of non-working people who use mental health services want to work[17] and yet only 64 per cent of people with a common mental health problem are employed.[18]

Mental health issues are on the rise, and that rise is being compounded by traditional working structures. It is in organisations' interests to address this problem – mental health issues such as anxiety and depression account for almost 70 million days off sick per year in the UK alone (yep, 70 million), the most of any health condition, and it's estimated that mental health costs UK businesses an unbelievable £45 billion a year.[19] It's so shocking we're going to say it again – mental health costs UK businesses £45 billion a year.

To have a positive impact on this vast issue, our model of work has to change. For those of us who face challenges with our mental health – whether 'common' or more serious – true autonomy over the way we work could be transformative. Life-saving even. For some people with mental health problems, working in a workstyle way simply makes the difference between being able to work or not. We have personally worked with workstylers who have PTSD, depression, anxiety and addiction issues. Some of them don't know how they're going to feel on any given day until they wake up that morning. It doesn't make them any less talented or incredible at the work they do, it simply means they cannot know when they'll be in the right headspace to work and when they won't. Workstyle gives them the freedom to fit their work around this.

 From the mouth of a workstyler: '*I joined the workstyle revolution because... as part of my ongoing mental wellness and therapy, I have to monitor my levels through different questionnaires and thought patterns. Today I learned that my positive wellbeing levels over the last three months have steadily increased to the highest they have been since I started treatment years ago. And the scores that pushed it up to those levels were in the area of work – starting from the exact time I created my own workstyle. So, from me to you, thank you. I know you wanted to change the world of work when you created workstyle, but you are also changing lives.' Katy, Northampton, UK*

Caring

Caring, the noun, is defined as 'the work or practice of looking after those unable to care for themselves, especially on account of age or illness'.[20] The adjective 'caring' means something different: it means 'displaying kindness and concern for others'. You can, of course, be a caring carer. :heart: But we think the distinction between the two definitions is interesting, particularly that the noun is about 'work'.

Caring is a paid career for many people. The caring profession envelops nursing, teaching and social work and is a wonderfully rewarding and sometimes exhausting one for those who choose it, but one that is also critical to having a well-functioning and supportive society. But for an estimated 63 million people worldwide, 'caring' means caring for a loved one.[21] Like Katerina's story at the start of this chapter, it is unpaid, and rarely an active choice. In the UK one in every eight adults cares for a member of their family or a friend.[22] Carers look after loved ones who are older, living with a disability or seriously ill and to varying degrees from a few hours a week to 24 hours a day, seven days a week. When it comes to employees, the proportion of unpaid carers is huge and often unseen: one in seven in any UK workplace – an estimated 4.9 million people –are juggling paid work with unpaid caregiving.[23]

Juggling is the operative word here. Looking after a loved one who needs us is no less rewarding because it's not paid, but the effect on our careers, our finances, our value and our self-worth in society can be significant. The responsibilities of caring are undefined, perpetual and unpredictable. For the majority the juggle of working and caring is untenable[24] – 2 million people in the UK have given up work at some point to care for a loved one and 3 million have reduced working hours for caring reasons.[25] For those who want to claim carers' allowance in the UK, this is possible only if they don't earn over a certain (low) threshold, which makes it almost impossible to pursue a meaningful career and also receive any financial contribution for caring responsibilities. For some, the stress of trying to balance work and care is too much. For others, it is the lack of formal policies, acknowledgement and support from employers that excludes this group from the workplace. In the UK just 18 per cent of private sector organisations have a formal written policy for supporting employees who are also carers[26] (note that we define carers as distinct from parents, who of course benefit from maternity and paternity policies), and you must work for an employer for six months before becoming eligible to request flexible working[27] (and you know how we feel about flexible working :eyes_rolling:)!

CARING

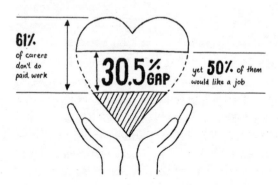

61%
of carers
don't do
paid work

30.5% GAP

yet 50% of them
would like a job

Those who do stay in work by taking jobs that fit around their caring responsibilities are often unfulfilled, isolated and live in precarious financial situations. Carers are far more likely to be vulnerable to physical and mental health problems, and an unbelievable 42 per cent of carers miss out on financial support through a lack of good advice or not identifying themselves as a carer.[28] This puts additional pressure on their careers and working lives.

For carers who have adopted workstyle, the difference can be staggering. Health and wellbeing is improved thanks to a sense of self-worth outside of caring responsibilities as well as the ability to fit work around each person's unique circumstances. Being able to work with people asynchronously in a community of supportive workmates gives the chance to do fulfilling work and earn an income around caring obligations. To those 2.6 million who have left work to care for someone,[29] workstyle gives you a way to come back but come back on your terms, fitting work around your caring responsibilities – it could change your life.

 From the mouth of a workstyler: *'I joined the workstyle revolution because... workstyle is important to me as it means I can care for my mother. I am very proud of her – she just turned 101 but she needs more care than the home she's in can provide. I'm her only child nearby so I have no backup, and I fit my work around caring for her. If I worked in a traditional way, I wouldn't be available to support her at the times she needs it – for example, her 2.30 bingo game on a Wednesday afternoon! We have always been close, and I'm really thankful I can devote the time to her when she needs me most. I regularly change my workstyle so I can be there for her, give myself time to catch up or prepare for a busier week devoted to her, and keep myself from burning out. She really loves hearing about what I do at work, and it tickles me that she is so interested.' Jane, New York, USA*

Neurodiversity

The term 'neurodiversity' was first used in the 1990s when an autistic Australian sociologist named Judy Singer[30] started talking about the fact that our brains are diverse in the same way that our physical attributes are diverse. We all have different eye colours, for example,[31] and our fingerprints and faces are unique. So, too, are our brains – each different and individual to us.

How neurodiversity is defined is varied and often contentious. It is frequently considered to encompass those who have a diagnosis such as ADHD, autism or dyslexia, but arguably should be considered more broadly to cover all varying neurological differences. Among neurodiversity, and those people who are neurodivergent, autistic people make up a significant number. One in every 100 of us is on the autism spectrum – around 700,000 people in the UK.[32] Neurodiverse and particularly autistic people process cognitive and sensory inputs differently and may be seen to communicate or interact with the world differently from neurotypicals[33] (those who are not neurodiverse), but the extent to which this is perceived as a deficit is dependent upon the efforts made by neurotypicals and organisations to be inclusive of neurodiverse people. Each person's differences are unique. Our strengths are also unique, and not having widely adopted neuro-inclusive ways of working means many people's exceptional attributes are, thus far, being radically underappreciated and underutilised.

NEURODIVERSITY

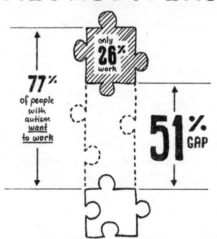

There are 450,000 autistic people of working age in the UK, and in spite of 77 per cent of autistic adults wanting to work,[34] only around 26 per cent are in any kind of employment, so the working 'gap' for this group is 51 per cent.[35] This is particularly startling when you consider the broad range of individuals this group encompasses and the much-needed, valuable skills autistic people have to offer the global workforce, if only it were to be more inclusive of them. :dreamteam:

The office environment and traditional recruitment practices are two of the barriers for autistic people in accessing and enjoying work. Half of all autistic people say their current job doesn't utilise all their talents.[36]

Shoehorning people into specific roles and focusing on job descriptions, hours and physical presence means that the uniqueness of each of us is being horribly underappreciated. Autism can mean above-average technical ability, high levels of concentration and great attention to detail – Penny's workstyle story in Chapter 22 is just one example of this.

Office cultures designed for more neurotypical employees can directly exclude neurodiverse people from work. Sensory overload caused by lighting and sound, communication issues in team meetings and long commutes are all significant barriers that would be resolved by workstyle. Not only do they intimidate or overwhelm some of those who are neurodiverse but they also don't help them to be at their most productive (or, in fact, neurotypicals, as we've seen throughout the productivity section of this book).

If we could collectively shift our thinking towards outputs and building the best teams with the freedom to work how each individual chooses, we would open up the working world to thousands of neurodiverse individuals who want to be a part of it. Curating teams that are output focused and accommodate all workstyles can directly make work more accessible to neurodiverse people.

For many organisations there is a commercial imperative to help create a more neurodiversity-friendly working world, but there is a societal obligation, too. In doing so, we can create a more diverse workforce across all areas and help move one step closer to the happier, more fulfilled society we seek. :open_arms:

 From the mouth of a workstyler: *'I joined the workstyle revolution because… after a change of country and setting myself up as a freelancer, I realised that some days I was able to work for hours without stopping – sometimes ten hours straight (not that I recommend it) – and other days I struggled to even work for two hours in a go. But I found out why when, aged 45, I was diagnosed with ADHD and Asperger's. I joined Hoxby in 2018 and realised there was a place where I could do the work I liked at the times that worked for me: they were calling it workstyle. What a revelation! I could work the way I wanted without having to fit into patterns that did not play to my strengths. By living and working this way, I show it is possible, and I am hopeful others will feel it is accessible to them, too.' Amelie, Kastrup, Denmark*

Illness

A staggering one in three people of working age in Europe and nearly 60 per cent of adults in the US are living with a chronic illness.[37] Forty per cent of the working-age population in the UK are expected to have some kind of long-term illness by 2030.[38] We're also an increasingly ageing population and, in addition to the unknown long-term implications of the coronavirus pandemic, one that is getting more unwell.[39] Heart disease, diabetes, stroke, asthma, arthritis and epilepsy are just some of the conditions affecting people with chronic conditions. These chronic illnesses are mostly incurable, life-long and, in almost all cases, have a detrimental effect on our quality of life.

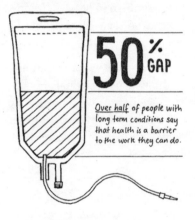

CHRONIC ILLNESS

50% GAP

Over half of people with long term conditions say that health is a barrier to the work they can do.

For many, these conditions are hidden. Ninety-six per cent of chronic medical conditions are invisible,[40] which raises a number of complexities around bias and stigma. With a hidden condition, there is often an expectation to carry on 'as usual' which forces challenging conversations with employers. :deep_breath:

The employed population and society as a whole face significant challenges because of illness. And businesses are losing out on a grand scale, too – the annual UK economic cost of sickness absence and worklessness associated with working-age ill-health is estimated to be more than £100 billion.[41]

When it comes to work, a chronic condition creates a plethora of emotional, physical and logistical challenges. Hospital and doctor's appointments, unpredictable emergencies and side effects of medication can all impact work and be hard to juggle with traditional employment. Financial stability is often threatened by illness, with long-term sick leave, childcare and sometimes healthcare costs to consider. Mental health, social connection and emotional resilience are also all impacted by illness. :working_from_chemo_chair:

When working in the traditional way, illness is a limiting factor for people's ability to have the career they want and deserve. Many employees affected by illness experience significant difficulties either staying in work or returning to work after a long period of absence. Where they can, as in Cat's story in Chapter 8, some people choose to retire early. But by stopping working because of illness, there can be a knock-on effect with increasing social isolation and mental health issues such as depression and loneliness.

For those excluded from work due to illness, focusing on contribution versus presence is crucial. Adopting workstyle and giving people with chronic conditions the autonomy to make decisions about when and where they work allows this excluded group to be in more control of their career prospects, gain financial stability and improve their mental health and social connection. We have seen this first-hand as well as experiencing it ourselves. Workstyle allows us to live healthier and more independent lives – attending medical appointments when we need and taking the time to manage our physical needs as our first priority. And all the while contributing to our society, our communities and our collective global workforce. :valued:

 From the mouth of a workstyler: *'I joined the workstyle revolution because... you never expect it to happen to you and can't possibly imagine the devastating impact it has on all aspects of your life, including your career and financial security. I am referring to cancer, and in my case a terminal diagnosis due to a rare and currently incurable form known as mesothelioma of the peritoneum. The cancer and treatment continue to leave me with multiple health challenges, including limited vision and other neurological issues as well as fatigue. Prior to my diagnosis, I had a challenging and demanding but fulfilling career in brand and marketing strategy. After the diagnosis I thought my career was over, but then I discovered workstyle and the option of a new way of working. It took something epic for me to be brave enough to embrace the world of workstyle but now I wish I had done it sooner. Being labelled when in work as a working mum and then, more recently, as terminally ill had troubled me. I want to be judged on my work and not my circumstances.' Hannah, Oxshott, UK*

Ageing

As people get older, they may require medical appointments and sometimes adjustments to the workspace, which can leave them excluded from work because they face similar barriers to people living with disabilities. But in the same way as those with disabilities do, older workers have so much to give the global workforce.

There are three ways to define ageing: 'chronological ageing' (how many years we have been alive), 'psychological ageing' (how old we feel) and 'biological ageing' (the way our bodies change as we get older). The first two can, and often do, cause discrimination, but the main cause of exclusion is biological ageing – the traditional way of working neither accommodates the individual needs of physically older workers nor recognises the benefits.

One example of this is that biological ageing affects the brain and can lead to memory loss as a common outcome, which could be a source of exclusion from work. However, while fluid intelligence decreases, crystallised intelligence increases with age.[42,43] Fluid intelligence is about logical thinking and solving problems independent of having acquired knowledge. Crystallised intelligence is about using skills and recalling prior knowledge and past experiences to solve problems. Recognising such benefits is key to understanding the value older workers, and intergenerational teams, can bring to the workforce.

As we highlighted in Chapter 4, we're living longer and retiring later. By 2050 the world's population aged 60 and over is predicted to total 2 billion, where the same age group was only 900 million in 2015.[44] We're excited to be part of that group, knowing that workstyle can give us access to meaningful work if and when we get there, regardless of what condition our bodies are in. :crystal:

The majority of people age well and live healthy and active lives. :running: :yoga: :cod_liver_oil: Scientific progress and better living conditions have helped not just the length but the quality of our later years. But work remains a problem. Only 39 per cent of retiring workers do so voluntarily; the majority would prefer to continue working in some capacity.[45] Working longer actually prolongs life and improves health,[46] slowing down biological ageing, the very thing that causes this group to be excluded. We must be able to do more to support this desire for continued working, for ourselves and for future generations to enjoy a fulfilling and rewarding, much longer working life.

As you might ex-
pect, we believe the
answer is to create a
world where work-
ers can access work
on their own terms
in order to fit this
around any specific
barriers to work-
ing they have with

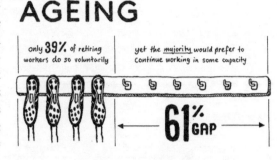

AGEING

only **39%** of retiring
workers do so voluntarily

yet the _majority_ would prefer to
continue working in some capacity

61% GAP

biological ageing. Imagine not retiring, or semi-retiring, but instead working as much or as little as you choose. In this future working world, where workstyle is the norm, there's the opportunity for financial stability, social connection, working satisfaction and happiness for the older generation. There's also the chance to work with others in an intergenerational working community and to learn from each other every day.

Workstyler Jane says learning is one of things she values most from working this way and in such a diverse group of people. She is not alone – in a 2018 survey that spanned 34 countries, 85 per cent of people felt they came up with more innovative ideas and solutions when they were part of an age-diverse team.[47] There's also a multitude of economic reasons to support older workers – wisdom, continuity, expert mentorship, unparalleled experience. As the age range of the workforce continues to widen, the opportunity for intergenerational working will become increasingly great. The individualised, workstyle way of working can create the same conditions for work for everyone within that workforce. It can unite us in our work like never before, avoid excluding those who are biologically ageing and break down barriers of age discrimination at the same time. Creating a working world that is inclusive of older workers today is to create a working world that will be inclusive of ourselves in the future.

From the mouth of a workstyler: *'I joined the workstyle revolution because... I want to continue using my brain, not stop just because I've reached a certain age. It's important to my sense of self-worth, as well as a necessary part of my income. I've just finished studying for a diploma in proofreading, so that rather than having a fixed retirement in a couple of years, I can continue to have an income through working in a workstyle way. Workstyle working removes the pressure on me to earn enough before I retire, and shows a route to continuing to work for all those who want to.' Julie, Scarborough, UK*

Parenting

For those who choose it and are lucky enough to have children in their lives, parenting is a joyous and rewarding thing. Caring for a child or children is raucous, chaotic and exhausting but also brilliant in a life-affirming and enduring way. :pleasure_and_pain: Our children are our future, and rearing, educating, nurturing and caring for them is what we do as a society, and as individuals.

Most of us have to work in some form. Having a career is what we aim for and aspire to through our educational years, in the hope that it will provide financial security for us to survive and prosper, and to fund our family's lives. :nesting:

Yet with the traditional way of working, being a happy, fulfilled parent and having a career can feel diametrically opposed. In the UK most parents work,[48] while both partners work in the majority of parenting couples,[49] and of those 55 per cent work full-time.[50] Yet working practices remain at odds with their needs and aspirations. More than half of working parents feel burned out due to work.[51] One in ten have refused a new job, and one in ten have said no to a promotion because of a lack of good work–life balance opportunities.[52]

Parents are also hugely valuable and effective workers: mothers and fathers of at least two children have been found to be the most productive members of the workforce.[53] You can understand why big organisations and governments have acknowledged the need to do more to support working parents – introducing improved family-friendly policies, for example – but fundamentally our working practices and culture are geared towards people without parenting responsibilities.

There is, in the first instance, a fundamental problem between parenting and work. :mismatch: When you become a parent you are responsible for your child 24 hours a day, seven days a week – not 5 p.m. to 9 a.m. School runs, medical appointments, mealtimes, bathtimes and bedtimes require the physical presence of an adult (or two depending on how many children you have and how challenging they're being!). Working in a traditional way often compromises our ability to do these most basic, immediate and urgent tasks.

A perfect storm is building here – parents are working longer hours and harder, but the system is lagging years behind being able to support them looking after, and enjoying, their children. This is particularly apparent in countries where there is no government-funded childcare until school age.

'Flexible working' is seen by many as the antidote to disgruntled and demoralised working parents, but, as we showed in Chapter 3, offering a slightly different working schedule to allow working parents to be part of an out-group doesn't solve the problem. Looking after children is rarely linear and predictable – and creating policies that cater to those pesky parents running to catch the school play is the kind of sticking-plaster approach we're fighting against :ninja: Workstyle, meanwhile, is a perfect fit for parents who want to work term-time only, align work with the school day, do projects during nap times or only in the evening, or want a very gradual return to work after maternity or paternity leave. When work fits around parenting rather than the other way around, we all prosper.

 From the mouth of a workstyler: 'I joined the workstyle revolution because... I wanted to return from maternity leave to a way of working that allowed me to live in a different city near the support network I

needed as a single parent. My request for flexible, remote working to match others in the company was declined on the basis of my length of service and, somewhat bizarrely, the value of my client portfolio. So, while juggling the feeding and sleeping of a tiny child, I resigned to instead look for work where I would still be respected for the experience and skills I bring, despite it being in different hours or from home. I want to align both worlds, to sacrifice neither my career progression nor my financial future, and now I want to make sure my children never have to face the discrimination I did. I want them to have freedom and financial success in a workstyle future.' Jessica, Brisbane, Australia

This will affect everyone

These seven groups may resonate with you and your circumstances, or remind you of friends, or may feel quite distant from your life at the moment. But the truth is every single person will be negatively affected at some point by maintaining a 9-to-5 office-based system of work. That includes you. Because no matter how well the system has worked for some individuals so far, it won't last for ever. Their lives will change – they may develop a physical or mental health condition, they might have children, or they could find themselves caring for an elderly relative. And even if none of these happens to them, what is guaranteed is that they will get older. If and when their lives change in any of these ways, they will find themselves cast among one of these broad excluded groups of people for whom traditional 9-to-5 full-time employment in an office simply isn't viable any more.

Whenever that time comes, people will crave the freedom to choose when and where they work because they will need it. When that change comes for us, whatever our circumstances, we will all want to feel like we can still work, make a meaningful contribution, earn income and be respected for what we do.

In the here and now, this means treating one another with that same respect and acknowledging that individual workstyles are fundamental to enabling fair access to work, so we know that, when we need it, we will be afforded the same.

Chapter summary

- While recognising that each person within a group is a unique individual, we see seven broad groups that are excluded from fully participating in work because of the prevailing system of work which defaults to 9-to-5, five days a week in an office.

- These 'excluded groups' are those living with physical disabilities, people with mental health challenges, carers, parents, older people, those who are neurodiverse and people living with chronic or terminal illness.

- For these groups, restructuring work to an individualised, workstyle-led system could be transformative for their inclusion in work.

- This affects all of us – the inevitable process of biological ageing will ensure we are all impacted at some stage.

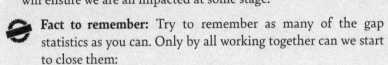 **Fact to remember:** Try to remember as many of the gap statistics as you can. Only by all working together can we start to close them:

  o Living with a disability – 82 per cent of people without disabilities work, but only 53 per cent of those living with disabilities do[54] – **a 29 per cent gap**.

  o Mental health – 43 per cent of people with mental health problems are in employment compared with 74 per cent of the general population[55] – **a 31 per cent gap**.

  o Caring – 61 per cent of carers don't do paid work but 50 per cent of those would like a job[56] – **a 30.5 per cent gap**.

  o Neurodiversity – 77 per cent of people with autism want to work[57] but only 26 per cent do[58] – **a 51 per cent gap**.

  o Illness – 50 per cent of people with long-term health conditions say health is a barrier to the work they can do[59] – **a 50 per cent gap**.

  o Ageing – only 39 per cent of retiring workers do so voluntarily, the majority would prefer to continue working in some capacity[60] – **a 61 per cent gap**.

- Parenting – 86 per cent of working parents want to work flexibly but only 49 per cent do[61] – **a 37 per cent gap.**

 And finally... During the writing of this book we have each aged chronologically (2 years), biologically (20 years) and psychologically (200 years). :wise_sage:

Play your part in the workstyle revolution

Reflect

☐ Are you in one or more of the excluded groups? If you are, reflect on how this has affected your career and how things might have been different if you had been able to work in a workstyle way.

☐ Do you know people, inside or outside work, in these excluded groups who you could better support to be fully included in work?

☐ Can you think of times in your career when people from these groups haven't been able to participate as fully as others in work because they have not had autonomy over when and where the work was delivered?

Act

☐ Introduce the idea of workstyle in your organisation, and encourage each person to create a 'workstyle plan' that outlines when and where they like to work and the things that help them to work in the most productive way.

☐ Speak to your colleagues about vacancies in your company or working community and how taking a workstyle approach would be more inclusive and attract more diverse talent.

☐ Take a photograph of the gap statistics and share it on your social media with a call to action to join the #WorkstyleRevolution to help close the gap.

☐ If you work at, or have contacts at, an organisation that supports any of these excluded groups and would be interested in a partnership to further workstyle working, please get in touch at lizzieandalex@ workstylerevolution.com.

Inspire

☐ Share more information with your team or whole organisation about the workstyle revolution. Discuss how you can start to implement the principles of workstyle in order to more fully include excluded groups.

☐ If you are from an excluded group and you feel comfortable doing so, be open about your circumstances and the barriers you face so others can learn from your insight. Support and encourage your colleagues or co-workers who come from traditionally excluded backgrounds to speak openly, too, if they are happy to do so.

☐ Suggest the creation of an advisory group made up of people from these excluded groups who could develop an inclusion action plan for the organisation if you don't already have one, incorporating workstyle approaches.

TWENTY-ONE

Workstyle has a lasting impact on society: ATTITUDES

Workstyle story: Yacob Cajee

Family man, equality activist, accountant, aromatherapist, hypnotherapist, writer and Nordic walking instructor

After 38 years as a qualified accountant working (in the main) in local government, I learned one Friday afternoon that my role was being considered for redundancy. Having uprooted from Devon to relocate to Pembrokeshire for work, hundreds of miles from friends and family, only 18 months previously, my wife Fiona and I felt completely devastated.

My initial response was fight rather than flight, but a few weeks later I had a stress-induced 'episode', causing a loss of vision in my left eye. Subsequently diagnosed as an ocular migraine, it was very frightening at the time, and a very good friend (who happened to be our financial adviser) convinced us that, for the sake of my health, I should accept redundancy and retire from full-time work a year earlier than planned. As well as our savings, we had our therapy practices (Fiona as a homeopath and me as an aromatherapist and hypnotherapist) and I had been doing some freelance writing over the previous three years, but his reassurance that we could make things work for the 12 months until my pension kicked in was a huge weight off our minds.

I'd had a generally successful career despite repeatedly experiencing racial discrimination. I heard comments on several occasions about 'the nigger in the woodpile' and I never heard the phrase challenged or condemned by my colleagues. Early in my career I was turned down for a job and told by a clearly embarrassed chief executive and head of HR that the councillors thought I was too young, despite my date of birth clearly stated on the application form from which I'd been shortlisted. This was in the 80s before age discrimination became illegal, so they could say I was too young because they couldn't say I was too Black. I was told by another head of HR that life would be so much easier if my name were John Smith. And twice I lost my job as a direct result of racial discrimination. I successfully took both cases to industrial tribunal but never heard if those responsible were disciplined or not. I was fighting racism one soul-destroying discrimination at a time.

I'd also had some great experiences, such as being part of the team that established the South Downs National Park, and I'd met some fantastic people along the way. However, my last couple of years in work had been less than enjoyable, and I needed to finish my working life on a more positive note.

I'd started doing some assessment work for the College of Policing, the first organisation ever to appreciate and welcome my equalities experience. Through the college, I met someone who told me about workstyle and pointed me to a community whose values were consistent with mine.

I'd always railed against the culture of presenteeism and distrust of staff that prevailed in every organisation (and there had been lots of them) that I'd ever worked for. I had colleagues who'd boast they had been up until the early hours rewriting the report they were due to deliver a few hours later, but were then surprised when clients questioned their facts or inadequate reasoning. I had bosses who insisted on recording holidays on both the HR system and a clock card system because they didn't trust staff to work their contracted hours. The workstyle revolution really appealed to my faith in people and my belief that performance should be measured by outcomes, not by the number of hours recorded on a timesheet.

The worldwide Hoxby community is more diverse than any other group of people I have worked with, making me feel much less isolated and giving me a greater sense of belonging. At the same time workstyle offers me the opportunity to use all my skills, whether in finance, equalities or as a writer (though not yet as a therapist), without ever being pigeon-holed. More importantly, it gives me the freedom to work when and where I want, fitting it around the other things that are important to me, whether playing golf or tennis, teaching Nordic walking, learning another language or spending quality time with family and friends.

Yacob's story is not unusual: there are variations of it throughout the workforce. It is inexcusable that, in spite of other human progress, discrimination at work is still so prevalent. More than a third of UK adults report having suffered workplace discrimination,[1] and the implications are far-reaching, not least for the individuals involved for whom the legacy of going through such an experience can be life-long.

In this chapter we are going to look at our second hypothesis for the impact workstyle can have on society:

2. **HYPOTHESIS TWO: ATTITUDES** – Workstyle is an attitude as well as a new structural approach to work. It is a mindset of seeing people as individuals that can help us to overcome many forms of discrimination.

While systemic change and widespread adoption of workstyle are absolutely fundamental to fully including everyone in work, changing the structure of work alone is not enough. Attitudinal change is also needed to create a truly inclusive world of work without bias. We believe that, implemented correctly, workstyle is an attitude as well as a new structure of work, and that this could help with reducing discrimination. :stand_together:

Seeing the monotype in each of us

In Chapter 8 we highlighted research showing how unreflective company boards are of society. When people surround themselves with others who are like them, which still happens in the vast majority of organisations, it often further exacerbates stereotyping, which in turn leads to discrimination and inequality. The traditional way of working benefits some at the expense of others based on characteristics that have nothing whatsoever to do with competence. In particular, traditional working makes it more likely that individuals are judged based on surface-level differences rather than innate abilities and individual contribution. Alongside shifts to individualised working structures, we need attitudinal shifts to change the way people think about each other and the way they work together.

The term 'stereotype' comes from industrial-age printing methods; it was the name given to a kind of printing plate that could be one of many. An original plate was used to create a mould from which multiple stereotypes could be cast from hot metal. The durable stereotypes could then be used over and over to print multiple identical pages. :copy_paste: The verb – to stereotype – means making assumptions about groups. Humans evolved to do this as a sometimes helpful way of simplifying the complex world in which we live, but it can also have life-changing consequences. For example, we know that both wasps and bees have a sting in their tail, and so we build a shorthand understanding that insects that are yellow and black are more likely to be dangerous. We're therefore more cautious around yellow-and-black insects than we would be around others. It is understandable but not strictly true – there are plenty more dangerous insects out there that aren't yellow and black but aren't as visible to us and therefore aren't in our hardwiring. We have carried this primitive shorthand into the way we design signage – yellow-and-black signs are most often used to denote a warning to our brains. :hazard_tape: Similarly, our brain makes shorthand assumptions about people on the basis of what we have seen, heard and experienced – it's how our brains work, but it impairs our ability to treat people objectively, without bias.[2]

You might have been raised to understand the importance of first impressions and not getting a second chance to make them. This is because it is our first impressions that form most of our implicit assumptions that then go on to influence our decisions. This is prejudice that we aren't aware of, and it is proven to cast across everything[3] from height to ethnicity, gender, accent and even someone's name, as illustrated in Yacob's story. It is therefore our responsibility to understand the assumptions that we are making and to make a conscious effort to overcome the ones that create bias. This starts with first impressions and purposely seeking to understand the person we are meeting (remotely or in real life) for the first time. The onus for first impressions is not on each of us to make them but on each of us to see others for who they really are. We need to go out of our way to not create the person's story for them but to let them share it with us. Teaching ourselves to look past stereotypes and at individual contributions enables us to treat one another more fairly, for who we really are.

As you might be aware, monotyping is a type of printmaking made by drawing or painting, typically on a copper etching plate. The image is then transferred onto a sheet of paper by pressing the two together, usually using a printing press. This process removes most of the ink during the initial press and so, unlike a stereotype, a monotype usually produces a one-off, unique print. :one_of_a_kind:

When we meet others in person, we are all prone to casting them into stereotypes because the information being received by our brains is overwhelming[4] – there is simply too much to take in all at once. This is one of the biases exacerbated by the office environment, but which is reduced by workstyle and the ability to work together asynchronously and remotely. In a thriving workstyle work environment, the nature of not meeting in person, nor having visibility of many of the factors that create bias at work, means we are more focused on the work itself than on the person. This frees us to appreciate the individual for their work and elevates collaboration to a cognitive level, rather than being shaped by our physicality or any of the other factors that create bias at work.

Workstyle working can only operate with this new attitude. We always try to deliberately consider each person as a monotype – appreciating the individual for who they are and understanding their workstyle as part of what makes them uniquely brilliant. One example of this is at Hoxby – when new workstylers join the community we encourage them to introduce themselves in 'The Meeting Room' channel on Slack. They can do this however they choose and include about themselves only what they are comfortable sharing – for some this is about their hobbies, families or motivation for joining the workstyle revolution; for others it is simply about their skills and passions and their careers. Most do so with a brief written introduction, removing many of the factors that might create bias from the equation at all. Letting individuals decide for themselves how they want to be perceived and the first impression they choose to give is an important part of the attitude that accompanies a workstyle system working brilliantly in practice.

We have found that seeing monotypes is something we can learn and improve at. By reading this book, we assume that you have a growth mindset – that you want to learn, grow and improve every day. We are hopeful that with the right attitude, anyone can start to see, and enjoy, the monotype in everyone.

We need to overcome our fear of the unknown, our fears of one another, of people we don't yet understand, because working with people who are like us limits our ability to learn new things from them and to grow as individuals as well as to produce better work. It will require a conscious effort to surround ourselves with people who are not like us, who can bring us out of our comfort zone and into a space where we can all learn and grow together.

We need to recognise and combat some of the biases and perceptions that our imperfect human brain instinctively puts on the world in order to make sense of it. And alongside this, we need to play our part in designing and embedding processes and systems (including new ways of working) that counter our biases and perceptions and help to create a more equal working world.

Geek box: Reshaping attitudes at work to reduce discrimination

By Dr Caroline Casey, founder of The Valuable 500

We all make judgements instinctively whenever we meet someone for the first time, look at their photograph or read their CV. Before we are consciously aware, we make social categorisations, cast stereotypes and define people as a homogeneous group (Abrams, 2010),[5] in effect writing the stories of others onto them even before they've had a chance to speak or do anything to confirm our judgement (Allport, 1954).[6] Our brains are then primed to look out for evidence or actions that confirm our initial bias (Wason, 1960).[7]

These biases can contribute to wildly disproportionate outcomes in organisations and in society, such as the gender gap, the hugely significant under representation of people with a disability, ethnic minorities and LGBTQ+ in FTSE 250 executives, for instance. People with disabilities make up an estimated 1 billion, or 15 per cent, of the world's population.[8] About 80 per cent are of working age.[9] The right of people with disabilities to decent work, however, is frequently denied. People with disabilities, particularly women with disabilities, face enormous attitudinal, physical and informational barriers to equal opportunities in the world of work. Compared with non-disabled persons, they experience higher rates of unemployment and economic inactivity and are at greater risk of insufficient social protection that is a key to reducing extreme poverty.

Undeniably, inclusion is difficult, but the first step is to acknowledge that balancing individual and collective needs requires us to share. We need to eradicate the psychology of scarcity and the notion that 'if I give to you, I take away from myself'. It has been proven time and time again that diversity has significant organisational benefits (Tsusaka Krentz and Reeves, 2019).[10] Inclusion is for everyone – you do not get to pick and mix inclusion; it's either in its entirety or not at all.

An important step towards changing implicit assumptions is to bring conscious awareness to the judgements that we habitually make (Lemos, 2005).[11] For this, we need to use data to highlight the truth of the disparity. By reviewing the make-up of our workforce at different levels within the organisation, disproportionate outcomes would highlight the need to change recruitment or promotion policies. In this new way of working, we need to have accessibility in our online and digital experiences. Moreover, in order to reduce prejudice, we need to consciously change our behaviours to practise 'conscious inclusion' (Lemos, 2005).[12] People make choices and in turn choices create culture. By actively developing our emotional intelligence skills and the way in which we communicate, this may result in implementing new accessible communication practices and allowing far greater freedom in employees' working arrangements.

As a society, we need to stop putting so much emphasis on labels because labels are for jam jars. We are extraordinary, different, wonderful people who are not defined by the box we tick. Currently, disability is often considered as something more akin to being weak or dependent, but there is a wealth of talent that is not being utilised for individuals' insight, innovation and potential. We need to move away from the emotional idea of weak or less than when it comes to the framing of disability. By moving past the medical model of disability and recognising the societal structures that serve as a barrier for many, we can truly begin to balance the playing field. Sustaining a reduction in prejudicial attitude change and conscious inclusion behaviours is a challenge that requires both continuous reinforcement and a long-term commitment to institutional and cultural change (Devine et al., 2012).[13]

Slowly but surely, things are changing. In this new post-pandemic phase of living and business, it would be a real risk to not prioritise inclusion. The next generation, people with or without disabilities will demand full inclusion from the companies they choose to spend or work with. 'Learning through doing' is more effective than simply being told that certain attitudes and behaviours are 'wrong' (McBride, 2015),[14] and a piecemeal approach to inclusion is unlikely to be effective if people see that there are no serious attempts to change the underlying structures and social realities that shape our organisations.

Changing attitudes to reduce discrimination

So, as Caroline's geek box shows, there is no single, simple solution to solving discrimination. Faced with growing social unrest, some companies have started to consider diversity in their leadership teams in terms of gender and racial background[15] or by putting blind recruitment processes in place (where the applicant's personal information is removed to try to reduce bias) or measuring and instigating equal pay policies between men and women (now a legal requirement in the UK for large companies). While these are important small steps in the right direction towards removing or countering the biases which groups have been subjected to in the past, they are happening far too slowly and the changes that are being made in many cases feel like tokenism. At the current pace of change it will take more than 135 years to achieve gender pay equality[16] and much, much longer to achieve full racial inclusion. Discussion in some areas such as transgender inclusion have only truly begun in the last decade.[17] Change simply isn't going to come about quickly enough by tweaking the old working system at the edges. Workstyle structurally changing access to work for excluded groups will not in itself solve the problem of discrimination, but we believe the widespread adoption of the attitudes that go with it can help speed up the pace of change. :kick_up_arse:

Discrimination comes in many forms, and a full book could be written (and many have) on each. However, it's important to give a few specific examples to highlight the problem. This is not by any means an exhaustive list but we hope it will serve to remind us all of why action, and a change of approach, is needed with regards to discrimination.

Gender discrimination is well known and age old. It's no secret that the traditional 9-to-5, office-based system has favoured men over the course of history.[18] Even if women are able to overcome the systemic biases inherent in their early career, a huge proportion are then faced with the juggling act of taking a period of time away from their work to become a mother and/or care for other members of their family. Women remain the primary caregivers in most societies – whether as parents or caring for elderly or unwell family members[19] – and women undertake about three times more unpaid work than men.[20] Currently, only 50 per cent of women of working age participate in work, versus 75 per cent of men.[21] Globally, that's 700 million fewer women than men—1.27 billion women versus 2 billion men.[22] This book was co-authored by Lizzie Penny and Alex Hirst equally. Unfortunately, it is likely to have been more successful if it had been authored by Alex Hirst and Lizzie Penny, such is the gender bias within the literary world,[23,24] the world of work and wider society. In spite of this, and to remain true to the change we are trying to create in the world, we agreed it should be authored by Lizzie Penny and Alex Hirst. It is our hope that this important decision might help to inspire more female writers and entrepreneurs to pursue their goals, regardless of how successful the book is. Perhaps by explaining this choice we may also inspire the kind of proactive decision making required by men like Alex who are in a position of privilege and whose actions have the power to determine whether we are ever to achieve gender parity at work and in society.

Race discrimination is finally getting attention around the world. In the UK 4 per cent of White people are unemployed, compared with double that number for Black, Bangladeshi and Pakistani people who had the highest unemployment rate – 8 per cent – out of all ethnic groups.[25] Many forms of race discrimination at work are in fact hate crimes. Thirty-one per cent of people have witnessed racist verbal or physical abuse in the workplace or at a work-organised social event,[26] and one in seven of those who had been harassed said racist treatment was the reason they had left a job.[27] Even over and above the argument that as a decent society we should be doing all we can to eradicate discrimination, there is an economic case for this, too. Baroness McGregor-Smith's review into race in the workplace concluded that full representation across the workforce from Black and Minority Ethnic individuals through improved participation and progression would be worth around £24 billion a year.[28]

Discrimination on the basis of sexuality continues to be so bad that 26 per cent of lesbian, gay, bisexual and transgender (LGBT+) people remain closeted, and almost half aren't fully open at work because they feel unsupported by their bosses.[29] Forty-two per cent of bisexual people hide or disguise their sexual orientation at work for fear of discrimination.[30] Eighteen per cent of LGBT people looking for work said they were discriminated against because of their identity while trying to get a job.[31] And 10 per cent of Black, Asian and Ethnic Minority LGBT employees have been physically attacked by customers or colleagues in the past year.[32] It's disgraceful.

All types of discrimination at work also have further knock-on effects for society. Take social mobility, for example. Seventy per cent of work internships are unpaid,[33] which directly excludes young people who cannot afford to work for free. And those people doing Britain's top jobs across areas including medicine, journalism and law are five times more likely to have attended a private school than the general population.[34] What's more, workers in those top professions who are from upper-middle-class backgrounds earn around 16 per cent more than those from working-class backgrounds in the same type of jobs.[35] And here again there is an economic case, over and above the obvious social need, to eliminate discrimination for social mobility. If social mobility in the UK increased only to the average level in Western Europe, our GDP would be roughly 2 per cent higher.[36]

There are other unseen areas that people don't traditionally associate with discrimination that could be causing hidden harm to significant numbers of the population. Menopause is a great example of this. In the UK alone there are 13 million women who are either peri- or post-menopausal.[37] Even though the number of employment tribunals specifically referencing the claimant's menopause is increasing, they are still rare, with only ten recorded in the UK in the first half of 2021,[38] when unbelievably a quarter of women consider giving up work because of menopausal issues.[39] Almost a million women in the UK alone have left the workplace because of menopausal issues.[40] These are all women who may have been able to stay if their work had been more individualised.

These examples cover just a handful of groups who suffer discrimination, but there are many others, not least the excluded groups we outlined in the previous section who are discriminated against. We believe, however, that the attitudinal change that goes hand in hand with adopting more individualised structures of work can help make much-needed progress. :step_by_step:

Creating a working world where everyone feels comfortable being their true selves and feels confident they won't be judged is key to helping reduce discrimination. An attitude of understanding and empathy for each individual can help create happier, more inclusive working cultures and in turn a more accepting and fair society. While we can't write with authority on the wholesale attitudinal change needed to eliminate discrimination, we do feel that the widespread adoption of workstyle attitudes can help. Through Hoxby we are constantly testing new ways of doing this and learning from them. These are a few examples.

Being empowered to present how you choose

When working in a workstyle way you don't need to identify your gender, race, sexuality, age, religion or background. Because you don't need to share these, and working is asynchronous and remote, everyone is empowered to choose how they present themselves, and also enabled to judge others based on their work outputs and how they collaborate in the community rather than other factors that create bias.

We accept each person as they are, as an individual, and as another member of the workstyle revolution – where we are all working together to achieve a shared goal. The application process to work on projects at Hoxby is anonymous. This makes it clear that we don't discriminate on the basis of gender, age, sexuality, race or physical ability – if you have the right skills (and a big dose of passion) for the opportunity, then you have every chance of being successful and being selected to do the work.

Creating a safe space

We work hard to make Hoxby a safe space for those who do choose to share more details about their personal circumstances or areas they have suffered discrimination in the past. We seek to support each other and encourage genuine openness about all the areas covered in this chapter, such that Hoxbies feel confident and comfortable to discuss their situation as much or as little as they choose. We have found many ask for advice or share experiences they have had with discrimination, anxiety, grief, caring for a family member or going through a diagnosis for neurodiversity, to name just a few.

We work hard to create an environment of psychological safety, with champions for different areas of diversity and dedicated safe spaces for these conversations where Hoxbies can discuss areas such as race, age, mental health, neurodiversity and disability. Hoxbies can connect with others, share experiences, find informal support, and also listen and better understand each other.

An attitude of autonomy and trust

We always start from a place of trust at Hoxby, and as I'm sure you've gathered, each of the Hoxbies working with autonomy is central to our working model and our belief system. We regularly reinforce the message of judging each other on our outputs rather than on any of the other factors that create bias at work, and we encourage everyone within the community to lead by example by illustrating these behaviours.

Understanding and listening to each individual

Working remotely is fantastic for helping us to overcome our unconscious bias. If we aren't in the same room, our brains don't leap to the same assumptions and instead we can understand one another as individuals in different ways.

Hoxby is also an environment that celebrates and recognises individuality wherever possible – whether that is understanding that some people work better late at night or helping the whole community to understand more about topics such as Windrush, menopause, autism or Braille – Hoxby is a place for people who are open to learning and accepting, both of which are important elements in the fight against discrimination.

Inclusive communication

Inclusive communication is critical to working in a workstyle way. This means dropping the office lingo for straight-talking, concise and jargon-free language. As well as culturally reinforcing this, we use Slackbots to help maintain this jargon-free environment. Hoxbies can expect a polite automated reminder every time they refer to a presentation as a 'deck'. :deck_chair:

Inclusive communication means talking openly and freely about our individual workstyles and being explicit – learning to be clear and say what we mean. We also have guidelines at Hoxby to ensure that accessibility needs are taken into consideration – whether it be subtitles on all the videos we share internally (of which there are quite a few), 'camel case' to capitalise the start of each word when using hashtags to make the individual words more apparent such as #BetterTogether, or recognising that mid-sentence emojis make it very hard for anyone using a screen reader, we are always conscious of the need to be as inclusive as possible in our communication.

While many organisations' 'values' are single words up on a wall near the coffee machine or in the lift, at Hoxby our values are phrases such as 'respect the workstyle', 'better together' and 'always improving' (along with, it won't surprise you to hear, emojis specifically designed for each :emoji_wordmoji:). We use them not only in our recruitment and selection of new Hoxbies but also in everyday conversations around the community so as to reinforce their meaning in practice.

Respecting each individual workstyle

At Hoxby we, and others within the community, make open and public declarations of our workstyles, truthfully sharing our motivations for our personal workstyles at that time (and, if we choose to, being open about what we do with life when we are not working too), thereby giving permission and encouraging others to do the same. Being authentic is one of the behaviours we ask of all the Hoxbies and an expectation we set around the community.

We also do our best to ensure everyone at Hoxby is as aware as possible of how to control their technology, such as turning off emojis and gifs within Slack if it suits their preference to do so, and encouraging everyone to turn off their notifications so as to be able to respect their workstyles without interruptions or temptations to work when they have decided not to.

True inclusion

It has been said that diversity is being invited to the party and inclusion is choosing the music (just don't ask Alex to choose the music unless you want back-to-back 90s Balearic beats :shell_suit:). Seriously, though, diversity is nothing if we don't also have the right culture and behaviours to genuinely include everyone. This cannot be about box-ticking but needs to be about truly bringing together teams of diverse people who can do their best work together.

There are different levels of diversity in different organisations, but in the workstyle world we seek bigger opportunities by going beyond the labels and categorisation that many diversity initiatives and efforts focus on to recognise minority groups today and focusing instead on the value of individualism, in order to structurally and attitudinally transform work to eliminate bias.

Changing norms doesn't have to move at a glacial pace, but incremental changes centred around a traditional approach to work mean that is exactly what is happening currently. :glacier: If we can ensure widespread adoption of workstyle attitudes at work, then we have the opportunity to accelerate inclusion and fundamentally address inequality, and all of society can benefit as a result.

Chapter summary

- Many, many people suffer discrimination at work, including on the basis of gender, race, sexuality and social mobility, to name just a few. New areas of discrimination such as for those going through the menopause are only just starting to be identified.

- We believe that workstyle can bring the necessary change of attitude to move forward more quickly than the glacial pace of change to date with reducing (and, ideally, eradicating) discrimination at work. We are testing new ways of doing this at Hoxby, including being empowered to present how you choose, creating a safe space, an attitude of autonomy and trust, understanding and listening to each individual, inclusive communication, and respect for each individual workstyle. We continue to learn and evolve the Hoxby community in the pursuit of creating a happier, more fulfilled society through a world of work without bias.

- Traditional, one-size-fits-all working perpetuates thinking in stereotypes. Workstyle recognises the uniqueness of individuals, treating them as monotypes. We believe that, in embracing the attitude as well as the structure of individualised working, workstyle can help reduce discrimination.

From the mouth of a workstyler: 'I joined the workstyle revolution because... I want to change the world! I want to be part of a revolution that takes us away from outdated ways of working that create inequality and instead create ways of working that allow people to be their unique selves.' Nicola, Leamington Spa, UK

Fact to remember: More than a third of UK adults report having suffered workplace discrimination.[41]

And finally... This chapter is where it all began for us in 2014, and the more we learned and understood, the greater our sense of injustice and outrage for the excluded and discriminated groups grew. This is what drives us. This is why we and all the Hoxbies are continually experimenting and seeking to improve the workstyle model. Closing these gaps and reducing discrimination is the legacy we hope to leave behind. :eulogy:

Play your part in the workstyle revolution

Reflect

☐ Consider whether there have been times when you might have inadvertently supported discrimination through the absence of action or because of your attitude. Reflect on what you could have done differently to be more inclusive.

☐ Are there certain scenarios in your work where more open-minded workstyle attitudes could positively impact everyone having an equal chance to participate?

☐ Consider how diverse your group of co-workers and colleagues is. Are you in a minority group? Think about what minority groups there are and what you can do to make everyone feel more included.

Act

☐ Be curious (but not intrusive) with others in your organisation who are different from you. Ask questions and really listen deeply to the answer. Try to better understand their world and their perspectives.

☐ Talk to co-workers about monotypes and discuss as a group how you can be better at seeing the monotype in each person.

☐ Suggest the creation of a diversity board made up of people from marginalised backgrounds who could develop a diversity action plan and conscious inclusion strategy for the organisation if you don't already have one.

☐ Read *Natives: Race and Class in the Ruins of the Empire* by Akala to learn more about systemic injustices and the role that attitudes play in changing things for the better.[42]

Inspire

☐ Start a discussion with your CEO, the HR team or your co-workers about how you can work together to create attitudinal change, including adopting an attitude of autonomy and trust throughout the organisation, facilitating better understanding and listening to each individual, and each and every person in the organisation being empowered to present how they choose.

TWENTY-TWO

Workstyle has a lasting impact on society: COLLECTIVE INTELLIGENCE

Workstyle story: Penny Kiley

Writer, editor, accessibility advocate, introvert, autistic person, older worker

I've always enjoyed my work but not always enjoyed my working life. During my 30-plus-year career I've worked – as a freelancer and as an employee – in a lot of different areas (newspapers and magazines, civil service communications, publishing) and often struggled to fit in. I am most comfortable in my own private space, just getting on with things. But that doesn't really work in noisy open-plan offices or in an extrovert corporate culture where being a 'team player' is all-important (but never defined).

All workplaces, whether public or private sector, are conformist in one way or another. Most of the time I didn't realise that I wasn't conforming, and I suspect that's true of many autistic workers. Our logical outlook means we tend to be outspoken – when I left my last job, a colleague asked: 'Who will say the things the rest of us are thinking when you're gone?' – and we also tend to take things literally. It's amazing how rarely neurotypical people (non-autistics) actually say what they mean but instead expect the listener to read between the lines. This can lead to misunderstandings.

So, communication in a typical office can be difficult. And so can a typical office itself because that environment isn't designed for the benefit of the people who work there. Open-plan offices are widespread, but I've yet to find anyone – neurodiverse or neurotypical – who likes them (and let's not get started on hot-desking). For autistic people, who are susceptible to sensory overload, such environments can be even more difficult. I hate background noise: it's uncomfortable and distracts me from working at my best. I hate open spaces, too: they don't feel safe.

Fixed working hours are also hard for everyone. I'd enjoyed flexitime in the civil service but my last job, in the private sector, was very 9-to-5. Except it was 5.30 p.m., and most people didn't take lunch breaks. Along with the heavy workload, I had the extra effort involved in trying to meet all the unspoken rules. I ended up burned out.

Over my working life I found ways to cope with all of this: claiming a corner desk and making a den (boxed in with filing cabinets), creating job satisfaction by learning new things and working hard, and finding people on my wavelength to make daily life bearable (yes, autistic people can be sociable). What I couldn't cope with was office politics and that's what finally drove me to go back to being freelance again. I was exhausted, confused and deeply unhappy. This time, I promised myself I'd never work for anyone else again – although, to be honest, I think it's unlikely even if I wanted to, given the ageism in the UK workplace.

I generally work remotely, so my clients don't know or care how old I am, and they don't care (or always know) that I'm autistic. What matters is what I can deliver, not how I do it. Instead of autistic 'deficits', I now have autistic strengths. I get great feedback because I'm good at what I do and easy to work with – and that is partly because of my autistic traits (logical, methodical, analytical, focused, honest and reliable). It's always good to hear that people value my unique contribution to a collective goal – to me, that is what being a 'team player' should genuinely be about.

My workstyle (I usually work from home) lets me control my working environment and my workload. And it has given me the freedom to choose. I can choose clients whose values align with mine: charities, non-governmental organisations and social enterprises. I can focus my energy on the work in hand without the distraction of an office environment or the cognitive burden of 'masking' to fit in. I can share online watercooler moments – or even real-life socialising (at times of my own choosing) – with like-minded freelancers. I even had the confidence to put a photo of myself with grey hair as my profile picture, after working on an age-positive project, as I knew I wouldn't be discriminated against for this in the workstyler community.

I sometimes wonder whether I'd have found a conventional career easier if I'd known earlier about my autism (I found out late, and it helped me to understand a lot that didn't make sense before). But I'd never give up the workstyle I have now – because it has given me the freedom to be myself.

At an individual level the way we work has a profound impact on the lives of people like Penny and the many other people we discussed in the previous two chapters. At a total level, we believe the mass adoption of workstyle could have the potential to unlock the cognitive diversity and collective intelligence needed to solve some of the world's biggest problems. :many_brains_make_light_work:

We believe that society stands to benefit from the improved collective intelligence that can be achieved by having a more diverse workforce and a more inclusive way of working. So, if changing the lives of millions of people by including them in work doesn't get you excited, hopefully this will. This affects all of us because our third hypothesis is not so much about individual lives but about what we stand to gain as a species if we bring the full spectrum of society together in the right way, and we believe that, thanks to workstyle, this is now well within our capability.

In this chapter we are going to look at our third hypothesis for how workstyle can have a positive impact on society:

3. **HYPOTHESIS THREE: COLLECTIVE INTELLIGENCE** – If brought together in the right way, the fully diverse workforce that workstyle can create could enable humanity to find rich new solutions to even our most complex problems.

To tackle this hypothesis, we will break it into three component parts:

1. Collective intelligence and the role of cognitive diversity.

2. How workstyle can improve collective intelligence.

3. Applying collective intelligence to solve the world's biggest problems.

1. Collective intelligence and the role of cognitive diversity

We're intriguing creatures, humans. We were given a pretty tough task just trying to survive on the African plains alongside a range of seemingly better-equipped animals with sharper teeth, longer claws and faster legs. On paper, in a head-to-head comparison with a tiger, we really didn't stand much of a chance. :running_scared: It was only when we banded together, sharing watch-keeping duties and hunting in groups, that we began to tip the odds in our favour. Of course, when we discovered how to make fire and could share this intelligence among the species, we changed the game for ever by being able to convert areas of dense, scary jungle into more open, defendable and understandable places. :campfire: But what anthropologists and biologists have also discovered through studying our ancient struggle to survive over the millennia is that this shared evolutionary experience has been codified in our genes.[1] :denim: The oldest, deepest parts of our brains are a relic of this era and something we still live with today. For instance, because we evolved in groups we are hardwired to fear being left out (as we were likely to die on our own in the wild). The bands our ancestors lived in were often small groups of eight to fifteen people, but they would occasionally come together as larger tribes – typically a maximum of 150 people. Research on primate social behaviour suggests that our brains can still only cope with maintaining stable social relationships with around 150 people – now known by the anthropologist who led the study as (Robin) Dunbar's number,[2] which Nienke highlighted in her geek box in Chapter 11.

So deep is this hardwiring that not only are we limited as to the number of people we can maintain a connection with but we also innately restrict that group to people who make us feel comfortable. We seek comfort and are drawn to what is familiar to us. In the case of our closest relationships, it's why many married couples look alike[3] and perhaps explains why some dog owners resemble their pets. :corgi: Extend this beyond our closest relationships and into our friendship circles and it's easy to see how tribes might have formed on this principle. Equally, we don't need to press our imagination hard to see how this hardwiring could have influenced the hiring processes for industrial-age factory owners and been perpetuated by the traditional system of work ever since.

Today we are no longer reliant on homogeneity and the safety of groups for survival, and science is already proving the benefits of thinking differently. Research shows that it is cognitive diversity specifically (the ability to think differently) that enables diverse teams to outperform homogenous ones.[4] Though their individual members may be of similar intellect, it is the diverse nature of their intellect and the way they collaborate that makes them collectively more intelligent.

Leading UK innovation agency Nesta defines collective intelligence as 'the enhanced capacity that is created when people work together, often with the help of technology, to mobilise a wider range of information, ideas and insights'.[5] This definition extends to include an example of collective intelligence in practice – compare the *Oxford English Dictionary*, which took almost 70 years of the 19th century to crowdsource 400,000 words for inclusion in its complete first edition, with Wikipedia which leverages technology and people's diverse knowledge towards a similar goal today but receives 1.8 edits per second and has more than 6 million new pages created per month.[6] :infinite_loop:

In his book *Rebel Ideas*, Matthew Syed makes a compelling case for collective intelligence through collaboration of diverse individuals being able to make more astute judgements, find more innovative and robust solutions to problems, think more creatively and overall facilitate us working more efficiently as a species.[7] Cognitive diversity is defined within the book as differences in perspective or information-processing styles. It is not predicted by factors such as gender, ethnicity or age and can therefore serve as a great leveller for the way we collaborate as a species. :spirit_level: Its invisibility to the naked eye helps to break through such barriers of prejudice that previously may have stood in the way of effective collaboration. What we know from our experience so far is that wherever there is undisputed agreement, similarity and homogenous culture, there is low cognitive diversity, often referred to as 'groupthink'.[8] And so it is in the act of disagreement that we see diversity of thought and the tensions of opinion that can take us beyond groupthink to find better answers more quickly.

Geek box: The evolution and principles of collective intelligence at work

By Geoff Mulgan, Professor of Collective Intelligence, Public Policy and Social Innovation, University College London

People have always tried to find ways to grow their collective intelligence – in small bands, groups and then societies, whether as farmers (National Geographic, 2019[9]) or craftspeople (Mark, 2011[10]), with work usually based around households where it was integrated with daily life.

With the industrial revolution the choices changed. Adam Smith wrote about the pin factory where a precise division of labour gave everyone a different role, working in a strict hierarchy.[11] In the 20th century Frederick Taylor achieved huge influence with his ideas of scientific management – which treated workers almost as robots, working under instruction by managers, measured and monitored.[12] His claim was that hierarchy, measurement and specialisation would best amplify the collective intelligence of the team.

But there was also a very different tradition. Robert Owen in New Lanark in Scotland showed how work could be organised in a more co-operative and egalitarian way – with just as much efficiency.[13] Today some 300 million people work in co-operatives, but the divide remains.[14] On the one hand, companies like Amazon are the modern-day equivalent of Taylorism with task segmentation, standardisation and a rigid division of work (including 'human exclusion zones'). On the other are the many examples of more open, flexible work organisation.

Two decades into the 21st century we can draw on the emerging science of collective intelligence which shows very clearly that teams work best when both individual and shared intelligence can be harnessed. In the second half of the last century Deming showed just how powerful these ideas could be when he helped transform Japanese manufacturing, tapping into what he called 'the gold in people's heads' and giving workers the right to stop or control production lines, in marked contrast to the rigid hierarchies of US manufacturing which fell badly behind.[15] In most knowledge-based and creative industries this is now obvious – too much hierarchy simply crushes ideas and creativity. Indeed, regular surveys of workplaces by the Organisation for Economic Co-operation and Development (OECD) consistently show that autonomy and productivity are closely linked.

This new science also has big implications for diversity. There is abundant evidence that it's easier to solve complex problems with teams that have a diversity of backgrounds, experiences and mindsets, especially when these can be combined with shared language, models and approaches. Meetings are a good example. Overly rigid and hierarchical meetings are not good for decisions. But the opposite extreme of structureless meetings can be just as bad. So the best options are structured so that the meeting's goal is clear, so that everyone gets a chance to speak, and so that there are clear roles (for example, to summarise the discussion or ensure follow-on actions).

The tech world has been working hard to develop better tools to help teams and groups work more collaboratively. Over the past 20 years there has been a deluge of digital tools designed to facilitate group work: Google Docs, Slack and Miro, to name a few. More recently we've seen the development of tools that combine artificial intelligence (AI) and collective intelligence (CI), that is, using AI to help groups think better together, for example by showing patterns of opinion in a group and guiding groups towards consensus.

While pure AI tools are often not very useful for tackling many of the problems societies face today, the potential is huge when they're combined with CI. In April 2019 Nesta announced its first 12 grants for experiments in this domain and has partnered with the Wellcome Trust, the Cloudera Foundation and the Omidyar Network making hundreds of thousands of pounds available to organisations interested in experimenting with AI/CI-based solutions (Nesta, 2019[16]). Many have also been used by the new United Nations Development Programme network of Accelerator Labs in 100 countries globally.

These methods are not yet mainstream and most organisations default to very traditional ways of organising themselves and their meetings, from board meetings to brainstorms. We are in the foothills of learning just what can be done to amplify the collective intelligence of a team of 10, 100 or 1,000. But we badly need to do this if we're to have a chance of tackling the biggest issues facing the world now – climate change, gender equality, malnutrition and, of course, global pandemics – all of which require a transformation of a magnitude even greater than that of the industrial revolution. They need us to become smarter, together.

2. How workstyle can improve collective intelligence

So, we know we are hardwired to want to feel part of a group and that we each maintain a number of relationships, to a greater or lesser extent, in order to do this. We also know that as a species, we feel most comfortable among people who are like ourselves and are often nervous to speak out in disagreement against a majority for fear of rejection from the group. Unfortunately, we also now know that this fondness for belonging to like-minded tribes comes at the expense of being able to draw on the knowledge of a broader, more diverse group and find more creative and robust solutions to problems. :power_of_many:

Organisations have traditionally sought to recruit talented people into their ranks based on their suitability for the job and their cultural 'fit' for the company and team rather than for diversity. Just looking at the process of submitting a CV in response to a specific job description shows how this matching process of person to job, team and culture restricts diversity of experience, thought patterns, information-processing styles and problem-solving methods. The issue has been further compounded by recruitment processes that are left open to individual preferences and biases, meaning organisations tend to recruit people in the image of those that have gone before and who share the same traditional working preferences. :mirror_mirror:

This limits access to cognitive diversity and ultimately reduces their collective intelligence, the benefits of which can't truly be explored while we continue to work in organisations that value homogeneity over difference.

Taking inspiration from Geoff's geek box, we can see how workstyle enables us to improve our collective intelligence in two ways: by increasing the cognitive diversity of the group and by creating the conditions for integration of such diverse minds. These two areas that make up the formula for collective intelligence were covered in the previous two chapters.

Our first hypothesis in Chapter 20 explored the ability for workstyle to open up work to be inclusive of the many groups of society currently excluded by the traditional way of working, illustrating how workstyle can improve the diversity of the workforce and with it increase cognitive diversity. It encourages us to pay special attention to the unique ways in which an individual approaches and succeeds at the tasks assigned to them. It arms us with the skills needed to build teams for culture-add rather than culture-fit. This radically transforms the group of people we can work with, from a small group of co-located, culturally similar people to a globally distributed, fully culturally and cognitively diverse community, working with a shared sense of purpose.

Our second hypothesis in Chapter 21 explored the attitudinal change that comes with an individualised system of work and how this can help with reducing discrimination. To reduce discrimination is to increase integration, and we believe that much of this stems from the attitudinal change that comes with the workstyle way of working. Workstyle enables, and in fact encourages, diverse groups of people to collaborate as their authentic selves. Understanding that we are individuals (with our own workstyle and value to offer) trains us to appreciate individuality in others – reducing discrimination and increasing integration.

Workstyle recognises and celebrates difference, creating an environment of trust where it is safe for individuals to question the status quo and metaphorically stick their necks out to find new, richer solutions to complex problems. This is the exact opposite of the tactics we would have adopted to keep us safe on the savannah, where thinking differently would probably have got us exiled from the group (or at the very least meant missing out on lunch). This trust is protected and perpetuated by the other key conditions that underpin workstyle (pop back to Chapter 5 if you need a refresher); digital-first and asynchronous approaches mean discord can be delivered in a positive, productive manner, which is at the heart of integration for collective intelligence. People are never caught out or put on the spot. Responses can be carefully considered and calibrated.

That Mahatma Gandhi viewed honest disagreement as a good sign of progress speaks volumes for the need for constructive debate and feedback. A readiness to question assumptions and a willingness to reject the way things have always been done is what will unearth revolutionary solutions to the world's problems. Research shows that higher levels of task conflict (arguments over how to solve a problem or make a decision), in a team that co-operates effectively, lead to better work outcomes.[17] This has resulted in companies with above-average diversity producing a greater proportion of revenue from innovation (45 per cent of the total) than companies with below-average diversity (26 per cent). This 19 per cent 'innovation advantage' also translates into better overall financial performance,[18] so there is an economic as well as a social case for collective intelligence.

The ability to work asynchronously gives workstylers the chance to put forward considered responses and delicately manage the tensions of differing perspectives towards the greater opportunity they present.

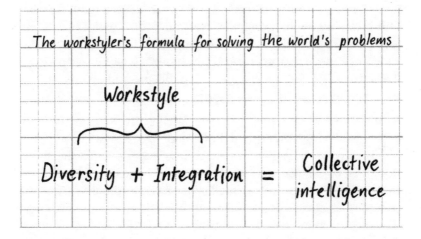

The workstyler's formula for solving the world's problems

Workstyle

Diversity + Integration = Collective intelligence

Having established a workstyle way of working within Hoxby, we have developed the basic operating system for collaboration between cognitively diverse people. Our next goal is to build a workforce that is as representative of wider society as possible. Not only will this set a new benchmark for diversity and inclusion at work for others to follow, it will also enable us to develop our understanding of how to apply cognitive diversity to the task of solving complex problems. Our ambition is to bring together the Hoxby workforce not only on the basis of individual excellence but also in order to become the most collectively intelligent workforce on the planet. :moon_shot:

Through Hoxby we have been applying collective intelligence theory to our workstyle-delivered projects as well as all manner of other subjects to understand what makes our teams collectively more or less intelligent. We've answered such trivial questions as 'What trick should our Christmas elf play on our children tonight?' to more profound ones like 'What are the key qualitative and quantitative measures for successful client collaboration with agencies?' (thanks, Patrick :wink:).

This constant form of live testing helps Hoxby to add greater value to each project it delivers for its clients, mostly through the way it assembles teams. Researchers at Hoxby are exploring how to curate teams for their cognitive diversity and therefore collective intelligence. This is not just about having the 'best' minds on a problem in terms of experience or skills – it's about the combination of their diverse knowledge and experiences that can be brought together in a positive, respectful way where each has equal confidence and opportunity to challenge, in pursuit of a shared goal.

Another area we've tested collective intelligence is in writing this book, where we quickly realised the limitations of our own intelligence and that you would need to hear from experts and workstylers along the way if you were to ever reach this exciting penultimate chapter. Applying collective intelligence has incredible benefits – it undoubtedly made this a more robust book. It also comes with new challenges – numerous, diverse perspectives made it a much more difficult book to write – but if we are to solve the biggest problems we face, then we need to first solve the challenge of effectively working together to draw on different perspectives.

3. Applying collective intelligence to solve the world's biggest problems

Workstyle drives a monumental shift in attitudes, away from a culture of sameness and towards a future that is globally inclusive, and thereby enables us to engage the almost incomprehensible cognitive capacity of our richly diverse, booming global population.

Our groupings for work are arguably one of the most significant ways in which we collaborate as a species, coming together en masse as human beings to work towards a goal. Organisations that create work are the entities that determine what the human effort is being directed towards in a co-ordinated and large-scale way. The ability for us to share our unique, individual expertise is therefore determined by the way in which our organisations enable us to collaborate. They give us a way to follow our purpose and passions and direct our efforts towards solving the problems that are most important to us.

Co-operating in new ways is already solving some of the world's most prolific problems, from traffic jams to hunger. Waze, the community-driven navigation app, combines GPS location data from the mobile phones of its 50 million members in over 200 countries to crowdsource information on accidents, hazards or speed traps to create up-to-the-minute traffic maps. The Breadline app allows food rescue volunteers in Hong Kong to see quantities of leftover bread at bakeries in real time, and the transparency it provides has led to a fourfold increase in redistribution of bread to help the homeless, refugee families and the elderly in Hong Kong. Victims of sexual harassment and abuse in Egypt are sharing their experiences with HarassMap to challenge stereotypes of victim-blaming to help create zero tolerance of sexual harassment in schools, universities and workplaces. The impact this holds for female empowerment across the globe has the potential to be much bigger than their current dataset. These are examples of human collaboration on a mass scale, but just imagine if we could harness cognitive diversity in the same way towards solving our societal and global problems. Projects such as the Centre for Collective Intelligence Design at Nesta are looking further at how we can respond collectively to challenges, and research looking at how technology and people can be combined at the MIT Centre for Collective Intelligence is making progress in helping us do this.

We are excited to think about what might be achieved when organisations bring diverse people together, working in a workstyle way. Whatever we choose to apply our newfound collective intelligence to, the way in which workstyle supports people, opportunities and choice can improve human development for society as a whole. In positively impacting human development, perhaps workstyle can increase our ability to solve some of the biggest global challenges of our time. Through a transformation of our working practices to a system that creates diverse groups that are collectively more intelligent, we believe we can also devise creative breakthrough ways to solve problems. It is entirely possible that we could find solutions that have escaped our species in the past, simply by changing the way we work together.

In 2015 all member states of the United Nations adopted the Sustainable Development Goals – a blueprint for peace and prosperity by 2030.[19] It is hoped that, if we can achieve these 17 goals, the world will be a fairer, more peaceful place for all. The goals span a range of global challenges. Workstyle can help to solve some of them directly: good health and wellbeing, gender equality, reduced inequalities, decent work and economic growth are all areas in which the worldwide adoption of workstyle could have a material impact. What is potentially exciting with this hypothesis is whether we can also use workstyle to improve our collective intelligence in order to direct more of the 7.9 billion brains on the planet[20] towards finding innovative new solutions and approaches for the remaining goals and, yes, change the world.

Such is the power of workstyle.

Chapter summary

- Humans are tribal by nature, but by grouping into like-minded tribes we miss out on the rich cognitive diversity within our species and on the huge possibility of collective intelligence to find more innovative and robust solutions to problems, think more creatively and work more effectively.

- We started Hoxby to prove the theory that a new way of digital-first working could create a more inclusive working world, but having seen the power of collective intelligence first-hand, we have become increasingly excited about the challenges that can be solved when diverse minds are brought together behind a shared purpose. Workstyle is an important enabler for this, as a structure to bring together diverse groups to co-operate in a new way.

- We believe that, if brought together in the right way, the fully diverse workforce that workstyle can create could enable humanity to find rich new solutions to even our most complex problems.

From the mouth of a workstyler: 'I joined the workstyle revolution because... I am always looking for agencies to create refreshing work, and the refreshing and original structure of Hoxby, and the collective intelligence that they can demonstrate as a result, is inspiring. Plus they give me so much energy to work with!' Patrick, Frankfurt, Germany

Fact to remember: There are 17 United Nations Sustainable Development Goals[21] and 7.9 billion human brains in the world whose collective intelligence could achieve them.[22]

And finally... We wrote this book with the help of more than 100 people. We're confident that this makes it a much better book than if we, Alex and Lizzie, had written it on our own. We really are better together. We did write all of the wordmojis, though, so we can take the blame for those. :rolling_on_the_floor_laughing:

Play your part in the workstyle revolution

Reflect

- ☐ What are the biggest problems that you think we are failing to solve as a species?

- ☐ What are the causes that organisations are failing to rally behind?

- ☐ Have you experienced collective intelligence in action? Was it a place for constructive disagreement? Did you get to a great outcome?

- ☐ How cognitively diverse are the teams that you work with? Consider how you could each increase the cognitive diversity of your team and the way you operate and integrate as a team in order to improve your collective intelligence.

- ☐ How could workstyle bring out the best of each individual's unique abilities in your organisation for the benefit of the collective?

Act

- ☐ Bring together a cognitively diverse group of people in your work or community in a workstyle way to solve a problem that feels insurmountable. Run it as a pilot so you can learn from it. Apply what you learn to other projects and tricky problems within your organisation or your life.

- ☐ Follow the work of Nesta and MIT on applying collective intelligence to some of the world's biggest problems and get inspiration for how you can help.

- ☐ Read *Rebel Ideas* by Matthew Syed for a brilliant overview of cognitive diversity and *Big Mind: How collective intelligence can change our world* by Geoff Mulgan.[23]

Inspire

☐ Offer your services to the United Nations to help solve one of the 17 Sustainable Development Goals with your cognitive diversity. Or, if it's easier, sign the pledge to join the workstyle revolution at WorkstyleRevolution.com and we'll contact them together. With enough of our diverse minds brought together in a workstyle way, we can change the world. :two_hands_making_w_symbol:

TWENTY-THREE

Change the world, and your life, today!

To make fundamental improvements to our wellbeing, productivity and society we need to make equally fundamental changes to the way we work together. By breaking free of the shackles that limit how we think work is done, and with a new understanding of how a more inclusive system could work, we can unlock greater human collaboration and perhaps even solve the world's most complex problems. All we need to do now is make it happen. :unite_behind_change:

Today it's on each and every one of us to challenge the cultural norms, working routines and unhelpful beliefs that are holding us back. We can either choose to stand by and watch people work longer and longer days, perpetuating inequality, harming their mental and physical health, and labouring through an unnecessary routine of commuting, or we can throw off the yoke of this traditional working culture and create something new that works for each of us in its own way and is fit for the digital age we live in.

We take heart from the fact that the highest value-added industries are based around human rather than physical capital. We constantly hear about organisations being in a 'war for talent' and that 'people are our greatest asset'. It all adds up to giving us great hope that many workers will have their demands met if only we ask for it (go on – make the case for workstyle with the accompanying hand gestures, too!).

There are huge benefits for organisations which can find the trust and have confidence to empower their workforce to work in their own workstyles. Having a truly autonomous, motivated and passionate team working in their most individually productive way can be transformative for organisations and individuals alike. For those organisations like Hoxby, which truly put workstyle at the centre of how they operate, there are innumerable benefits to reap.

To do this we each have to get to know ourselves as individuals and tailor our way of working to ensure every one of us has the best possible workstyle for any given time in our lives. This is not a one-off project but an ever-changing journey for all of us.

The time has come for us all to act. Your future, as well as equality and progress for society as a whole, is in your hands. We need to take back control of our lives and ensure the freedom to choose when and where we work for ourselves.

Having the freedom to decide our lifestyle and design our workstyle together is no easy thing. The removal of constraints introduces difficult choices and newfound responsibilities. Ultimately, however, this freedom is the key to living a more fulfilling life. We've done it, as have more than 2,500 other workstylers since 2014 who have helped to shape the advice, guidance and tools that are available to support new workstylers keen to embrace this revolutionary way of working.

The overwhelming advice from them is to **set**, **project** and **respect** your workstyle. Begin by setting a workstyle of your own – that fits your work around your life. Feed all of the insights you have gleaned from this book into a workstyle of your own choosing. Write it down in a 'workstyle plan'. :pen_and_paper: Then share it with people – project your workstyle to as many people as you can and commit to it. Workstylers make a point of projecting our workstyles to the people we live and work with. :public_address_system: You can see examples of them online, too. This hugely important stage in the process helps us to articulate our workstyle to other people and also speak it into existence. The informal contract we enter into with others and with ourselves is often enough to hold us to account[1] and you can also add it to your email signature and your profile page if you have one so that people know when you're working next and have a broader understanding of your workstyle. After that, it's up to you to respect your own workstyle. :person_bowing: This can be the most difficult part of the process – being strict with yourself to switch off, learning to say 'no' and considering how best to collaborate with others. Knowing when to hunker down and when to take it easy, knowing where to find your rhythm and where to feed your soul. You can do it, but if you get stuck then the workstyle revolution community is always on hand with advice, support and tools to help you.

We are in this together. You have taken the first step towards change simply by picking up this book and taking a week to read it. :parkinsons_law: By understanding how an individualised system of work can revolutionise our lives and our world, hopefully your workstyle journey can begin. Thank you for reading our case for workstyle and why we feel radical reform in working structures is needed, right now. If you're feeling inspired to do more, then we highly recommend you make time to take these three steps, if you haven't already:

1. Set, project and respect your workstyle to become a workstyler.

2. Sign the pledge at WorkstyleRevolution.com to join the revolution.

3. Recommend this book to someone you think needs workstyle in their life.

This book is the start of the conversation, written to prick the imagination, question the status quo and hopefully be the start of a revolution that moves us out of industrial-age thinking and into a new digital age way of working that can transform our wellbeing, productivity and society.

In order to create positive change, we can't sit back and wait for organisations to lead us. They won't. Individuals within and outside those organisations need to take action. If enough people believe in the transformative power of workstyle, our collective action can change the world.

We love a good chat about workstyle

We would love to hear from you. Whether you are a passionate believer in workstyle, want to join our longitudinal study, are part of a charity or organisation that would like to collaborate with us, are a business that wants to embrace the benefits of workstyle for wellbeing and productivity, or if you simply want to say 'hi', :wave: please do get in touch at lizzieandalex@workstylerevolution.com.

Otherwise please visit WorkstyleRevolution.com for more tools, support and information, or follow us online @the_workstyle_ revolution.

Thank you

This book quite simply wouldn't have been written without the help of all our supporters inside and outside Hoxby who have helped us on this journey. In addition to testing workstyle, we set up Hoxby to see how diversity and collective intelligence can be combined to create something magical, and this book is a living example of the truly monumental power of that in practice.

Thank you to Ben Foulkes, who helped Alex with the early work on the book while Lizzie went off suddenly for cancer treatment, and whose research and insight were invaluable. To Josh Edson for the beautiful illustrations, and to Annika Hart, Qiulae Wong, Anna Hollaway and Clare Fleerackers for their contributions. To our amazing support team who help us in every way, especially Victoria Shaw and Fran Bailey, as without them this book simply wouldn't have been written. Thank you to everyone who so generously and openly contributed their workstyle stories to the book – Cat, Ed, Ursula, Katy, Anneli, Auws, Sophia, Sam, Laura, Shigeri, Katerina, Yacob and Penny. To all the academics, experts and leaders who contributed geek boxes and case studies – thank you for being our champions, supporters, challengers and teachers and indulging our inner geeks throughout the process. Thank you to Jane Hunter for reading the first draft and giving us the confidence to write the second, as well as for all her support along the Hoxby journey. And for our other reviewers, especially Vicky and Adrienne, to whom we are so grateful for their insight, constructive criticism and support.

Thank you to all of you for coming with us on this journey and making it so much fun. We are proud to have this book as our legacy and will forever remember the joy of writing it with you.

Writing a book can be a lonely and daunting experience, as can starting a revolution. We are lucky to have had each other throughout the process and also feel very fortunate to have had the unwavering support of our families who have been with us through the highs and lows since that fateful night in the pub when the word 'workstyle' was first uttered. We very much hope our children are able to benefit from the revolution we have started.

And finally, thank you to all the workstylers out there who have inspired us that there really is a better way to work. You have stood alongside us to prove that it can be done. Every workstyle story we have heard has been inspirational in its own way.

Let's hope this book will inspire many more.

The references we have cited throughout the book can be found at:

WorkstyleRevolution.com/Endnotes

Appendix I

A summary of the hand gestures, for in the pub with your mates :beers:

Workstyle – easy to remember as both hands spell out the letter 'w'.

The Triangle of Opportunity – Ageing, Technology and Independence – which came together in 2014 to create the conditions for wholesale systemic change to the way we work.

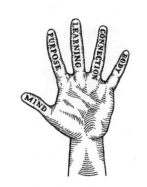

The Five Elements of Wellbeing – Mind, Purpose, Learning, Connection, Body – that improve your wellbeing thanks to workstyle.

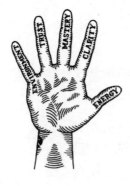

The Five Elements of Productivity – Energy, Clarity, Mastery, Trust, Environment – that improve your productivity thanks to workstyle.

The Three Hypotheses – We believe that Inclusion, Attitudes and Collective Intelligence are the three ways that workstyle can be transformative for society.

Workstyle can create a better world.

Appendix II

A workstyler's guide to setting your workstyle :refreshing:

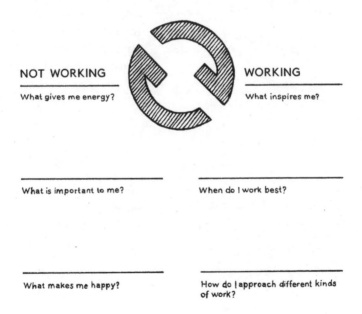

A WORKSTYLER'S GUIDE TO SETTING YOUR WORKSTYLE

WORKSTYLE

What would my ideal workstyle week be?

How might my workstyle change?

How will I set, project and respect my workstyle?

NOT WORKING

What gives me energy?

WORKING

What inspires me?

What is important to me?

When do I work best?

What makes me happy?

How do I approach different kinds of work?

Is it not the interest of the human race, that everyone should be so taught and placed, that he would find his highest enjoyment to arise from the continued practice of doing all in his power to promote the well-being, and happiness, of every man, woman, and child, without regard to their class, sect, party, country or colour?

Sir Robert Owen, in his Paper Dedicated to the Governments of Great Britain, Austria, Russia, France, Prussia and the United States of America *(1841), 17th of '20 Questions to the Human Race'.*